Straight Answers
ON THE
New Age

BOB LARSON
Straight
Answers
ON THE
New Age

THOMAS NELSON PUBLISHERS
Nashville

Published in Nashville, Tennessee, by Thomas Nelson, Inc. and distributed in Canada by Lawson Falle, Ltd., Cambridge, Ontario.

Printed in the United States of America.

Scripture quotations are from THE NEW KING JAMES VERSION of the Bible. Copyright © 1979, 1980, 1982, Thomas Nelson, Inc., Publishers.

Library of Congress Cataloging-in-Publication Data

Larson, Bob.
    Straight answers on the new age / by Bob Larson.
      p. cm.
    Bibliography: p.
    Includes index.
    ISBN 0-8407-3032-2
    1. New Age movement—Controversial literature. I. Title.
BP605.N48L37 1989
133—dc19

89-3026
CIP

6 7 8 9 10 — 96 95 94 93 92

Contents

Straight Answers on New Age Psychic Phenomena

Parapsychology
Psychics

Straight Answers on New Age Divinatory Devices

I Ching
Tarot Cards
Tasseography
Chiromancy
Nostradamus
Water Witching
Astrology
Biorhythms
Auras
Dreamwork
Runes

Straight Answers on New Age Consciousness

Mysticism and Enlightenment

Straight Answers on New Age Media Manipulation

New Age Music
New Age Periodicals
  New Age Journal
  East West
  New Realities
  Yoga Journal
  Windstar Journal
New Age Books
  Dancing in the Light
  It's All in the Playing
  Out on a Limb

Muller, Robert
Naisbitt, John
Price, John Randolph
Ram Dass
Spangler, David
Sutphen, Dick
Yogananda, Paramahansa
Zen Master Rama
Places
Arcane School
Association for Humanistic Psychology
Astara
Chidvilas Foundation
Club of Rome
Esalen Institute
Hunger Project
Institute of Noetic Sciences
Findhorn Foundation
Ken Keyes Center
Perelandra
Planetary Citizens
Planetary Initiative
Windstar Foundation
World Goodwill
Practices
Affirmations
Aikido
Art
Astral Projection
Biofeedback
Brain/Mind Development
Chakras
Feldenkrais Method
Isolation Tanks
Massage
Near-Death Experiences
Numerology
UFOs
Past Lives Therapy
Plant Communication

Rebirthing
Reiki
Self-Healing
Self-Hypnosis
Yoga

Preface

I continually confront the New Age Movement on my syndicated, live-by-satellite talk show. Since "TALK-BACK with Bob Larson" started January 3, 1983, dozens of shows have catalogued the movement's influence on business, education, and popular culture. My research files are voluminous on everything from Aquarian occultism to New Age holistic health.

Prominent New Age personalities have debated me, including Tolly Burken, who introduced firewalking into America; extraterrestrial walk-ins, publicized in psychic Ruth Montgomery's book *Aliens Among Us;* and Benjamin Creme, forerunner of Lord Maitreya and proponent of the New Age Movement. Since more than half my audience professes no religious affiliation, those committed to Aquarian ideas are frequently called to defend the New Age Movement.

As I started to write this book, it seemed ironic I hadn't done so sooner. Yet I hesitated to launch this project, knowing of the many other excellent books on the subject. How does *Straight Answers on the New Age* differ from other perspectives on the subject? Much of this book isn't editorialized; I simply report what's happening. (In the "Straight Answers" and "In My Opinion" sections, you'll find what I think about each aspect of the Movement.) By presenting a comprehensive and historical document on the New Age, I hope Christians and New Agers alike will consider more seriously the movement's ideas and implications.

Other evangelical books evaluating the New Age Movement have focused on conspiratorial or demagogical aspects. *Straight Answers* means to serve as a handbook, encompassing in one volume virtually everything you need to know about the New Age. Each chapter stands alone, describing particular aspects of the Movement. The detailed index permits quick referencing of any New Age topic.

Straight Answers also reveals the pervasiveness and inclusiveness of the New Age Movement, a scope often underestimated. Considering New Age eccentricities, it's disconcerting to realize that fifty million Americans are hard-core enthusiasts and sympathizers. If you are a New Ager, you'll gain a valuable perspective on why the Movement attracts so many who were disillusioned with organized religion. Evangelical Christians will find reason for concern about the Movement's interest in occultism.

Whatever your motive, check out the table of contents, and read what interests you most. Then read the book cover to cover. I suspect you, too, will find it eye-opening.

Chapter 1

LOOKING OUT FOR NUMBER ONE

Straight Answers on the
Human Potential Movement

His employees were taught to break twelve-inch planks with their bare hands. They also walked on burning coals while chanting mantras. Larry Kendal employs fifty-five people, and his real estate company, The Group, Inc., sold more than $90 million worth of property last year. He's also president of the Fort Collins, Colorado, Chamber of Commerce. Larry says, "Our goal is to maximize the potential of each member of the organization, and then maximize the potential of the entire group. Unlimitedness is our natural condition."[1]

Farther east, in Washington, D.C., a group of sober men declares in unison, "I direct my thoughts to the world of my inner being. I see world leaders, friends, and adversaries joining together in fellowship to resolve issues, forgiving each other." The assembly of seventy-five people isn't a New Age conclave of spiritualists or higher-consciousness seekers, but a band of Pentagon employees meeting for their weekly Pentagon Meditation Club. The club president advocates a new form of SDI, a "spiritual defense initiative" that will protect humanity by the "unified force" of a human "peace shield."[2]

At the dawn of the computer age, "Don't fold, bend, staple, or mutilate" was the magnetic card instruction humorously applied to people. At the advent of the New Age, seeking "transformational values" of "human potential" became the battle cry of assorted higher-consciousness devotees. Through intuitional therapy, professional training courses, public education, and personal experimentation, a constituency has developed that believes mankind has a cosmic destiny. And through mystical examination and psychic development of one's human potential, superior beings who have undergone spiritual reconstruction will supposedly emerge as the new vanguard of the human race. (Some human potential training is nonspiritual, but such training is in the minority.)

Everywhere in the New Age, the same buzzwords and underlying values are found: human potential; practical spirituality; progressive politics; feminism and matriarchy; organic foods; and grass-roots activism. Apart from the New Age Movement, these terms are spiritually neutral. Within the Movement, they assume inherent definitions which convey a distinctive ideology. New Agers have utopian dreams of a world in which all humanity lives in harmony with earth and the cosmos. Instead of an apocalyptic Second Coming with dire events from without, the New Age is emerging from within. Even young children are being influenced by New Age philosophy.

The third graders concentrated intently, their little eyes squeezed tightly, their small brows furrowed. You could almost hear them thinking, *I wish I may, I wish I might.* But the power of imagination being employed had nothing to do with standard nursery rhyme fare. These diminutive students were on a journey of the mind to inhibit their negative behavior.

The teacher had told them to imagine tiny vultures living inside them. If they lost emotional control and were bad, the vultures would grow. If they learned to minimize conflicts with their fellow students, the vultures would diminish. Innocuously called an Autonomous Learner Model, the course had been developed as a New Age adjunct for children, teaching youngsters the mind's power to create reality.

Instead, it created a furor among parents. One mother reported her daughter couldn't sleep at night because she feared vultures were flying about her room. Another parent declared his son was imagining all kinds of monsters for the malevolent purpose of punishing his peers.

HUMAN POTENTIAL UTOPIANISM

The thrust of the Human Potential Movement, unleashing latent powers and abilities within man, is both socially utopian and spiritually idealistic. It supposes there are boundless capabilities in the human psyche and unlimited powers latent in the human spirit. All the dilemmas of mankind, from war to the environment to dysfunctional relationships, can be solved by an immense change in human consciousness. And the subconscious is the key. Subliminal and self-hypnosis tapes, along with visual stimulation devices, can unlock the solution to personal happiness and the power of the soul we're told. Through positive reinforcement and restructuring the perceptual processes (that is, changing the way we look at the world), the innate force of the subconscious will conquer all foes and resist all negativism.

At the core of the Human Potential Movement is humanistic psychology, which places humanity at the center of the universe and denies the concept of original sin. Emotions are paramount, and traditional concepts of deity give way to "self-realization." A movement trademark is the eclectic borrowing of various disciplines, including Gestalt awareness, transactional analysis, sensory awareness, Primal Therapy, bioenergetics, and biofeedback.

In business, traditional economic formulas such as time management, strategic planning, and carefully monitored cash flow are shunted aside in favor of "self-talk" and "centering." The market for New Age business techniques is so lucrative that the Maharishi Mahesh Yogi's Transcendental Meditation Program (TM) has been adapted for corporate consumption under the name "One, Incorporated."

Scientology established the World Institute of Scientological Enterprises and Sterling Management to invade the workplace with its science of the soul called Dianetics. Silva Mind Control counsels business people to solve work problems by projecting themselves out of their bodies. They are also told to envision their work environment complete with imaginary "counselors," entities who assist with improved profit-loss statements.

John Naisbitt, best-selling author of *Megatrends,* has adopted a New Age approach to entrepreneurialism. As a highly paid lecturer, Naisbitt explains that mankind is shifting to a global economy. To assist the unwary, he and his wife have created their own metaphysical foundation called Bellweather. Naisbitt says, "We consider ourselves to be New Age entrepreneurs. Bellweather supports people creating new morals and new directions" (see Chap. 12).

Some New Age ideology infiltrates corporate America through "wellness" programs. The Long Island Lighting Company spends $200,000 a year for a biofeedback consultant. Weeden & Company, a Wall Street trading firm, hired International Health Systems, a massage clinic, to give on-the-job acupressure to its staff.[3]

Innovation Associates of Framingham, Massachusetts, charges $15,000 for a four-day seminar designed to strengthen executives' commitment to a common purpose. Hoy, Powers, & Wayno, a New York firm, uses meditation, imaging, and intuitive thought to instill creativity and leadership among managers. At the Stanford Graduate School of Business, a professor uses Zen, yoga, and Tarot cards as part of the instructive curriculum for the course "Creativity in Business."[4]

New Age consultants bill themselves as providing "stress management, employee assessment, and integrated strategies." One such consultant offers a psycho-therapeutic assessment of professional potential by observing employees' "auras." Another "business analyst" advises Fortune 500 clients and trade associations with the assistance of channeling and psychic cosmic consciousness. New Age consulting companies also offer "life affirming direction" and advice on "death and dying." One New Age public relations firm offers "mainstream coverage for New Age ideas."

Typically, human potential groups meet for a weekend of training, which expands to a program designed to achieve personal growth and kindle latent abilities. Total attention is given to body awareness and impassioned feelings of the here and now. The purpose is to cultivate a less judgmental attitude about relationships and a less critical stance on conventional values.

In the beginning, the Human Potential Movement attempted to emphasize credible leadership and cautious concern for group dynamics. That began to change in the mid-1970s, when the movement flourished in the western United States and adopted the Eastern mysticism popular in California. The goal of overcoming dull routines of everyday existence gradually evolved into pursuit of "self-transcendence" by merging with ideals of cosmic consciousness. Self-discovery for improvement of personal esteem unfolded into a form of metaphysical "self-actualization."

The roots of the Human Potential Movement can be found in nineteenth-century Theosophy and Emersonian transcendentalism, as well as Eastern mysticism. Biblically, Paul's letter to the Colossians addresses some pre-gnostic ideas similar to New Age beliefs. What's different today is the mass marketing and widespread acceptance of once esoteric experiences. Today, discovering how to look out for number one is easily and cheaply available. American business people speak as effortlessly of Kroning, The Forum, and Lifespring as they do of quarterly reports and bottom lines. In fact, the New Age Human Potential Movement is not only an adjunct to big business but is, itself, a big business. Human potential training courses take in more than $4 billion annually from American companies. Human relations seminars feature touchy-feely gurus in pinstripe suits lecturing corporate captains on the merits of out-of-the-body experiences.

NEW AGE BUSINESS TECHNIQUES

In a competitive world market, where rumblings of trade wars cloud the horizon, boosting company productivity and creativity takes a high priority. Many manufacturers are desperate to boost morale, spur inventiveness, and enhance profits. As a result, businesses are constantly looking for a new edge, and New Age mind control techniques are the latest fad to captivate corporate America. More than half the 500 largest United States corporations, including Proctor and Gamble, IBM, and Singer, have adopted some form of New Age creativity training. These companies willingly pay anywhere from a few thousand dollars to a half million dollars for product development sessions designed to reprogram employees' thinking.

In an article entitled "New Age Training in Business: Mind Control in Upper Management?"[5] Richard Watring, director of personnel for Budget

Rent-a-Car in Chicago, carefully categorized the kinds of New Age intrusions into the workplace. Meditative techniques are used as part of stress-management strategies, including TM, self-hypnosis, guided imagery, yoga, and centering. Some techniques enhance intuitive creativity, such as visualization, Silva Mind Control, Dianetics, and focusing. Certain techniques heighten self-esteem by incorporating biofeedback and affirmations. Other techniques encourage shared responsibilities, including The Forum and Lifespring. Though the goals are laudable, critics raise serious questions about the techniques used to achieve them.

"Visualization" is a key word with many New Age business advisers. Employees undergoing training are told they must acknowledge their dreams and commit to realizing them. They're instructed to relax, take slow, deep breaths, and visualize a spacecraft taking them to another planet. Once there, the workers are to look back on earth to sense a oneness with the cosmos. The resulting visualization releases them from past limitations and restrictions.

Psycho-technologies have invaded the work force with the intent of "self-actualization" (otherwise known as "enlightenment" or "contacting one's inner divine nature"). Most New Age influence enters through the human resources development department of large companies. A representative of Digital Equipment recently warned, "I see the training industry being used to proselytize New Age religion under the deceptive marketing of increased productivity, self-actualization, and self-improvement. As trainers, we must sound the alarm to this covert missionary work."[6]

In California, Pacific Bell spent $175 million on something called Krone Training for its 67,000 employees. Krone Training is also euphemistically known as "Leadership Development." During one portion of training, employees are asked to consider "a purpose that is beyond self." Critics say this technique is an obvious introduction to theological concepts of universal unity consciousness. Christian critics in the ranks of Pacific Bell went to court, prompting an investigation by the California Public Utilities Commission. In Albany, Georgia, the manager of human resources for the Firestone Tire and Rubber Company was fired when he refused to implement New Age techniques. Manager William Gleaton claimed New Age seminars constituted a form of secular humanism he was unwilling to promote.[7]

A Boston firm called Synetics offers to take employees on "mental excursions." Other New Age entrepreneurs encourage businessmen to discard jackets and ties to promote equality. Personnel might play with crayons, make up stories, or merely daydream. Programs like Transformational Technologies use meditation and hypnosis to promote common corporate visions. Employees are encouraged to think of themselves and the company as one, a unitary consciousness idea borrowed from Eastern mysticism.

Transformational Technologies is the stepchild of Werner Erhard's est and its successor, The Forum. Trans Tech sells its services apart from The Forum through fifty franchise operations that cost up to $20,000 each. A recent year's billing hit $15 million, with clients including RCA, Scott Paper Company, and Boeing Aircraft.[8]

EST

More than a half million graduates have been charged hundreds of dollars each to discover, in est's words, "You are part of every atom in the world, and every atom is part of you . . . the self itself is the ground of all being, that from which everything arises."[9] Such are the assertions of est, Erhard Seminars Training.

At age eighteen, Jack Rosenberg had an experience during which he says, "I lost the kind of consciousness that locates one in a certain place. I became the universe."[10] Later, while driving his wife's Mustang down a freeway, he declared, "I got it." What he got was a new name, Werner Erhard, and a system of New Age philosophy rooted in yoga, Dale Carnegie, Mind Dynamics, Silva Mind Control, Scientology, and Zen Buddhism. Erhard's arrogance led him to say, "How do you know I'm not the reincarnation of Jesus Christ?"[11]

Such preposterous claims lie behind what some disgruntled ex-members say is a confrontational style of indoctrination that destroys moral and emotional standards of coping. A former est worker now claims, "They said it was all right to sleep with your friend's husband because you can create the feeling of being guilty or feeling fine. You are your own God."[12]

Apparently, you can also choose your own appellation. After reading an *Esquire* magazine article about West Germany, Rosenberg borrowed the names of physicist Werner Heisenberg and German economics minister Ludwig Erhard. For more than a decade, he explored the then-developing Human Potential Movement, Zen Buddhism, hypnosis, Scientology, and California's Esalen Institute.

Erhard's seminar system involved a calculated process of breaking down the inductee's personality and rebuilding it by harassment and intimidation. The trainer verbally abused the audience with repeated obscenities. All ego defenses were ridiculed by hurling demeaning epithets at anyone who resisted the trainer's tactics. After hours of such manipulation, participants were supposed to "get it." For some, "it" became a way of overcoming introversion to assert themselves. For others, "it" was just another trip on the consciousness-raising express.

Celebrities who jumped on the bandwagon included Valerie Harper, John Denver, Jerry Rubin, and Cloris Leachman. By the time Erhard abandoned est in the mid-1980s, hundreds of thousands of graduates had been told that all religious ideas are meaningless. One's reality could be chosen at will, and gods could be invented as needed.

THE FORUM

"An expression of a breakthrough in transformation achieved by est"[13]: that's the self-congratulatory way The Forum describes itself. Unlike the est training format of lectures punctuated by personal confrontations between trainers and participants, The Forum is more casual and involves dialogue between leaders and audience. Whereas early est sessions prohibited bathroom breaks and involved verbal abuse, The Forum is more upscale than est and targets a corporate clientele. It even has a juvenile division, known as Young People's Forum, for children between six and twelve.

The Forum aims for "healthy, successful people, who are already effective in their lives."[14] Critics say that translates into those who can afford $525 for four sixteen-hour sessions about "making it happen." Erhard assures participants that once they realize the benefits of The Forum, they will consider the cost "a joke."[15] According to Dr. Jack Mantos, director of research for Werner Erhard and Associates, The Forum evolved out of The Forum Satellite Events, a series of addresses Erhard broadcast via private satellite.

Apparently, Erhard sensed a different mood among people in the 1980s. By his estimation, people in the 1970s concentrated on "getting it together." Citizens of the New Age seem more interested in "making it happen." Some observers believe The Forum is merely a maneuver to repackage est training to counteract a decline in enrollments. Whatever the motive, interest from business leaders has paved The Forum's way with gold.

The Forum has convinced chief executive officers that workers will produce more if they can contact their "sense of being." How is this achieved? The Forum ambiguously states that "being" is inexplicable, the "magic" of being trained in The Forum.

LIFESPRING

The U.S. Surgeon General's office once declared Lifespring "has considerable potential for emotional harm."[16] A Pennsylvania woman whose husband got a large settlement after suffering a severe psychotic reaction to Lifespring sessions said trainers told participants to slap the person with whom they felt closest. One session involved playing "Life Boat," a game in which trainees decided who deserved to enter a small boat to be saved from a sinking ship. Such criticism contrasts strongly with Lifespring's claimed benefits of "increased clarity on career direction, a deeper understanding of self, enhanced joy in relationships, and more fun in life."[17]

Founder John Hanley had been a trainer with Werner Erhard in Mind Dynamics courses during the early 1970s. Today, his brand of self-awareness training takes people through guided meditations and communication exercises. Hanley has achieved financial success, but all is not well at Lifespring. When ABC-TV's "20/20" did an exposé, serious claims were leveled that Lifespring's "psychodramas" were morally questionable. Reporter Geraldo Rivera cited one case in which an ex-nun was told to go to a seedy bar and proposition the first man who spoke to her. On another occasion, participants were told to discuss their sex organs and describe their most bizarre and humiliating sexual experiences.[18]

When he founded Lifespring in 1974, Hanley presented his first training to 23 persons. Today, he has centers in more than a dozen major cities. His expense budget exceeds $10 million, and he employs a full-time staff of over 100.[19] Hanley had left Alexander Everett's Mind Dynamics because he felt it emphasized too many abstractions and was too reflective. Hanley wanted to compel people to pursue a state of passion and "aliveness."

Hanley readily pays homage to est and Erhard. He believes that est paved the way for the transformational training business. Hanley says, "The est course was a quantum shift in 'being' with people. We're all in Werner's wake." Any differences with est? "The est training focused on the fact that people were robots and on automatic pilot, while Lifespring was more concerned with personal relationships,"[20] he says.

Lifespring is unashamedly anti-intellectual. Feelings and experience are all-important. It is also strongly influenced by the ideas of Abraham Maslow, the late humanist psychologist. More recently, Hanley has explored the notions of philosophers Sören Kierkegaard and Martin Heidegger. Other theories might eventually be included as well, since Lifespring's basic idea is that "personal growth and effectiveness are paramount," so that one may continue having "expanded choice, creating options, and providing a supportive atmosphere for the examination of values and systems."[21]

Lifespring's goals are achieved through Gestalt awareness, encounter training, psychosynthesis, and Eastern meditation. Experimental learning methods include two people engaging in "communication exercises," guided meditations, and a variety of group exercises. Trainers present brief "lecturettes," suggesting ways of testing beliefs and habits. The forty-five-hour Basic Course, sixty-hour Advanced Course, and ninety-day Leadership Program focus on personal power, self-understanding, sexuality, communication, wellness, intuition, and spirituality.

LIFE TRAINING

Would you like to free your life of the fears, decisions, judgments, expectations, and beliefs that have "made your life into a drama, a series of habitual, automatic reactions to your problems"? Then Life Training is for you. Just devote seventeen-hour days on the weekend, from 9:00 A.M. to 2:00 A.M., to "processing" the experiences of your life. Why so much time so quickly? To quote a promotional piece, "The Training is designed to go very deep, very fast. . . . It is this depth and rate of discovery that distinguishes this experience from other educational programs."[22]

Potential clients are told they will ease the effects of life's disorders by living in a new and "awakened" manner. How? By nurturing the "SELF . . . the capacity that the great religions have called the Soul."[23] Trainees are told that no particular religious belief system will be emphasized, but that Life Training is "spiritual . . . because it develops the capacity to live out of your spirit."[24]

Life Training was created in the late 1970s by two Episcopalian priests in San Jose, California. They borrowed the rational-emotive therapy of Albert Ellis, a noted humanist psychologist. His theory states that all suffering stems from irrational thinking. But those who have participated in Life Training and are also familiar with est readily notice the similarities in the two-weekend format, the size of the groups, and the use of neutral hotel facilities. Other est resemblances include a controlled environment in which trainers verbally berate audiences, use of transformational buzzwords, group manipulation, and public exposure of painful past experiences. And as with est, the ultimate yardstick of all truth is the measure one takes of oneself.

Life Training sessions are so carefully designed that detailed instructions suggest how to be seated, when and how to talk, and what to do in the event of drowsiness during the marathon sessions. Watches, chewing gum, and outside reading materials are prohibited. Specific curse words are allowed in place of certain unacceptable epithets. The names God, Jesus, Christ, and Buddha are forbidden. Results of the training are held as confidentially as is information divulged to a priest.

MISCELLANEOUS HUMAN POTENTIAL SEMINARS/ORGANIZATIONS

Insight Transformational Seminars (ITS): Founded in 1978 by John-Roger.[25] John-Roger was born Roger Delano Hinkins in a small Utah town. He says that in 1963, while in a coma, he became inhabited by a spirit identified as "John the Beloved."[26] John-Roger currently claims to be the embodiment of the divine Mystical Traveler Consciousness, and heads the Los Angeles-based Movement of Spiritual Inner Awareness (MSIA).

His Insight Seminars brought in $8 million in one year.[27] His ministers have run productivity seminars for U.S. government offices and major corporations. Among MSIA's celebrity ministers are actresses Sally Kirkland and Leigh Taylor-Young, and singer Carl Wilson of the Beach Boys.[28] Every year ITS presents an "Integrity Award" to "outstanding world citizens." Past recipients include such New Age advocates as the late R. Buckminster Fuller and former United Nations official Robert Muller.[29] MSIA's annual Integrity Days have given away as much as $10,000 to the favorite charities of celebrity honorees, such as Mother Teresa, Desmond Tutu, and Ralph Nader, most of whom are not actively associated with John-Roger or his organizations.[30] Featured events are "Awakening Heart Seminars," costing $450, and "The Opening Heart Seminar" and "Centering in the Heart Seminar," which cost $775 each.

John-Roger states, "In awakening the heartfelt energies, you can't help but discover your own self-worth, your own magnificence." The targeted energy is defined as God, or "whatever you want to call it."[31] Mystical aspects of Insight Transformational Seminars are underscored by the financial support of such groups as the Holistic Center for Therapy and Research and the Prana Theological Seminary.[32] (Prana is the Hindu concept of vital energy.)

Disaffected members have accused John-Roger of brainwashing his followers, seducing young male staff members with promises of promotion for sexual favors, and using electronic listening devices to preserve his reputation as a clairvoyant.[33] Former MSIA members report campaigns of hate mail and vandalism directed against them and their families.[34]

Institute of Human Development: Offers a complete collection of metaphysical and self-improvement tapes for use in guided meditation, guided visualizations, and positive reprogramming. Complete freedom from sickness, fear, worry, and financial problems is promised. An additional "Cosmic Odyssey" offers the secret "why's of life and the universe" and the "highest New Age teachings." Tapes teach psychic self-defense against demon possession and negative energy fields, plus tutoring in past life regression, future life projection, Cabbala, awakening kundalini energy, developing ESP, commanding financial success, hypnotizing others by mental telepathy, Aquarian Age techniques of controlling the environment, universal binding laws of Egyptian mysteries, automatic handwriting from higher entities, talking with animals, and how to become a Christ Master.

Institute of Transpersonal Psychology: A Ph.D. program located in Stanford, California, offering bodywork, spiritual work, or psychological work that requires three to four years to complete. Courses include T'ai Chi, Aikido, Sensory Awareness, Zen Meditation, Hinduism, Astrology, the Tao of Physics, Arica, Hatha Yoga, Feldenkrais, Healing and Hypnosis, and Parapsychology. The Institute claims to be on the frontier of psychology, uniting concern for the body, mind, and psyche. In addition to studies, daily one-hour sessions are set aside for yoga and jin shin jyutsu.

Arica: Named after a Chilean town where a Bolivian mystic named Oscar Ichazo lived. He founded what was called "scientific mysticism," borrowing from Hinduism, Zen, and Tibetan Lamaism (a form of occult spiritualism). Students are taught to hear music through their feet, develop breathing exercises, and engage in "mentations" (concentration on various organs of the body for specified time periods). Ichazo currently promotes Psychocalisthenics, a series of twenty-three movement-breathing exercises designed to awaken vital energy.

Esalen: Michael Murphy and Richard Price met Frederic Spiegelburg, professor of comparative religion at Stanford University, through whom they were introduced to the concepts of Eastern philosophy, yoga, and other subjects which eventually shaped their lives and work.[35] They founded the Esalen Institute in 1962 at Big Sur, California.[36]

One element that made Esalen seem daring and sensual was its coeducational hot water, mineral baths in the 1960s. Exposed on one side to the sky and stars, some bathers experienced feelings of oneness with the Universe that they claimed changed their lives.[37]

The Esalen Institute preceded the Human Potential Movement and promoted early experiments with encounter groups and sensitivity training. In

27

1962, according to Michael Murphy, "humanistic psychology was just beginning to take root. Gestalt therapy was virtually unknown outside narrow professional circles. Attending to the needs of one's body was reserved for athletes, dancers, and so-called 'health nuts.' Meditation had not been assigned a role in maximizing human potential, and anyone studying or claiming psychic insight was considered, at best, to be on the fringes."[38] All these disciplines were explored at Esalen.

By the mid-1960s, the Esalen seminars had shifted from ordinary didactic sessions to a newer kind of "experiential seminar," during which emphasis was placed on experiencing the theory being discussed. Psychotherapist Robert Gerard led his students in visualization exercises, while discussing the theory of psychosynthesis.[39]

Fritz Perls, the founder of gestalt psychotherapy, resided at Esalen when he was in his seventies. He disagreed with analytical explorations of a client's past, and advocated a kind of therapy that concentrated on the present. Clients were encouraged to exaggerate emotions, such as anger and fear, in a group environment.[40]

Sensory awareness courses required following a series of relaxation exercises designed to increase physical and mental awareness.[41] Bodywork, or "therapeutic manipulation," remains a staple at Esalen, where "skillful touching" is used to alter "the structure, the chemistry, the feelings, and the behavior of a human being."[42]

Today, the Esalen Institute defines itself as "a center to explore those trends in education, religion, philosophy, and the physical and behavioral sciences which emphasize the potentialities and values of human existence." Activities include seminars, workshops, and residential programs, as well as research and consulting.[43] Costs vary between $270 and $530, depending upon the program's length.[44] Participants in Esalen therapy are taught Eastern-style mystical concepts, allowing them to vent their "true emotions."

Michael Murphy and the Esalen Institute became involved in attempts to help Soviet citizens "recognize the power of the human consciousness."[45] In 1979, the Esalen Institute Soviet-American Exchange Program was organized, resulting in projects such as the first live satellite teleconference between Soviet and American scientists on the topics of Chernobyl and Three Mile Island, a project that involved multiple downlinks in the Soviet Union and audiences in four Soviet cities.[46]

Further examples of "citizen diplomacy" included visits by Esalen founder Michael Murphy and some followers to Russia, where they met with Soviet citizens of mutual interests.[47]

As Esalen celebrates its twenty-fifth anniversary, its commemorative catalog acknowledges the contributions of such well-known figures of the twentieth century as Aldous Huxley, Arnold Toynbee, R. Buckminister Fuller, Abraham Maslow, B. F. Skinner, and Joseph Campbell to Esalen's thought and growth as the precursor of human development movements.[48] It must be remembered, however, that Esalen Institute's past has also included burnouts, freakouts, and several drug deaths and suicides.[49]

STRAIGHT ANSWERS

Q: *What kind of New Age courses in school should concern parents?*

A: Yoga, relaxation techniques, guided imagery, and visualization are a few buzzwords. Children may be asked to invent imaginary playmates or envision "helpers" who assist them in expanding their powers of fancy. They may lie on the floor, arms and legs outstretched, and pretend to become interrelated with each other or imagine they are animals in the forest or birds in the air. Such techniques are designed to separate their minds from their bodies, practices that can lead to occult, out-of-the-body experiences.

Q: *What's wrong with cultivating a child's imagination to expand his creativity?*

A: Childhood imagination rooted in fantasy is different from metaphysical experiences encouraged by psycho-manipulative techniques such as mind-body separation. Creativity based on an abstract relationship to reality is one thing, but inducing altered states of consciousness through occult methods opens the door of the spirit, which leaves younger children unprotected by barriers of biblical knowledge.

Q: *What should an employee do if his company requests he enroll in a New Age mind-training course?*

A: In several similar circumstances, employees have registered grievances with their state labor board and have won some suits in civil court. How far one might pursue retaliatory action is a personal matter. Obviously, every reasonable course of action to abstain because of personal convictions should be pursued. Under no circumstances should one participate in a technique or practice that might be spiritually compromising.

Q: *Is there anything inherently wrong with the idea of developing human potential?*

A: Scripture teaches that humanity in its fallen state cannot achieve reconciliation with God, and that salvation cannot come from works. The Human Potential Movement is a system of salvation that depends on what we can do for ourselves, not what God's grace can accomplish by faith in the redemption of Christ. The movement is humanistic, with humanity at the center of its hope to avoid fear and failure instead of centering on the help of the Holy Spirit. "I can do all things through Christ,"[50] the apostle Paul declared, the philosophical antithesis of developing human potential.

Q: *Are human potential techniques to be trusted when they claim no indoctrination of any particular belief system?*

A: No! If human potential advocates admitted the truth about their goals, trainees would be suspicious from the start. The belief system of the training is never overtly stated, but an occult or metaphysical purpose is inherent in the training techniques. The true intent of the techniques isn't revealed until the student has made a financial commitment and is in a controlled environment that lowers his ability to think critically.

Q: *Are New Age seminars nonreligious, or is that claim a ploy to avoid discriminatory accusations?*

A: A Christian businessman who required his employees to attend a church retreat or prayer meeting would be sued instantly. New Age seminars hide behind language chosen to obscure their religious nature. Such seminars make all the claims of religion, such as offering "transformational encounters" and "magical experiences." But to avoid the wrath of the IRS and the penalty of antidiscriminatory statutes, trainers consistently claim they offer no specific religious agenda. Any knowledgeable observer can readily recognize the Zen orientation of groups like est and The Forum, as well as the Hindu concepts underlying the "cosmic consciousness" sought by human potential groups.

Q: *Are human potential concepts newly devised therapeutic tools, or are they historically rooted in ancient heresies?*

A: That answer can be given in three words: syncretism, Gnosticism, and Pelagianism. Syncretism, the melding together of unrelated ideologies, errs by failing to distinguish between God, his creation, and Christianity versus other religions. Just as early heretics sought to combine elements of paganism, Christianity, and philosophical thought, human potential groups use a variety of occult and mystical methods. Gnosticism, a heresy in the early Church, was based on esoteric knowledge of the divine mysteries unavailable to the uninitiated. This information could be obtained if the seeker were properly guided by an intermediary. Groups such as Life Training and Lifespring carefully guard their group sessions and allow no public inspection of inner proceedings. With the aid of a gifted teacher, the training supposedly provides an awakened understanding of life. In the fifth century, Pelagianism denied the transmissible corruption of Adam's sin to all mankind and therefore held that human nature alone is capable of fulfilling the will of God. The idea of self-discovery and self-betterment found in human potential groups extends this ancient idea.

Q: *Is there any affiliation between New Age human potential ideals and traditional mystical religious concepts?*

A: Yes. Werner Erhard is an excellent case in point. He claims that in founding est, Zen Buddhism and Scientology were his most powerful influences. Erhard has also given grants to Buddhist groups such as the Naropa Institute of Colorado, the Nyingma Center in Berkeley, and the San Francisco Zen Center. Additionally, he has sponsored presentations by the Dalai Lama, head of Tibetan Buddhism.[51]

Q: *What are the central spiritual errors of the Human Potential Movement?*

A: The Human Potential Movement teaches that the mind/soul nature of man is God. Scripture teaches that God is the Creator of reality, not that He is our minds. All that exists was spoken into being by God, and we cannot deny or rearrange our objective material existence by a mere mental redefinition. Second, our misconduct cannot be justified by human efforts to do good. Only the grace of Jesus' redemption can provide atonement for erroneous action (sin). Finally, it is the Holy Spirit who progressively sanctifies us, not self-actualization facilitated by visualization procedures.

Q: *Since most New Age motivational training establishes no goals, what commitment is there to succeed?*

A: To the New Age seminar trainer, the very idea of commitment to a concrete conclusion is irrelevant. The procedures are so individualized that no one who completes the training knows objectively what kind of transformational breakthrough he has achieved. Thus, the results are in the eyes of the beholder. By maintaining this mystique, the originators of human potential courses claim that they are not accountable for the consequences of their training. Attendees and graduates are on their own, left to draw their own conclusions.

Q: *Why are courses like The Forum so ambiguously explained by their representatives?*

A: If you don't know what you are being trained to do, you automatically lay down your logical defenses. In the pursuit of "being," you forget reason. Furthermore, if you don't know what "it" is, how can you know when you've attained "it"? There is no way to evaluate quantitatively the time and expense of the training. This is a clever marketing device that sells snake oil to the company buying the course and gives its employees whatever they think they received, a sham for participant and purchaser alike.

Q: *Do courses such as Lifespring have any theological beliefs about original sin?*

A: They avoid the inclusion of religious terms, but their teachings have profound doctrinal significance. For example, Lifespring teaches "our conscious intentions and knowledge can be trusted."[52] That departs from the biblical stance that man is a fallen creature whose heart is "desperately wicked."[53]

Q: *Does the past matter, or is it relatively inconsequential, as Lifespring suggests?*

A: Failing to learn from the past sentences one to repeating the failures of history. Lifespring says the past has no meaning when redefined by the present. That is a convenient way to elude moral guilt. It creates a universe that is unaccountable for sin and needs no conversion. The Christian concept of redemption is unimportant if one needs only to rethink and re-create past misdeeds. This concept also flies in the face of conventional psychology, which says neuroses are often rooted in past trauma. Lifespring irresponsibly declares, "It is never too late to have a happy childhood."[54]

Q: *How limitless are the possibilities of unleashed human potential?*

A: Human potential philosophy teaches that the idea of fixed possibilities is a product of our culture. Transforming the self makes feasible new ways of being. This notion presents several dangers. It is a man-centered approach to reality that displaces God's sovereignty in human affairs. It also opens the door to exploration of psychic phenomena, allowing for possible satanic intervention. Finally, it supplants Christian conversion with a "transformational ideal" that can't change reality but does alter perception of facts, a hazardous form of emotional escapism.

Q: *Why do some human potential courses use humiliation and embarrassment?*

A: This is a form of brainwashing, or "brain rinsing," as one human potential advocate put it. Both fascism and communism exploit the fact that human values cannot be remolded until all self-esteem and the protective emotional defenses of individual identity have been eradicated. Humiliation destroys the coping mechanisms that surround the soul and sense of self. Once these have been eliminated, the person can be indoctrinated without intervention of critical thought.

WHO'S WHO AND WHAT'S WHAT

Awareness: An "exalted" state of consciousness, usually achieved by meditation, in which one becomes aware of entities and spiritual energies.

Bodywork: Rather than simple development of the outer musculature, this approach to fitness aims to reduce muscular tensions in search of "psychic freedom" by using complex yoga-like physical exercises and postures.

Cabbala (also Kabbalah): Ancient Jewish occult form of mysticism by which rabbis sought to decipher esoteric meanings in Scripture by assigning numerical values to letters and words.

Erhard, Werner: Founder of est, a mind-expansion cult that teaches reality can be intuitively experienced because "being" is more important than "doing."

est: Acronym for Erhard Seminars Training, a process of "getting it" by "direct intuitive acquisition" after long hours of deprivation and verbal humiliation.

Feldenkrais: System of bodywork founded by Moshe Feldenkrais, teaching that emotional and spiritual balance is achieved through functional coordination, body awareness, and stipulated movements (see Chap. 12).

Hubbard, L. Ron: Science fiction writer (1911–1986) and founder of the Scientology cult, which believes humanity descended from an extraterrestrial race of omnipotent gods known as Thetans.

Jin Shin Jyutsu: A Japanese occult healing discipline involving body manipulation at specified points; similar to acupressure.

Krone Training: New Age motivational teachings, developed by Charles Krone, that critics say are based on the occult teachings of the Armenian mystic Gurdjieff.

Kundalini: According to Hindu yoga teaching, spiritual energy at the base of the spine, in the form of a serpent (Hindu goddess Shakti), that seeks ascension to the brain to form a psycho-sexual union with the Hindu god Shiva, resulting in "enlightenment."

Lifespring: Motivational training technique, founded by Mind Dynamics graduate John Hanley, that declares, "We are intelligent and well-meaning beings. . . . There is nothing that needs to be fixed."[55]

Life Training: An imitation of est started by two Episcopalian priests; involves the rapid "processing" of painful past trauma.

Maslow, Abraham: Founder of the Association of Humanistic Psychology, he also coined the New Age terms "peak-experience," "synergy" (mutual cooperation), "self-actualization," and "humanistic psychology"; considered the founding father of the Human Potential Movement (see Chap. 12).

New Age Movement: A spiritual, political, and social phenomenon networking many occult/metaphysical organizations and groups intending to transform individuals by means of "mystical enlightenment" so that a new age of unprecedented prosperity, peace, and harmony can be introduced on earth.

Silva Mind Control: "Mind expansion" techniques developed by Jose Silva to control one's future and fortune through self-hypnosis and the alteration of reality by mental supposition.

T'ai Chi: Chinese martial art of slow physical movements used with meditation to develop self-discipline and spiritual awareness; part of bodywork.

Transpersonal Psychology: Technique for psychologically exploring the spiritual aspects of human nature; developed by Abraham Maslow.

Transformational Technologies: New Age business training program begun as an offshoot of The Forum; uses hypnosis, positive thinking concepts, visualization, and yoga exercises.

Transcendental Meditation: A variant of Hinduism expounded by Maharishi Mahesh Yogi, a "god-realized" guru who teaches that the constant repetition of a Sanskrit (the ancient language of sacred Hindu scriptures) word or phrase allows the mind to transcend to a state of "bliss consciousness."

IN MY OPINION

The idea of developing human potential has invaded our culture. The United States Army slogan, "Be all that you can be," owes its concept to the New Age Movement. When MasterCard asks you to "Master your possibilities," the company offers more than plastic power. It also unwittingly participates in a global conspiracy of self-deification.

This cultural milieu erupted from the idealistic fervor and narcissism of the 1960s, but it is now encountering a midlife crisis. Suddenly, the limits of human mortality must be faced. Exploration of the spirit is a way of denying the reality of death by reconstructing materiality. No matter that rational decision-making processes are ignored. So what if the lessons of history are disregarded? New Agers believe humanity's unlimited potential and human nature can be remolded. One need only read a brief chronology of homo sapiens to see how unscrupulous, charismatic leaders have exploited such naiveté.

A dangerous pragmatism underlies the New Age search for human potential, as evidenced by its acceptance of such eccentric practices as "trance channeling." For example, New Age exponent and mystical guru Baba Ram Dass was asked about the well-known trance-channel Pat Rodegast, who serves as conduit for the entity Emanuel. Is Emanuel a spirit from beyond or a part of Rodegast's mind? Ram Dass answers: "From my point of view as a psychologist, I allow for the theoretical possibility that Emanuel is a deeper part of Pat. In the final analysis, what difference does it make? What I treasure is the wisdom Emanuel conveys."[56] Ram Dass concludes what many New Agers believe: reality and truth are negotiable.

The onslaught of New Age training in corporate America may signal its demise. Whatever short-term goals are achieved, future U.S. enterprise may be bartered away. New Age business techniques may temporarily increase sales, but unsuspecting individuals will be more vulnerable to altered states of consciousness and potential demonic possession. Placing mankind at the center of one's personal and corporate universe is blasphemy, a sacrilege promoted for corporate profit. Such pretentiousness may accelerate productivity momentarily through ego gratification, but eventually the idea that higher profits can be thought into being will be considered infantile.

Some New Agers honestly admit that their goal of "unitary consciousness" and mass global "spirituality" can be achieved only if all hindrances to human potential are removed. New Age author and theoritician John Randolph Price, in his book *Practical Spirituality,* describes the elimination of two billion people with lower "vibratory rates."[57] Such apparently genocidal intent contrasts sharply with the claims of human potential champions. The reality of New Age propaganda is not global harmony and enlightened masses, but death, destruction, and the aims of the Antichrist.

A common theme of New Age human potential cults is the supposed power in each of us to create our own reality. In Lifespring, participants are told past events can affect us only according to the current meaning. In effect, the trainee is told that reality is not what happened, but what one *thinks* happened. In contrast, Christianity teaches that the past is powerful and affects who we are today. Sinful deeds are not eradicated by ignoring them. They are forgiven by repentance and faith in Christ (1 Pet. 2:24).

The underlying principle of the Human Potential Movement is that life must be experienced, not understood. In this psychological system, there is no right and wrong, only "what is." Thus, New Agers seek to assuage their consciences by re-interpreting reality. But avoiding the penalty for sin takes more than a few days at a seminar. It requires the blood of Christ and his death on the cross (Eph. 1:7). Human potential philosophies may transform who we think we are and what we think may have happened. But the future of heaven or hell is an objective reality, and the judgment of God is an actual future event that cannot be wished away.

Chapter 2

FIRED UP FOR
THE NEW AGE

Straight Answers on New Age
Mind Control Techniques

The pulse of rock rhythms blares from a speaker in the background. Dozens of people stand in obvious anticipation. Some breathe heavily. Others chant repeatedly, "Cool moss, cool moss." Finally, the group's leader steps onto a ten-foot-long path of glowing coals. The embers range in temperature from 1,200 to 2,000 degrees Fahrenheit. "We can do anything we want," the leader exclaims as he briskly traverses the fiery path.

Like lemmings, the others follow. Why not? They've shelled out $125 each and were told during the preceding five hours, "You can change fear into victory, limitations into freedom, doubt into certainty, and fatigue into energetic power." By the end of their sweltering stroll, they will believe the words of their firewalking instructor, who told them that every time someone creates a miracle, like firewalking, he transcends the accepted laws of the physical universe.

Firewalking began as a religious practice in the South Pacific and among the Hindus of India and other, assorted idolaters around the world. Today's firewalkers are exploring psychological frontiers of the New Age Movement. They promise neophytes the ability to lose weight, conquer smoking habits, spell better, read better, and even achieve superior orgasms.

Manipulating the mind by orchestrating reality is one way New Agers hope to acquire "transformative" states of consciousness. To do so, they must overcome certain inhibitions of the normal mindset, which include reserve and fear. Of the latter, a well-known firewalking teacher says, "Fear is just random energy. By changing our frame of reference, fear's power becomes personal power, the power to get things done."[1]

Power is much of what New Age ideology is all about: power to transcend time and space; power to defy presumed moral laws and known physical laws; power to do anything with one's mind; in short, power to become a god. In the words of one advertisement for a firewalk, "Experience a personal triumph, a deep belief in your ability to take action, to do what *you* want to do."

Will Noyes believes it. Crippled with arthritis, he couldn't stand straight or walk without crutches. After four months of firewalking, Will says he can walk upright and has taken dancing lessons. But professional medical journals illustrate different consequences. There are scores of documented hospitalizations and even foot amputations resulting from firewalking. At a recent convention of record retailing executives, 370 people were invited to march across twelve feet of burning coals to the theme from "Rocky." An ambulance had to be called in, and many participants spent the rest of the conference on crutches after suffering second-degree burns.[2]

For the traditional firewalker in India or Asia, sacred devotion is part of the process. The walker may precede his feat by fasting, celibacy, and ritualistic purification. Western New Age walkers make no such preparations. Instead, they speak of "anchoring, disassociation, and neurolinguistics." But a professor of anthropology observes of classical firewalking, "To my knowledge, there is always some supernatural overtone, some kind of relationship to a higher spirit. They're invoking a higher spirit or power and aligning themselves with this greater power. It almost always has cleansing properties."[3]

How can people walk on fire without injury? One firewalker claims that perspiration on the soles of the feet provides protection for a brief duration. The so-called Ledenfrost theory says the feet secrete an unidentified substance that shields them from injury. An instructor of firewalking claims that glands in the brain release protective chemicals called neuropeptides, and that positive thoughts about the walk encourage the secretion of this substance.

In the fall of 1984, Bernard J. Leikind, a physicist, and William J. McCarthy, a psychologist, both from the University of California at Los Angeles, attended a firewalk led by Tony Robbins of the Robbins Research Institute. Both men succeeded in crossing the bed of hot embers without injury, though Leikind had not attended the prefirewalk seminar, which was advertised as being crucial to the accomplishment.[4]

Their conclusions were that firewalking can be explained by a combination of physics and psychology. Leikind wrote that the secret to firewalking lies in the distinction between heat and thermal energy, the conductivity of different materials, and that "just knowing the temperature is not enough to decide whether something will burn us."[5]

Though firewalkers cross beds of the glowing embers, they are light and fluffy carbon compounds. Leikind reported darkened footprints where people had passed over the embers and pressed them down, cooling them so that the risk of injury was lessened. Even when the embers are glowing yellow—the hottest intensity—the thermal energy is not likely to burn a

firewalker's feet. Serious injuries at firewalks have occurred when participants have spent more than the average 1.5 seconds needed to cross the
bed of embers or have walked upon deeply piled, hotter embers.[6]

Leikind concedes that the Ledenfrost effect is a scientifically-based explanation, since moisture does act as an insulator, but, he says, that it is "likely
to be helpful but not necessary for firewalking, provided the heat capacity,
thermal conductivity, and temperature of the embers or rocks is suitably
low."[7] He discounts various other explanations offered by firewalk theorists,
ranging from protection by correct beliefs to a bioelectric field surrounding
the walker as being "totally unsupported by any direct experimental data."[8]

McCarthy has theorized that psychology may explain why firewalkers
sometimes feel no pain or heat. "Distraction can reduce the pain that people
experience, because they can attend to only a few things at once."[9] At one
firewalk, instructions were given beforehand that "actually seemed calculated to distract our attention from the sensations of our feet. Concentrating
on the 'mantra,' looking up at the sky, hearing the applause and shouts of
elation, and breathing in an artificial and forced manner, all served to distract the walker."[10]

Firewalking is scientifically possible without participating in mind-over-
matter self-improvement classes. Firewalk instructors say that a person's
subconscious mind may be at work even if the person is a doubter.[11] But
skeptics point out that if the instruction is not vital to the act of firewalking,
then it is all a deception.[12]

NEUROLINGUISTICS

New Age firewalkers agree that a successful fire walk demonstrates at-
tainment of a higher consciousness. It's mind power at work at its most
dramatic. That's why many firewalking instructors also teach neurolinguistics. Practitioners say they can cure phobias in minutes and enable clients to
overcome any inhibition. Salesmen of the art claim they can induce an
almost trance-like state in a potential client, causing him to respond affirm-
atively.

Neurolinguistic programming (NLP) is the brainchild of linguist John
Grinder and Dr. Richard Bandler, a computer expert trained in Gestalt therapy. It was developed at the University of California, Santa Cruz, and uses
sophisticated techniques to establish rapport with a patient. The therapist
scans a patient's body language and word patterns in search of underlying
patterns. Hypnosis may be used, though some say the patient-therapist relationship itself can induce a natural trance-like state.

Dr. Bandler says NLP "teaches people to run their own brains instead of letting their brains run them."[13] The application of NLP also uses some techniques of so-called Ericksonian hypnosis (named after Dr. Milton H. Erickson). Erickson taught that psychotherapy could bypass client resistance by imbedding therapeutic messages during presumably casual conversations.

Some NLP therapists use a technique called "anchoring," the careful manipulation of voice changes and body movements for hypnotic effect. The use of hypnotic reinforcement is also prominent among NLP therapists. For example, a shy person may be asked to remember a time when he felt confident. He is then touched on the shoulder to imbed or "anchor" that confidence. The mainstream psychological community is skeptical, viewing NLP as too manipulative. Studying how a person looks and sounds and treating him like a machine is considered too behavioristic and devoid of empathy between counselor and client.

VISUALIZATION

Visualization is yet another mind game played by New Agers. It also goes by other names such as "guided imagery," "dynamic imaging," or "positive imaging." The intent is the same: creating or recreating physical realities with the mind's perceptual powers. Its roots are in Hinduism and modern Science of Mind sects. Hindus have a word for it: *maya*. All the universe is maya, or illusion, they say. Only spirit is substantive. Therefore, what common sense interprets as objective reality is really a figment of the mind. And if reality is an illusion, mental powers can alter it by visualizing something different.

The manipulation of maya is one way yogis seek to achieve union with their god, Brahman. For modern mystics, the purpose is more practical. Groups such as Christian Science and Unity teach that sin, sickness, disease, and failure are all products of the mind. None of these have tangible existence; they are only thoughts that can be dispelled by proper alignment of the mental processes.

Creative visualization involves a mind-body synthesis, beginning with relaxation techniques, followed by breathing exercises. Self-hypnosis procedures may also be employed. First, the desired image is centered in the mind and enforced with repeated affirmation. Contradictory thoughts must be allowed to float only fleetingly through the mind. At this point, any doubts about the visualized goal must be suspended. No outside authority is allowed to intervene, not even a transcendent God. At this moment, the one visualizing is thought to be in touch with his Higher Self, a projection of God, and therefore no harmful or selfish visualization is possible.

How does visualization differ from positive thinking and the homilies of Norman Vincent Peale? In brief, it is a big step beyond. It's more than mind over matter. Visualization claims to produce an entirely new reality. The message of its benefits is carried in workshops, seminars, books, cassettes, and videos, all available in scores of New Age catalogues and retail outlets.

In some cases, visualization is used in attempts to cure disease by activating the immune system to increase the number of white blood cells. For example, the patient may be told to envision his cancer as a snake in his body being attacked by a giant eagle, which kills and carries it away. To assist the mental voyage, New Age entrepreneurs provide subliminal voice recordings and consciousness-altering musical sounds of surf, wind, and rain.

The health application of New Age visualization has been its most readily received message. A promotional device marketing books and tapes to enhance visualization advertises: "Mentally and physically, begin the transformation you desire, whether it be improving appearance, alleviating illness or injury, easing discomfort from allergies or pain . . . whatever you personally wish to alter and improve."[14]

Critics of visualization raise logical questions about its validity, even apart from the fantasies it engenders. Suppose two different people visualize competing realities? Which is entitled to preference? What structure of priorities guides such mental faculties? Suppose the reality sought is control over the lives of others? Who determines what selfish considerations are unfit for visualization? What kind of unconscious guide can circumvent self-indulgent goals? What if a critically ill patient tried to think away his condition instead of seeking appropriate medical advice? And for the Christian, what differentiates faith from visualization, since the former is declared in the Bible to be "the evidence of things not seen"?[15]

MEDITATION

He's a professor at Harvard Medical School and the author of the best-selling book *The Relaxation Response*—impressive credentials for someone who wants you to think yourself warm on a cold day. But Herbert Benson has done his research. Benson investigated Tibetan Buddhist monks in a cold Himalayan colony in the north of India. In deep states of what the meditative monks called "heat yoga," the devotees raised the temperature of their fingers and toes as much as fifteen degrees without changing their bodies' core temperature.

What other powers over mind and matter does meditation offer? Some New Age advocates of the ancient art of meditation claim it can grow more brain cells, allow you to embody the consciousness of the true Messiah, and even enter the bodies of others to assist their spiritual quest. For eight dollars, one popular New Age yoga instructor offers a course entitled "Contacting the Tree of Life and the Tree of Knowledge." A promotional brochure states: "While meditating with another person, you die and enter the Garden of Eden. You see the Tree of Life and the Tree of Knowledge, surrendering to the great evolutionary intelligence to give you what you need."

To most, meditation means prayer or deep contemplation. Others see meditation as an extremely private religious ritual. But the New Ager who speaks of meditation seeks something far more tantalizing. He wants nothing less than to totally alter his state of consciousness in order to obliterate any sense of differentiated, or individual, self. The core experience to which he aspires may be called "detached alertness" or "passive volition," but the desired result is the same—achieving a state of unconcern toward all surroundings. Only then can the meditator hope to merge his mind with that of the "Universal Mind."

One New Age periodical explained, "Meditation is a technique for developing a tension control so that worry, fear, anger, and all the other thoughts and feelings and concerns that seem to constantly hassle people are dealt with in a firm but calm manner."[16] Critics say, however, that it comes at the price of a dissolved ego and hours of sitting cross-legged in the lotus position.

Several universally applicable techniques are used to enhance meditation. Some meditators suggest concentrating on the mystical "Third Eye" at the point midway between the eyebrows that supposedly coincides with the pineal gland. Some advocate riveting one's mind on the navel, representing a point in the abdomen about two inches below the navel, where the center of life is said to reside.

Another method involves using the yantra, the visual equivalent of a mantra, a geometric design on which the meditator can focus his attention. Other frequently used objects are an inscription, a flower, a statue, or a candle flame. Some use the mandala, typically a square or circle drawing designed in many colors, symbolizing unity of the macrocosm of the universe with the microcosm that is man. T'ai Chi, meditation in motion, is profusely practiced by the Chinese, who perfected the art. The purpose is to place the entire body and mind in harmony with the macrocosmic forces of the universe.

What are New Age meditators getting for all those hours with eyes closed, concentrating on each breath and chanting mantras? Ardent advocates say it decreases tension, anxiety, and aggressiveness without use of drugs. Edgar Cayce, the occult mystic, described meditation as "an emptying of all that hinders the creative forces, rising along the natural channels of the physical man to be disseminated through those centers and sources that create the activities of the physical, the mental, the spiritual man."[17]

Whatever the side benefits, New Agers readily admit that meditation is one pathway by which they seek "god-realization." Descriptions abound of what it's like to achieve that state. Meditators depict the ultimate consciousness acquired by their quest as a condition of unutterable bliss. Critics argue that such supreme detachment from reality might have such qualities, but part of the benefit comes from escaping all accountability for one's conduct and any responsibility to others. In fact, say the most vociferous detractors, that is exactly the kind of indifference one often finds in the contemplative countries of the Far East.

STRAIGHT ANSWERS

Q: *Can firewalking be removed from religious considerations by treating it as a mental and physical feat?*

A: Deuteronomy 18 refers to pagan fire purification ceremonies when it declares that one who "passes through the fire" is committing an "abomination." Though devotion to an idol and spiritual purification may not be present during a westernized New Age fire walk, the inherent motivation is identical. New Age firewalkers worship the idol of self and seek to purify their insecurities and fears without turning to Christ, whose perfect love casts out fear. A study of the occult reveals that certain ceremonialism attracts evil spirits. Since fire purification ceremonies have been associated with entity possession and control (e.g., voodoo rituals), one can assume that a fire walk could be a denizen of demons.

Q: *Is there a natural explanation for the phenomenon of firewalking without receiving burns or blisters on the soles of the feet?*

A: Several theories have been proffered. The major firewalking advocate, Anthony Robbins, claims the mind creates electrical fields that cause a glandular secretion inhibiting the effects of the fire. Other explanations postulate that perspiration or air pockets insulate the soles of the feet. Each of these assumptions has been carefully studied by scientists. To date, the evidence is inconclusive. Perhaps all or some of these explanations may play a role. Still, firewalking has traditionally been practiced as a religious ceremony crediting supernatural powers for success, so one should not dismiss the possibility that a nonrational event occurs with assistance from spiritual forces.

Q: *Can hypnosis alleviate the pain of firewalking?*

A: Hypnosis could explain the absence of pain, since its acute neurosensory response could be disassociated. But that could not explain the absence of blisters and burning experienced by some walkers whose faith apparently protects them. This seems to indicate a religious aspect, since "believing" is crucial to avoidance of harm. Hebrews 11:6 says it is impossible to please God without faith. Satan, who wishes to be "like God" (see Isa. 14), may extract a commitment of "faith" to protect firewalkers and thus keep "true believers" from harm.

Q: *What is the pagan purpose behind firewalking, and how does it differ from New Age intents?*

A: The pagan specifically dedicates his walk to a particular deity and, before stepping on the coals, performs lengthy acts of obeisance to an idol of the god. Certain aesthetic standards are observed. After the ceremony, a successful walker is deemed to be sanctified. Though the terminology concerning New Age firewalking may be altered, the same results are sought. New Age walkers also enter a condition of altered consciousness, after which they are presumed to be revitalized and able to face situations they were previously incapable of handling.

Q: *If neurolinguistics can cure certain ailments or remove some phobias, doesn't such benefit outweigh possible misuse?*

A: New Agers sacrifice the sanctity of the mind through various techniques of thought control. They violate the privacy of one's personhood by assuming that each of us is an undifferentiated part of all others. Therefore, they have no qualms about breaching another person's integrity by hypnotically manipulating that individual for his supposed benefit. The person may not know it or even want it, but a decision has been made without his permission.

Q: *What harm is done if the symptoms of a disease can be visualized away and comfort brought to the patient?*

A: Visualization techniques open doors to the mind and spirit that the Lord intends to remain closed (see Gen. 1:27–29; 2:19–20). Adam apparently possessed incredible powers of intellect. But after humanity's fall, there is no indication God condoned the cultivation of psychic powers to alter reality. As for healing, visualization is particularly dangerous because real symptoms of serious illness could be ignored. Wishing away an organic disorder by psychosomatic manipulation could place the patient in greater danger as the disease progresses.

Q: *Is it possible for the mind to activate the body's immune system?*

A: "For as he thinks in his heart, so is he," the Bible declares.[18] According to some medical studies, the emotions may profoundly affect the body's ability to recover from disabling illness. Evidence suggests that some cancers may be brought into remission through positive mental attitudes. Furthermore, studies show that those with a negative outlook on life are more prone to accidents and illness. These general, as yet scientifically unsubstantiated observations, however, do not endorse the idea that specific immune responses can be activated mentally as substitutes for appropriate medical treatment.

Q: *Can reality be created or manipulated by the mind, or are such attempts invalid?*

A: God alone is the Creator of all that exists. Satan is the master deceiver who manipulates our perception of reality. In Eden, he began this technique by tempting Eve with the question "Has God indeed said?"[19] In fact, God had not said what Satan suggested, but his implication distorted Eve's conception of God's character. New Agers substitute visualization for repentance. They pretend that transgression does not exist, that evil and sin are unreal, to avoid facing their iniquity. Instead of seeking God's will, they rearrange unpleasant incidents. Rather than allowing grace to make "all things work together for good,"[20] they make arrogant assumptions about situations in life and try to amend whatever they find unacceptable.

Q: *If Eastern meditation can be relaxing, is there any real danger in practicing it?*

A: Some psychotics are relaxed and at ease with life. They have detached themselves from reality and are insulated from all that is unpleasant or perplexing. Yet, they are considered mentally insane. Likewise, certain meditation disciplines may detach one from truth and create a fictional sense of serenity. The question is not how peaceful one feels, but whether that composure leads to constructive action. No one was more peaceful than Christ. But instead of retiring to a cave for contemplation, he actively sought instances of human need and "went about doing good."[21]

Q: *Are the techniques of mystical meditation dangerous, or is religious intent the main concern?*

A: Certain techniques of inducing the meditative state may cause effects that should be avoided. For example, some yoga positions seem to attune the body's psycho-neurological systems automatically to facilitate altered states of consciousness. Thus, merely practicing the postures could trigger undesirable results. Of course, if the motive is to affect the mind mystically, the outcome could be even worse. Some techniques, such as candle-staring or chanting, could disassociate the mind from reality to the extent that mental illness may result. That is why Christ warned against "vain repetitions"[22]—not only because of its uselessness in pleasing God, but also because it shuts down the mind and increases vulnerability of the spirit.

Q: *What are the essential differences between Eastern mystical meditation and the biblical form of meditation?*

A: Christian meditation is the natural process of constantly acknowledging God's Word by focusing on the Lord's nature and his intervention in our lives. New Age meditation seeks to dull the senses and curtail the mental processes, to worship the self as an inner manifestation of the divine.

WHO'S WHO AND WHAT'S WHAT

Anchoring: A neurolinguistic process of enforcing hypnotic suggestions by implanting positive experiences or messages into the subconscious.

Christian Science: A cult founded in 1879 by Mary Baker Eddy, who wrote *Science and Health with Key to the Scriptures*, which teaches death is an illusion, God is Divine Mind, and disease can be removed by right thinking.

Disassociation: Avoiding pain or unpleasantness by redefining reality with other mental associations, such as thinking firewalking coals are "cool moss."

Firewalking: An ancient, idolatrous ritual in which one seeks spiritual purification by walking on super-heated coals to prove one's confidence in the god's protection.

Guided Imagery: A form of visualization in which specific images are constructed in one's imagination, as suggested by a therapist or New Age counselor.

Mantra: A word or phrase believed to have the power of concentrating one's attention beyond distractions of the external world to facilitate a meditative mindset.

Maya: A Hindu teaching that the only reality is the deity Brahman, the Supreme Absolute, and that all else in the material world is an extension of Brahman's thoughts and therefore illusory or transitory.

Meditation: The mystical process of stilling the mind and senses so that sensory stimulation is limited and awareness of internal essence becomes acute.

Neurolinguistics: A behavioristic form of motivational training and therapy, it supposes that observing body language enables a counselor to help a client overcome his phobias, learning disabilities, and insecurities.

Peale, Norman Vincent: Pastor and author who pioneered the positive thinking concept and from whose premises certain New Agers have drawn inspiration.

Positive Imaging: A form of psychological reinforcement that seeks to replace negative mental images with carefully constructed positive ones, out of which a new reality can be created.

Unity: A cult that denies biblical doctrines of sin and salvation, yet uses Christian terminology to promote a unity of non-Christian beliefs while claiming a reverence for Jesus as a great teacher (full name: Unity School of Christianity).

Visualization: New Age practice based on the concept that thoughts have the power to create objective reality and that by visualizing circumstances in an altered frame of reference, one can literally transform fancy into reality.

Yantra: The visual equivalent of a mantra, supposing that a meditative state can be induced by staring at a colorful diagram of concentric or geometric design.

Yogi: Practitioner of yoga, which means "union with God," achieved by aesthetic physical disciplines designed to subjugate the body and free the spirit.

IN MY OPINION

Firewalking, visualization, and meditation seem dissimilar, but there are penetrating similarities that involve manipulating the mind and reality. Each denies reality and attempts to change objective facts.

The heat of firewalking coals is a fact of physics that no hypnotic suggestion can alter. Likewise, life's problems are real, and attempting to visualize them away is an escape mechanism of denial. The difficulties of existence can be conquered through God's grace without meditating to elude responsibility for one's own failures.

Christ reminded Satan of God's warning, "You shall not tempt the Lord your God."[23] Yet firewalkers do just that by suggesting they can think away the potential danger to which they subject themselves. God does vow, "When you walk through the fire, you shall not be burned."[24] But God's promise applies to inadvertent adversity.

God is faithful, but he is not obliged to intervene on our behalf when we frivolously place ourselves in jeopardy. The firewalker who seeks to alter his phobias and insecurities by threatening his own welfare blasphemes God, who offers his Holy Spirit for strength in our weakness and courage for our fears. Trust in God's Word is a more reliable guide to overcoming adversity than hot coals and hypnotic chants. God offers promises you can stand on without getting your "soul" burned.

As a sales technique or a means of overcoming a negative self-portrait, a positive outlook is acceptable. But a fine line is crossed when mental depictions of success are sought by reconstructing reality. Visualization as a spiritual tool can become an Aladdin's lamp. It is particularly dangerous if one uses selfish mental fantasies to alter actualities. The Almighty becomes a mere spiritual vendor, dispensing products to the religious consumer upon demand, that our will instead of his might be done.

Once the visualization process begins, what authority will limit its application? Will a hazardous disease be thought away while the debilitation continues? Will financial failure be ignored while the visualizer dreams his way to riches and hastens the summons of the bankruptcy judge? Will Christ become an idealized icon, conveniently pictured in one's mind according to the human will rather than the prerogative of divine sovereignty? Could a visualized Jesus actually be a manifested evil spirit, invading one's mind with masquerading intentions?

Suppose a disease is caused by improper diet, unwarranted emotional stress, lack of faith in God, or personal sin. Can it simply be visualized as nonexistent, thus avoiding the penalty for sinful actions? Jesus offers mountain-moving faith, which is quite different from the New Age entreaty of visualization that says, "The mountain isn't really there." One has confidence either in a technique to alter what is, or in reliance on a higher power to take what is and render it as if it were not there. One's faith is in God, or one's faith is in faith.

Meditation is not antithetical to biblical Christianity. In fact, the words *meditate* and *meditation* appear numerous times in the Old and New Testaments. But the Scriptures do lay down strict guidelines for meditation. The root word of *meditation* implies a process of slowly digesting God's truths, using concentrated thought patterns focused on the laws, words, and precepts of God.

In contrast to the mystical methods of meditation designed to still the senses and empty the mind, biblical meditation heightens the intellect. Christianity teaches that the mind is an avenue by which God reveals his laws and his love. The Christian meditator isn't trying to empty his mind but seeks to fill it with the knowledge of God without resorting to rigidly aesthetic disciplines. According to the Bible, meditation isn't an encounter with an overactive ego, but a natural flow of attention to the things of the Lord throughout the day.

The mystical meditator seeks a direct experience of "god-realization," achievable by circumventing the intellect's conceptualization processes. In that state, the answers to all life's questions will supposedly be intuitively revealed. This fourth state of consciousness is thought to be a higher condition of mind, offering uninterrupted communication with the divinity of one's higher self.

But the meditator may get more than he bargained for. Ironically, the Stanford Research Institute International, which often espouses New Age ideology, published a study warning against the dangers of intense meditation disciplines, such as Transcendental Meditation. Researchers found that a form of psychological desensitization may occur, endangering those who are unable to control the release of large amounts of anxiety. Another study by the Illinois State Psychiatric Institute of Chicago concluded that certain forms of meditation are far less therapeutic than simply sitting daily and thinking about the expectation of relief.[25]

Christian meditation differs from New Age meditation in its methods, motives, and result. "Let the words of my mouth and the meditation of my heart be acceptable in Your sight, O Lord,"[26] the psalmist said. Christians don't need to hyperventilate or encourage an insensible irresponsibility. Those who worship Christ eschew seeking an inner manifestation of self as God. They meditate instead on the transcendent God, who lifts us above our dilemmas to commune with him. The kneeling position is not only more comfortable than the lotus position, but also more spiritually satisfying. Contemplating a risen Savior is considerably more uplifting than gazing at one's innie or outie!

Chapter 3

THE WHOLE TRUTH ABOUT HOLISM

Straight Answers on New Age
Holistic Healing

The patient lies on his back, naked from the waist up. First he engages in a series of breathing exercises and guided meditation. Then the healer begins the ancient art of laying stones. More than a hundred crystals are placed at various positions and angles on the patient's body. The healer says crystal power can soothe the mind, calm the spirit, and cure disease.

Just as modern science uses quartz crystals to drive watches and tune in radio stations, some psychic healers believe crystals are a powerful light force that can penetrate subconscious blockages in the body. They also work with other stones in the quartz family, including agate, flint, fossilized wood, onyx, opals, amethyst, and amber.

Desperate from pain and suffering, disillusioned with modern medicine, thousands turn to extraordinary healing techniques. American health care is increasingly seen as desensitized and impersonal. Doctors are viewed as part of a disease-oriented, technologically callous, and authoritarian health care system. Consequently, nontraditional forms of healing are making amazing inroads. A major New York medical center refers AIDS patients to spiritual healers. Many who are skeptical about the high cost of modern medicine turn to Dr. Feel Goods, throw away their medicine, and wait for the healing hand of some unseen force.

Evidence of supernatural healing processes can be found in pictorial scenes on the walls of caves dating back 15,000 years. Egypt, Babylonia, Tibet, India, and China are among the cultures that adopted apparently effective means of nonrational healing. The modern trend toward holism had its genesis at the turn of this century. The New Thought movement introduced metaphysical healing, based on the idea that bodily ills are the result of mistaken belief, a concept borrowed from Mind Science churches such as Christian Science.

Critics of New Age holism say that, extravagant claims aside, no practitioner has yet opened blind eyes or cured an AIDS victim. Psychiatrists argue it's not unusual for a fleeting sense of well-being to follow an exotic healing procedure. They claim autosuggestion plays a big role in a temporary sense of euphoria. What worries doctors is that after the novelty wears off, the organic problem will once again be evident, and the person may be nearer death than before.

The diversity of New Age healing practices is astounding. Through visualization, healers teach terminally ill cancer patients to unleash their immune system by imagining the body's white blood cells as voracious sharks attacking cancer cells, envisioned as small, frightened fish. Some have adopted the Chinese practice of pulse diagnosis, by which the internal temperature of the body and the condition of five major organs are supposedly detected. Reiki, a laying-on-of-hands therapy, is based on the belief that healing can be psychically projected to distant locations (see Chap. 12).

The holistic health movement is based on the belief that all beings consist of cognitive, physiological, emotional, and spiritual qualities. Each of these must be integrated properly to bring health to the whole person. The universe is viewed as a supportive organism with a harmonious balance that can be duplicated in the body. By soothing body, soul, and spirit, holistic healers hope to restore that balance between the macrocosm of the universe and the microcosm of each individual's body.

This view contrasts sharply with traditional medicine. Historically, medical science viewed the human body as a biological machine, powered by energy released in the digestion of food. Health was considered the absence of pain and dysfunction. Sickness was thought to be the appearance of these symptoms. It was believed that illness usually originated from a single pathogen, such as bacteria or a virus, that invaded the body from without. The purpose of medicine was to identify and isolate the pathogen and destroy it with drugs or remove it by surgery. But New Age holism changed that perception for millions.

CRYSTALS

Of all popular New Age healing methods, none has stirred more interest and controversy than crystals. Some keep crystals in their refrigerator to prevent food from spoiling. Other sleep near crystals to facilitate pleasant dreams. Crystals are believed to be conduits of cosmic energy with the ability to cure Parkinson's disease, arthritis, chronic back pain, and even blindness. Psychics offer their services to program crystals so they will emote whatever qualities the users desire. As one New Age healer explained, "Your body is crystallized thought. Patterns are stored in the bones, and vibrations from crystals can replace a bad pattern."[1] A New Age authority on crystals wrote, "Quartz originates as a thought form in the universal mind on higher levels of light, and it's projected down to the earthly substance that quartz is. Crystals are an access tool to other planes of awareness."[2]

Such reverence for crystals has raised the price of these pet rocks. Crystals go for as much as $15,000 if they are quality gems believed to have healing power. Herb Alpert of Tijuana Brass fame is the proud owner of a 750-pound slab of quartz he purchased at a Manhattan mineral shop. Alpert says, "It makes me feel good to be around it. Since it's from God, you have to like it."[3]

Smaller portions of crystals will soon be available through mass marketing techniques. Robert Vanosa, the artist who created the distinctive tea boxes for Celestial Seasonings, is scheduled to develop packages for twenty-one types of crystals. Each rock will sell from $20 to $100 and will come with its own pedigree and a pamphlet explaining its origins and healing power.

Though several kinds of rocks are used to channel "biocosmic" power, most New Age crystal champions prefer clear quartz. Because they are composed of silicon dioxide, a common component of the human body, quartz crystals and human beings are equated as brothers in earth's family. The clarity of crystals is thought to be a manifestation of their perfection. Their six sides represent the six chakras of the body's psychic energy as proposed by Hinduism. New Age crystals represent nothing less than a symbol of alignment with cosmic harmony.

Potential uses of crystals are bound only by the imagination. Some bathe and sleep with crystals. Others lie silently on their backs with crystals strategically placed on their forehead, limbs, solar plexus, and chest. True believers in crystals have managed to stop smoking with their assistance. There are even mixing guides to crystalline nectars. Finely ground quartz is stirred into a glass in appropriate proportion with a liquid to bottom up and bliss out.

Crystals worn as pendants supposedly increase one's "auric field" (a New Age term referring to the body's emanation of psychic energy). But they must be removed nightly or these "perfect" stones will pick up one's energy imbalances. During the night, crystals should be placed on top of a dish of dry sea salt, since salt provides an environment for the crystal to clear its energies. During the day, one supposedly can plant proper energies in his crystal by mental visualization. Affirmations are also used. One New Age crystal patron suggests, "My life is one of total oneness with the God-force and Christed energies."[4]

ELECTROMAGNETIC HEALING

Electromagnetic healing operates on the basis of the "unified field theory," which postulates that a subtle form of electrical stimulation occurs by the laying-on-of-hands. In Sweden, a well-known radiologist treats lung and breast cancer with electricity. Robert Becker, M.D., author of the book *The Body Electric*, envisions a day when electromagnetic healing will allow amputees to grow new arms and legs. English electromagnetic healer-psychic Kay Kiernan claims to have treated Queen Elizabeth II for a strained shoulder.[5]

Occult healer Olga Worrall claims to be a Christian and a carrier of healing energy. She says, "A healer is so constructed biologically that he or she transforms para-electricity into an energy that can be used by all living systems."[6] A New Age psychiatrist hypnotizes people to test the immune system's responsiveness to suggestion. He believes cancer cells can be confused by mental imagery and rendered incapable of defeating an attack by the immune system.

Until now, Western medicine has been based on technological therapies in conjunction with the latest pharmaceutical wonder drugs. Today, many are turning from mainstream medicine to New Age healers, who offer alternative cures based on exotic beliefs rooted in Eastern mysticism. To those who question whether the source of a healing art should be considered before accepting any therapy, a famous psychic surgeon replies, "If the devil can relieve pain and remove an ulcer, then I prefer the devil."

ACUPUNCTURE

Actress Jaclyn Smith had whiplash. James Garner had pain in his knee. Robert Wagner wanted to quit smoking. Merv Griffin was exhausted. What did they do? Each went to see Zion Yu, Hollywood's leading acupuncturist. Yu jokes he has needled more people than Don Rickles and Rona Barrett combined.

Shortly after the normalization of relations between the United States and China in the early 1970s, the practice of acupuncture began sinking its roots into American soil. Physicians traveled to China to study this ancient therapy, dating as far back as 2600 B.C. Some acupuncturists began hanging out shingles in the United States. One acupuncturist developed computer software that displays video charts of the human body, indicating acupuncture points for 627 medical problems that range from abscesses to yawning. The medical community took a cautious, grudging look at the effectiveness of inserting needles at specified points to relieve stress, cure inner ailments, and induce analgesia. But it took the New Age Movement to propel acupuncture into the foreground of the crusade for holism.

Knowledge of acupuncture goes back nearly 3,000 years in Chinese literature. Primitive societies practiced it hundreds of years earlier. Its most notable ancient description is in *The Yellow Emperor's Classic of Internal Medicine,* dated in the fifth century B.C. One legend claims that acupuncture arose when villagers noticed that a warrior's long-standing maladies were mysteriously cured by spear wounds suffered during a battle.

The term acupuncture comes from the Latin *acus,* meaning "needle," and *puncture,* which means "to prick." Originally, stone, bone, and bamboo needles were used. Ceramic, gold, and silver needles were introduced later. Their use is based on the philosophy of Chinese medicine, which is rooted in the religious tenets of Taoism. The primal energy of the cosmos, dubbed *chi* by Taoists, is thought to permeate all phenomena and instill life, vitality, and health in every living thing. Chi exists in the essence of yang, an aggressive male principle, and yin, a yielding female principle. Both flow through the body in defined pathways known as meridians.

Ideally, yin and yang are balanced in the body, but when a state of disequilibrium is introduced, the flow of energy is disrupted and disease occurs. Traditional Chinese physicians were not concerned with the symptoms of an illness, but turned their attention to constantly tuning up the energy balance. They believed that needles inserted at the proper points could disrupt the flow of yin and yang and thus restore a harmonizing balance to revitalize health.

Critics suggest otherwise. They insist that neither diagnostic nor therapeutic data proves that a special relationship exists between hypothetical acupuncture points and the function of internal organs. If nerve pathways were an explanation, why are the insertion points on acupuncture charts in epidermal areas completely unrelated to the afflicted organ? Fueling suspicion is the fact that the present system of acupoints numbers 365, based astrologically on the number of days in a year. Skeptics also ask how two separate dysfunctions can apply to the same point, such as the *zusanli* point, which is the accepted treatment point for both diarrhea and constipation.

Dr. Charles A. Fager, chairman emeritus of the Department of Neurosurgery at the Lahey Clinic in Burlington, Massachusetts, is an outspoken opponent. Dr. Fager argues,

There is not the slightest shred of evidence to show that acupuncture produces any real physiological changes. The only people helped by it are those with pain and functional disorders. These people are very suggestive, and their cures are totally psychogenic in nature. There is no physiological reason why, if you stick a needle in somebody's ear, a pain in the small of the back will go away. The anesthesia is simply hypnosis. Acupuncture is basically a form of deception and fraud and should be against the law.[7]

Koreans have experimented unsuccessfully with injecting liquid radio-isotopes into acupuncture points to trace the meridians. Kirlian photography has been used without convincing proof. Others have suggested that the needles stimulate secretion of cortisone, an internal pain killer. Additional research has focused on endorphins, internally produced neurotransmitters that can ease pain and create a feeling of euphoria.

One theory claims that human connective tissue forms a continuous network of molecules, which are semiconductors passing along energetic electrons. Collagen, which makes up the fascia (a layer of tissue below the skin), is a fibrous protein with enough crystalline structure to rapidly conduct electricity. Thus, meridians may be pathways of low electrical resistance in surface tissue, conducting a form of electrical energy the Chinese have called chi.

Meanwhile, several branches of acupuncture have developed. Acupressure supposes that intense pressure applied to a point using a thumb or elbow causes stimulation similar to an inserted needle. Ear acupuncture is based on the idea that all meridian channels meet in the ear. By triggering these points, such as putting a staple in the ear, the reflexes are triggered and the body's healthful balance of chi is restored. Critics, however, are persistent in claiming that the effectiveness of acupuncture requires an element of expectation on behalf of the patient, indicating that self-hypnosis may be the real effect of needle insertion.

THERAPEUTIC TOUCH

One branch of holism teaches that the body is a manifestation of energy and illness is the condition of poorly distributed quantities of this energy. Therapeutic touch suggests that a healer passing his hands over the body surface in a circular, flowing motion can redistribute this vital energy. Such techniques have already been introduced into the curricula of nursing schools and medical colleges. New York University has accepted four doctoral dissertations on therapeutic touch in recent years.[8] Currently, the university accepts therapeutic touch as part of the master's curriculum in nursing.[9]

Belief in a nonphysical energy responsible for health and healing is common among occult healers. Rolling Thunder, a well-known American Indian medicine man, declares, "The Great Spirit is the life that is in all things—all creatures, plants, and even rocks and minerals." This power is said to be similar to the circulatory system. When it is unbalanced, illness results. The healer's job is to realign this energy with the equilibrium of the cosmos.

The practice of laying-on-of-hands seems to serve two purposes. Some believe it draws energy toward the hands as they move across the body, so that balance is restored. Other holistic advocates suggest that the healer injects a kind of psychic energy into the patient. Most healers believe they are embued with a kind of power. Psychics assume that the same power responsible for touch therapy is also the source of psychic phenomena.

Dr. Delores Kreiger, founder of the therapeutic touch movement and professor at New York University, believes anyone can be taught to sensitize himself to the "unnamed and unmeasured energy." She insists that no religious faith is required by either the patient or the practitioner. Critics note, however, that Kreiger developed her theory after delving into Eastern philosophy and yoga.[10] While she claims no specific doctrine, she does admit application of therapeutic touch is similar to the ancient Hindu principle of prana, the so-called vital energy force of life.

MUSIC THERAPY

Background music has long been used to reduce stress and provide a placid environment. Now, some New Age healers say the right music can cure depression, diagnose mental illness, and reduce the effects of surgery. Their ideas are based on the theories of Pythagoras, the ancient Greek philosopher and mathematician. He taught his students to cleanse themselves of fear, worry, and anger by daily singing. Another example cited by music therapists is when King Saul's despondency was soothed by David's harp.

New Age music therapists consider sonic vibration the creative force of the universe. Thus, appropriate application of specific tones, frequencies, and harmonic intervals is thought to evoke healing forces. The applications are many: reducing pain; inducing altered states of consciousness that release internal healing forces; accelerating the brain's directives to facilitate healing. Organs, bones, and various body parts are said to have certain vibrations responsive to relevant healing sounds.

Today's sound healers see themselves fulfilling Edgar Cayce's prediction that sound would be the medicine of the future. Some New Age artists have written and recorded therapeutic music based on crystals, runes, tantric harmonics, and so-called spirit sounds. Dr. John Diamond, a holistic doctor and spiritualist healer, teaches that different pieces of music have the ability to raise one's "life-energy" and enhance the function of the thymus gland. Diamond combines his theory with acupuncture to stimulate certain meridians with particular tunes.

One psychic uses music therapy to treat headaches, stomach upset, and depression. The sound is directly applied to the body on the theory that each part of the physique vibrates at an audible frequency. Consequently, transmitting the correct frequency to a diseased organ supposedly restores its proper vibration. Because music is nonverbal and passes through the auditory cortex directly to the mid-brain network governing our emotions, it is considered a short circuit that unleashes the healing powers of the mind. It is also considered helpful in regulating blood pressure and heart rate. Music therapy is believed to stimulate endorphins, natural opiates, and to alter the brain's alpha waves to produce deep relaxation.

PSYCHIC SURGERY

Andy Kaufman, the mechanic on the TV show "Taxi," is dead. He might be alive today had he not watched a prime time TV special on the paranormal. It was hosted by Burt Lancaster and featured a sequence on psychic surgery in the Philippines. Kaufman flew to Manila, where psychic surgeons operated on him. Two months later, he died at the age of thirty-five.

Psychic surgery presumes to be a bloodless method of operating without a scalpel. The patient lies on a table, and the surgeon makes an imaginary incision in the abdomen with his bare hands. Suddenly, some internal tissue appears, it's discarded, and the wound closes without scarring. The patient walks away without sedation or anesthesia.

One patient described his ordeal this way:

> We attended a service with a hymn sing and a sermon, stressing the power of belief. We were taught a mantra to chant during the procedure. When they operate, they part the skin, stretching a pore. Their fingers are like laser beams. They feel the damaging clots, lumps, and scar tissue, and within 30 seconds they scoop them out, right in front of you. I got off the table, into my wheelchair, and had lunch. I felt fine.[11]

The Philippines is not the only place you can find psychic surgeons. A book entitled *Arigo: Surgeon of the Rusty Knife* heralds the feats of a Brazilian peasant who operated with an unclean pocketknife without pain, bleeding, or stitches. Those who observed him say he could stop the flow of blood with a verbal command. Arigo is also said to have had the ability to read blood pressure without instruments, though he never went beyond the third grade. Over 300 patients visited him daily. The Brazilian claimed his powers came from the spirit of a German doctor who died in 1918 and returned to possess his body. Unfortunately, before scientific investigators could test him to their satisfaction, Arigo died in 1981.

Arigo was not alone. Brazil boasts thousands of psychic surgeons, some of whom are medical doctors. They believe they can contact the spirits of deceased physicians who operate through them, providing special skills. Most of their surgery is done in a trance state without using anesthetics or antiseptics. Though the practice is officially illegal, it still thrives. Brazilian healers are usually members of Cardecism, a spiritualistic sect. Unlike their Philippino counterparts, they seldom perform deep body operations, preferring instead to work on early breast cancer, skin tumors, and fleshy membranes over the eyes.[12]

Adept magicians, such as Henry Gordon, have easily debunked some psychic surgery. Gordon demonstrated for television cameras how he removed a huge piece of diseased tissue from the upper arm of a man, while a camera watched from two feet away. Gordon admitted later the "tissue" was a piece of chicken liver. The blood came from a tiny plastic vial broken at an appropriate time. Gordon's fingertips had pressed into the soft flesh so they disappeared from view, appearing to penetrate the skin without actually doing so.

PYRAMID POWER

Those not yet confident in the potency of crystals may opt for the power of pyramids. Not only can these triangular shapes be placed on one's body, but under a hollow version you can sleep more soundly, eat more nutritiously, and even achieve superior orgasms, say advocates. The philosophy of pyramidology is based on the idea that the ancient Egyptian pyramid of Cheops was built according to precise geometric measurements and alignments to channel an unexplained biocosmic force or electromagnetic field. Its power is said to work best when the pyramid is aligned along a north-south plan, either true north or magnetic north.

In 1970, Sheila Ostrander and Lynn Schroeder wrote a best-selling book entitled *Psychic Discoveries Behind the Iron Curtain*. Their speculation about the power of pyramids began fueling a fad that has long interested occultists. Since the Greek historian Herodotus visited Egypt in the fifth century B.C., mysteries concerning the ancient land of the Nile have fed speculation that the early builders of the pyramids were privy to secret forces that could be harnessed by mankind.

In the philosophy of pyramidology, the triangular sides represent perfection, the square bottom embodies the four elements in Egyptian mythology (earth, fire, air, water), and the apex signifies deity. New Agers who believe in the potency of pyramids say their form constitutes an amulet that provides precognitive and postcognitive knowledge. It may also be a point of contact with the world of higher consciousness.

Occult legend has it that Egyptian priests were initiated into their religion by spending a night inside a pyramid. In the morning, they exited, supposedly possessing the powers of a god. One promoter of pyramids suggests writing down what you desire on a piece of paper. Then place it under a pyramid for three to nine days. If your thoughts are properly focused during this time, the power of the pyramid will somehow psychically reply. Others claim to tell the past and future by placing a mirror under a pyramid.

Advocates of pyramid power claim proper use of these geometric forms can also sweeten water, mummify bodies, maintain the fragrance of flowers, sharpen razor blades, prevent foods from molding, and actually alter molecular structure. How? Pyramids are believed to be antennae that pick up frequencies of universal energy. The power is said to be most effective when the substance to be affected is placed a third of the distance below the apex.

The healing power of pyramids is supposedly based on the prismatic effect of certain rocks and the tiny electrical charge they emit when rubbed. Thus, rubbing a rock pyramid produces an electrical field that combines with the body's electrical forces to change cellular structure. The pyramid may be an open or closed structure composed of stone, wood, plastic, or metal.

STRAIGHT ANSWERS

Q: *Isn't medical science too disease-oriented and impersonal, whereas holistic healers are more sensitive?*

A: Technological advances have altered the bedside manner of physicians so that it is often detached, peering at patients through reports instead of a stethoscope. But the fact that New Age techniques seem more personalized does not necessarily mean they are more effective. The ultimate issue regarding health care should not be the patient's emotional comfort but the quality of the treatment he receives.

Q: *If some holistic healing is in the mind, how dangerous is the placebo effect?*

A: From a natural standpoint, there is danger a patient will accept the apparent absence of symptoms and presume a cure has been effected. Spiritually speaking, if the therapy is of the occult and administered by a healer under mystical influence, the encounter could result in psychic oppression.

Q: *Isn't holistic health more biblical than traditional medicine, since it considers the soul and spirit?*

A: Recognizing people have a soul and spirit does not mean those elements are properly acknowledged or treated with sanctity. New Age healers revere the spirit because they believe it is a spark of the divine, not because they honor biblical warnings against clairvoyant practices. Holism in medical treatment is good if conducted by a Christian therapist who treats the spirit as the eternal aspect God breathed into man.

Q: *When considering a healing therapy, how crucial is it to consider its historical source?*

A: Job 14:4 warns us, "Who can bring a clean thing out of an unclean? No one!" James 3:11 adds, "Does a spring send forth fresh water and bitter from the same opening?" In some cases, a practice may be divorced from its pagan historical roots and redefined within a newly applicable frame of reference. If the practitioner makes no such distinction, there may be serious harm in store for those who are spiritually vulnerable. For example, an acupuncturist who is a devout Taoist and inserts the needles with occult intent is historically consistent despite his contemporary use of the treatment. Thus, the advisability of receiving care from such a person is questionable.

Q: *If crystals have vibratory properties, isn't it reasonable to assume they would resonate with the body's energy?*

A: The vibratory capacity of crystals is a fact of physics, but the concept of the body's compatible vibratory response is mere inference. Science has yet to prove that measurable electromagnetic or biocosmic forces resonate in the body. Thus, any suggestion of a sympathetic reaction between a quartz rock and human flesh is conjectural.

Q: *How are the various uses of crystals explained?*

A: None of the claims made by advocates of crystals has been accepted by the scientific community. Validation for such assertions rests solely on the questionable proof of personal testimony. It must be assumed, therefore, that the power of crystals is in the mind of the beholder. Anticipatory autosuggestion has a way of fulfilling self-made prophecies. If a person thinks a crystal will do a certain thing, in all likelihood such expectations will be satisfied, even if it means altering circumstances to produce "proof."

Q: *Why are so many well-informed and famous people buying crystals if there is nothing to them?*

A: Celebrities often suffer poor self-esteem and become fascinated with fads to sublimate their need for personal identity. Whatever the latest rage may be, they tend to hop onto the bandwagon. They are often exploited by those who realize celebrity endorsement carries weight in the marketing arena.

Q: *Can the use of acupuncture be divorced from its pagan and occult background?*

A: That depends on the practitioner's motives. Any act rooted in the occult and executed with that purpose opens one to spiritual danger. Certainly, one should not seek an acupuncture treatment from a Chinese Taoist, who could unwittingly invoke evil supernatural forces while attempting to bring physical relief. It is best to avoid such therapies as acupuncture until the medical community has had ample opportunity to perform further research. In the absence of any collectively acceptable anatomical explanation, the risk of engaging in an occult act suggests caution. Anyone desiring to pursue acupuncture therapy should consult a licensed practitioner, preferably one who professes faith in Christ and applies the technique on a purely medical basis.

Q: *Of the various theories explaining acupuncture, which is the most logical and widely accepted?*

A: None has preeminence, although the so-called nerve-gate theory is popular. This hypothesis suggests that needle stimulation affects synapses, the nerve junctions where pain impulses are transferred. Deriving a comprehensive hypothesis that accounts for both the remedial and analgesic benefits of acupuncture is difficult. Scientists are puzzled that a simple needle insertion seems to halt pain and also heal an organic disorder. One possible explanation with serious implications is that the force of chi is a form of alien supernatural energy that is invoked by a Taoist acupuncturist.

Q: *Is there any spiritual danger in seeing an acupuncturist to cure an ailment medical doctors have not treated successfully?*

A: The practitioner may be a mere technician, inserting needles according to a meridian chart with no commitment to a Taoist view of yin and yang. In that case, the risk is minimal, and the "remedy" may be psychosomatic. Danger is involved if the acupuncturist pays homage to the spiritualist tradition of his craft.

Q: *What kind of energy do healers manipulate when they claim to redistribute an electromagnetic force in the body?*

A: In most cases, the energy is a figment in their minds. Psychic healers are elixir salesmen, dispensing hope in the form of exotic maneuvers of the hands. But it cannot be discounted that transcendental powers can be conjured, since occult healing aligns philosophically with the forces of Satan's kingdom.

Q: *If therapeutic touch healing requires no faith or religious commitment, what harm can it inflict?*

A: Even if religious overtones are absent, that doesn't mean an act is irreligious. Contact with the spirit world doesn't depend on explicit overtures to demons. That's why biblical passages such as Deuteronomy 18 sternly denounce divinatory practices. Participation in such occult deeds may open one's life to deception. Consequently, if a healer is laying on hands in similar fashion as commanded in James 5, but without the restriction of a defined petition to Christ as Lord, the danger of acquiring demonic assistance is very real.

Q: *What is wrong with music therapy if David played his harp to soothe the despondency of Saul?*

A: The curative power of David's music had nothing to do with the vibrations of notes on the shepherd's harp resonating with Saul's mind and emotions. Scripture plainly tells us that the king's desolation resulted from the influence of an evil entity. It was the God David worshiped and the Holy Spirit his music invoked who calmed King Saul's restless soul. Christianity recognizes the power of music to lift the human spirit in praise to God. But nowhere in the Bible is music presented as a sacred science to orchestrate health. This is an occult idea. Today's advocates of music therapy are sonic shamans who use musical magic.

Q: *Can psychic surgeons place their hands inside a patient's body?*

A: The phenomenon has never been demonstrated satisfactorily to critics. Such surgery is usually performed in dimly lit conditions where a high sense of expectation inhibits critical analysis of the event. Various kinds of witch doctors and shamans have claimed such abilities, and there is no reason to assume all of them represent a collective conspiracy of lies. Perhaps some occult practitioners possess the powers of materialization and dematerialization and can insert their hands into a person's body to remove something without signs of scarring or bleeding. Most psychic surgeons, however, probably rely on sleight of hand to accomplish their deeds.

Q: *So long as his cure is not considered final, is it harmful to visit a psychic surgeon?*

A: A suffering person is in an emotionally vulnerable condition. He desperately wants help, and it is unfair to tamper with his feelings by offering false hope. Most psychic surgeons operate under the influence of spirit guides, and submitting to their strategies could result in various forms of spiritual bondage.

Q: *Is the form of a pyramid sacred, or is it merely a geometric figure without spiritual or supernatural significance?*

A: There is no evidence in Scripture or physics to suggest that the shape of an object inherently imbeds it with supranormal powers. Shapes have an effect only if the one attaching such significance really believes power resides in forms. In that case, the convictions of the adherent produce effects, not the shape of the objects.

Q: *Why have Egypt's pyramids been credited with so many different kinds of powers?*

A: Because of their size and age, pyramids engender awe. After all, they are the oldest surviving man-made structures on earth. In addition, the religion of the ancient Egyptians was integrally tied to the pyramids, lending an aura of mystery. Thus, those involved in New Age and mystery school cults assume pyramids have secret powers known to the Egyptians of old and experienced by us today, though we cannot explain their power.

WHO'S WHO AND WHAT'S WHAT

Acupressure: The practice of using pressure applied by fingertips to activate acupuncture points without inserting a needle.

Acupuncture: An ancient Chinese healing art, based on the theory that physiological health is present only when the life energy force of the universe flows uninterrupted through the body, an equilibrium that can be maintained by the twisting insertion of needles at specified points.

Chi: According to mysticism, the life-giving energy force of the cosmos, composed of opposites known as yin and yang, which flow in all living things and enter the human body through channels known as meridians.

Clairvoyance: A psychic phenomenon whereby one possessing such abilities receives extrasensory information about events or circumstances of the past, present, or future.

Cosmic Energy: In metaphysics, an undefined force in the universe by which all living beings have their subsistence, the presence of which ensures health and welfare.

Crystals: Quartz rocks possessing highly predictable vibratory properties that make them useful in science, thus leading to the assumption they can sympathetically effect similar vibrations in the mind, body, and emotions of an individual.

Ear Acupuncture: A form of auricular therapy based on the concept that the ear is shaped like a fetus-in-utero and is a microcosm that contains reference points by which the body can be affected.

Electromagnetic Healing: The theory that an electrical force animates the body, and that its proper stabilization contributes to health and healing.

Kirlian Photography: A technique developed in 1939 by a Russian electrician and amateur photographer named S. D. Kirlian. It uses photographic plates to register invisible phenomena, such as the corona of an aura surrounding the human body or a portion of the body, such as the hand.

Kreiger, Delores: Originator and popularizer of the therapeutic touch theory.

Meridian: In acupuncture, a pathway in the body similar to the circulatory system, through which the universal life-energy flows.

Mind Science: A religious philosophy based on the ideas of Ernest Holmes, who denied orthodox Christian doctrines in favor of promoting the possibility of "Christ-realization" by all men.

New Thought: A late 1800s philosophy of mental healing promoted by Warren Felt Evans, who influenced Mary Baker Eddy, founder of Christian Science, and Charles and Myrtle Fillmore, who founded Unity.

Prana: The power whereby everything in the universe exists, known as chi in Taoism and vital breath in Hinduism.

Psychic Surgery: The practice of bloodless surgery done without scalpels and incisions by means of the healer's placing his hands inside the patient's body to repair damaged organs or remove diseased tissue.

Psychometry: The clairvoyant art of deriving information from inanimate objects, such as a psychic's locating a lost person by holding an object he wore and picking up the vibrations of where he can be found.

Pythagoras: Ancient Greek mathematician and philosopher who developed theories on the inherent mathematical structure of music and its power to affect emotions.

Reiki: An occult form of healing by laying hands on a person to send the forces of recuperation to another person at a distant location (see Chap. 12).

Taoism: A Chinese religious philosophy founded in the sixth century B.C. by Lao-Tse, who taught that the *tao* ("the way of virtue") is an eternal, all-pervasive harmonizing force in the universe.

Therapeutic Touch: A form of spiritualistic healing asserting that by properly passing hands over a patient's body, his energy can be properly distributed to acquire health and long life.

Unified Field Theory: A concept of physics suggesting that an underlying principle guides all physical phenomena and is embodied in a single force that ensures stability and peace in the universe.

Visualization Healing: A form of New Age consciousness intimating that the natural healing processes of the body can be accelerated and activated by right thinking.

Yang: One half of the chi force, representing male, light, positive qualities.

Yin: One half of the chi force, representing female, dark, negative qualities.

IN MY OPINION

New Age healing techniques are increasing in popularity. More than one million patients a year in Great Britain consult some form of psychic healing. In fact, 1,500 English hospital administrative boards have granted permission for spiritualist healers to enter hospitals and render healing services to patients.

The preposterous claims of New Age healing arts were previously relegated to the realm of charlatanism or shamanism. Today they are often accepted by medical doctors who are concerned about alleviating suffering and who have abandoned their commitment to empirically proved therapies. Thus, they experiment with the nonrational so long as it seems to improve health. But rational evaluation must once again become a trademark in medicine.

Doctors must recognize that since creation is the manifestation of a rational Creator, the healing processes he lovingly provides will also work rationally. Further, doctors should not ignore the penalty humanity pays for disregarding moral law. Instead of recommending massage therapies and exotic cures, physicians should tell people to quit smoking, curb their appetites, shift from fat to fiber, exercise sedentary bodies, cut out alcohol, and honor the Lord who made them. Scripture also tells us that improperly discerning the Lord's body results in much sickness. When have you heard a doctor ask if you had properly examined yourself spiritually before taking communion?

Before seeking a non-Christian source of supernatural healing, an important question should be: "Where did the sickness originate?" While not every sick person has fallen under the attack of the devil, some sicknesses result from direct satanic assault. The Bible also points out that since in a broad sense all sickness is a result of sin, all disease is thus indirectly the work of the devil.

Acts 10:38 tells us Jesus healed all that were "oppressed by the devil." Their relief came not by redistributing some form of bioenergy, but by removing Satan's domination over their bodies. Scripture says Christ healed because "God was with Him."[13] Before letting anyone lay hands on them, patients seeking solace should find out what god is with the healer and the source from which the psychic solicits healing.

The psychosomatic link between the body and mind is unquestionable. Thus, there is nothing inherently wrong with considering a "holistic" approach to healing, if by doing so one recognizes the trinitarian nature of man, knowing that healing must touch every aspect of one's life. Proverbs 17:22 says, "A merry heart does good, like medicine." But Christ did more than preach positive mental imagery. He didn't use autosuggestions to eradicate symptoms. Christ wasn't a placebo for the diseased and dying. Matthew 4:23 tells us he healed *all* forms of illness.

While there is nothing intrinsically evil about holistic healing, its New Age application is suspect for Christians. For example, one occult healer described holism as "a point of view about the universe . . . the joy of creativity, the knowing of consciousness, the fulfillment of self-actualization."[14] Obviously, the anatomical investigation of organic causes of illness has nothing to do with this philosophically stylized approach to health.

Supernaturalism has long been an arm of false religion. Jannes and Jambres withstood Moses with their miracles. The apostle Paul, in 2 Timothy 3:8, used these occult magicians as an example of those who "resist the truth." Thus, no matter how beneficial the deeds of New Age healers seem, they ultimately oppose God's truth about the origin of illness and the identity of man's true Healer. They may call their healing arts holism, but the Bible calls it sorcery (see Deut. 18:10, 11).

Satan is prepared to promise physical health in exchange for disobedience to God. In Eden, he offered the ultimate incentive to Eve: "You will not surely die."[15] But Satan's pledge of health and healing is bogus. He temporarily relieves physical affliction by transferring the malady to the emotional, psychic realm. Those who have been to New Age healers often experience assuagement of physical pain, but usually it is followed by emotional torment or an accentuated interest in the occult, drawing them deeper into the devil's snare. Thus, New Age healing, which denies Christ as Creator, Redeemer, and Healer, merely exchanges an adversity on the organic level for torment on the spiritual level.

Certainly, some nonorganic illnesses can be cured by suggestion. Even the symptoms of serious diseases can be temporarily alleviated by holistic hocus-pocus. But those who accept these healing practices seldom investigate how the same patients might have done with conventional medical care.

Chapter 4

EYE, EAR, AND FOOT DOCTORS

Straight Answers on New Age Medical Methods

"I had AIDS and healed myself."

The voice belongs to Wil Garcia. The sound comes from a small color TV sitting on the altar of a United Methodist church. Then the face of Wil's lover, George, appears on the screen. "I've never had more energy. I've never been happier with my life," George says.

Wil and George are part of a crudely constructed video about overcoming AIDS with holistic self-healing and mental imagery being shown to an audience of more than 250 people. In the five-minute video, prelude to a full-blown documentary, the two homosexuals say they were cured by New Age visualization processes and meditation sessions, during which they imagined the AIDS virus leaving their bodies.[1]

The newest information on New Age healing methods is as current as the latest trip to a New Age bookstore. *Superimmunity, Who Gets Sick (How Thoughts and Beliefs Affect Your Health), The Mind as Healer (The New Heresy), Heal Your Body (The Mental Causes for Physical Illness and the Metaphysical Way to Overcome Them),* and *Imagery in Healing (Shamanism and Modern Medicine)* are just a few of the titles on the shelves. New Age alternative health therapies run the gamut from facial brushing (to cure headaches) to discerning the "psychospiritual" nature of disease. The "psychoimmunity" of illness is sought, and dandelions are eaten to cure kidney stones.

New Age healing theories are based on several suppositions. First is the idea that the body will always naturally heal itself. No matter what the disease, restoring the body's energies to a proper equilibrium allows natural healing to occur. Second, New Agers concur that negative physical realities are the result of projected thoughts. The particular therapy is not as important as the belief in its efficacy. In the words of one New Age healer, "We have to work with both body and mind, so that the nonmaterial concept of health is manifested in our material being."[2]

Approaches to New Age healing can be summarized in several categories:

Self-Healing: The patient's perception is considered more important than the viral nature of the disease. Laughter, courage, tenacity, and control are emotional factors governing the body's ability to self-heal. Maladaptive tension puts the body into a state of imbalance. Proper relaxation rebalances the body without intervention of outside chemicals.

Prevention: Proper diet is a major consideration, including some exotic advice. Many New Agers borrow from the Edgar Cayce readings and ingest ragweed for improving elimination and liver function. Dandelion leaves and roots are considered nutritive herbs. Three times as many vegetables that grow above the ground should be consumed compared to those that grow below the ground. New Agers also say that mixing certain food types is taboo. For instance, meat and starch should never be eaten at the same meal.

Imagery: Just as placebos trigger positive mental attitudes toward certain therapies, so it is believed that an adjusted perspective can affect biochemistry. Simply said, the power of suggestion was the secret of shamans and the best way to facilitate the body's positive powers of health. Disease is seen as a necessary karmic force to teach those unprepared to leave the earthly plane of existence. Those who are ready to realize their personal responsibility for choices, including the option to accept the divine within, may no longer have need of sickness and can dwell in a continual state of wellness.

Nutrition: "You are what you eat." That adage guides the New Age approach to cooking. Avoiding chemically treated foods and retaining nutrients in preparation are cardinal considerations. Packaging procedures, canning processes, and freezing techniques are all carefully monitored. The yin-yang quality of each food is also analyzed to examine its spiritual constituents.

Bodywork: This New Age term refers to the necessity of an appropriate balance between the body and mind for continuing health. Its extreme form promises agelessness and youthful vigor. The body is seen as a reflection of life's experiences and spiritual progress. Techniques such as massage, yoga, aikido, T'ai Chi, and psychostructural balancing of the body are said to permit one's internal physiology to retain health.

MACROBIOTICS

"Some kind of world government could enforce law on the international level, resolving relationships between countries and blocs, then that would relieve world tension."[3]

That sweeping conclusion isn't unusual for a New Age theoretician. But it is in this case. The words were spoken by Michio Kushi, foremost proponent of the macrobiotic way of life. In fact, Kushi sees an active interplay between diet and government. Kushi was a confidant and adviser to President Carter's late sister, Ruth Carter Stapleton, and declared her cancer would be cured by application of his visualization and macrobiotic techniques.

In Kushi's words, "What is necessary in order to create one happy, peaceful world? That question is the subject matter of macrobiotics, the study of the Unifying Principle . . . that deals with yin and yang, or balance, the basic order of the universe on all levels—spiritual, social, individual, and biochemical."[4]

Food as the way to world peace? That astounding assumption is the root of macrobiotics. In essence, macrobiotics is an Oriental approach to eating organically. It comes from two Greek words: *macro,* meaning "large," and *bios,* referring to the science of life. Thus, macrobiotics proposes to blend eating with the macrocosmic order of the universe by carefully controlling food selection, preparation, and consumption.

Philosophically, macrobiotics is based on the idea that all energy in the universe alternates harmoniously between opposites—night and day, male and female, light and dark, yin and yang. This Taoistic approach supposedly applies to foods, harmonizing spirituality through diet. Preventing Illness and arresting degenerative diseases are just two of the presumed benefits. There have been claims of heart disease and cancer cures.

Macrobiotics is more than a way to eat. It is a way of life. Its deference to ecological balance presumably achieves a oneness with the environment. This unity is precursory to a dynamic balance with other areas of life, including psychology, education, politics, and economics. The ultimate goal is world federalism and planetary unity. In the words of one macrobiotic proponent, "Planet Earth is surrounded by and immersed in a vibrational body of energy, which is conscious. The foci are 'power points' . . . sacred places, such as the pyramids, Stonehenge, etc." Eating macrobiotically places one in harmony with this "etheric web of consciousness."[5]

Macrobiotics suggests that 50 to 60 percent of the diet should consist of whole grains. Another 5 to 10 percent should include beans, bean products, and sea vegetables. Foods should be grown without chemicals and used in their natural state. This diet must be accompanied by daily exercise and spiritual practices of meditation and prayer, along with an appreciation of nature. In Michio Kushi's estimation, this will establish a "peaceful, universal mentality," because macrobiotics "provides a universal compass, yin and yang." According to Kushi, you can then "become an angel or a devil, as you wish."[6]

HOMEOPATHY

George Guess was an M.D. until the North Carolina board of medical examiners revoked his license to practice medicine. A graduate of the Medical College of Virginia, Guess became the first American physician whose license was rescinded because of practicing homeopathy.[7] The result was a head-on legal collision between the medical establishment and this centuries-old therapy.

The principle of homeopathy is the paradoxical law of similars. Each physical condition is treated with a substance that, given in large quantities, could cause the condition. Most homeotherapeutics avoid antibiotics and allopathic drugs in favor of the more than a thousand remedies of minute doses of natural substances from the plant, animal, and mineral kingdoms. Although considered a fringe form of medicine, homeopathy supports twenty-two homeopathic schools in America and is recognized by law in three states.[8]

Other countries have adopted a more favorable attitude. The English royal family consults homeopaths. In the 1930s, King George was so enamored with homeopathy that he named one of his racing horses Hypericum, the name of a popular homeopathic medicine. Today, Queen Elizabeth II is the patron to the Royal London Homeopathic Hospital. In Germany, the practice has been popular since the early nineteenth century. In France, over 6,000 physicians actively practice homeopathy, and at least 18,000 pharmacies sell homeopathic medicines. The Brazilian government requires schools of pharmacy to teach homeopathy. Two medical schools in Mexico offer complete homeopathic curricula.[9]

An eighteenth-century German physician named Samuel Hahnemann discovered that, if too much of a substance caused a symptom, a minute dose of that substance sometimes cured the symptom. Under his care, patients who were dying (after receiving traditional medical assistance) were cured. It was Hahnemann who coined the Latin phrase *similia similibus curentur* ("Let likes be cured with likes"). It became known as homeopathy from the Greek words *homoios,* for "similar," and *pathos,* for "disease."

Homeopaths say their practice isn't unusual. Even medical science knows that inoculations against smallpox, measles, and polio involve small doses of the offending viruses. In homeopathy, other natural substances are used to stimulate the body into healing itself. The usual dose is either 6x or 30x, the x referring to the number of times the substance has been diluted in a ratio of one part remedy to ten parts distilled water. The trick, say homeopaths, is finding the right medicine for each case. Also crucial is potentization, an exacting method of dilution that involves successive thinning of the substance, accompanied with vigorous shaking.

Unlike allopathic medical doctors, who see illness as a negative intrusion, homeopaths believe disease is a positive fight for health, the natural effort of the body to maintain a homeostatic balance. According to homeopathy, treating symptoms is bad because it suppresses the body's natural healing responses. The homeopath prescribes a catalyst that imitates the body's defenses and stimulates the body's responses. Unlike conventional drugs, which have a direct effect on the physiological processes related to the patient's systems, homeopathic medicines are thought to work by stimulating the immune system. Homeopaths also deny that a single virus is responsible for illness. Instead, they look to the holistic integration of mind and body to cure all physical and emotional states.

REFLEXOLOGY/IRIDOLOGY

"This little piggie went to market, this little—" Just then, your mother pulled the tip of your toe and you sneezed. Know why? Reflexologists have an answer. Your sinuses correlate to the reflex points on the extremities of your toes. If you believe that, there are even more fantastic accounts to dazzle your mind and tickle your toes.

Envision the sole of the foot as a microcosm of the body. Beginning at the big toe (the head), follow down the foot as if it were a corresponding replica of the thoracic and abdominal regions. Near the ball of the foot are the lungs. Farther down come the liver, gall bladder, and colon. Then assume that each sympathetic location of a body organ has a nerve ending at the exact representational spot on the sole. If the kidneys are near the arch and the coinciding nerve endings leading to the kidney are located there, a renal dysfunction can be treated by massaging and stimulating this part of the foot. This system is known as reflexology.

Iridology follows the same microcosmic principles. In this case, the eye's iris supposedly displays the status of every internal organ and records past and present states of health and disease. Though practiced in ancient societies and popular in Europe in the nineteenth century, Americans ignored iridology until the 1904 publication of *Iridology, the Diagnosis from the Eye* by Dr. Henry Lahn. Until then, iridology had been considered irrational, akin to palmistry and phrenology. Today, it is a staple of naturopaths and many chiropractors and has gained considerable popularity among New Age healers.

Like reflexologists, iridologists consider the iris representational of all organs of the body. The top of the head is exemplified by the top of the iris, and the foot by the bottom of the iris. Other areas of the body are appropriately arranged with respect to their positions in the human physical structure. Instead of employing biopsies, blood tests, X-rays, and exploratory surgery, the iridologist says he only has to examine the eye to pinpoint specific organs needing treatment.

Both reflexologists and iridologists are forced to admit there is no physiological basis for assuming that corresponding nerve pathways lead from the eye or foot to relevant body parts. How, then, are diagnoses made? Dr. James Carter, a noted iridologist, who has researched the practice for fourteen years, says some conclusions are paranormal. Carter declares that perfecting the technique involves the use of "intuition . . . a kind of hyperconscious or ultraconscious state."[10]

Just how is the microcosmic representation and the corresponding organ or body portion connected? No one knows. Some kind of invisible pathway is assumed usually on the philosophical basis that all is God and God is all. But from the standpoint of neurology, such a pathway has never been confirmed. In spite of all this, reflexologists and iridologists concur that certain zones of the body (hands, feet, ears, eyes) are the loci for diagnostic intervention that circumvents intrusive, traumatic methods of traditional medicine.

POLARITY THERAPY

The patient lay on a cushioned table with pillows under his head and knees. Slowly, the therapist pressed his thumbs into the subject's feet, ribs, head, and stomach. At times, he used slow massage. Occasionally, his hands seemed to float over the patient's body. The practitioner explained, "Energy flows through your body, and energy controls the metabolism and the structure of the body. The body has an energy field around it. In Polarity Therapy, what we do is balance that energy."[11]

Polarity Therapy, "acupuncture without needles," was started by Dr. Randolph Stone (1890–1981), Chiropractor and Doctor of Osteopathy, who declared, "The art of the true healer must be to balance man with Nature, tune him into the greater energy field, so all the elements can flow and function. That is how Nature heals."[12]

In Polarity Therapy, the head and feet are considered positive and negative poles. Various other organs and tissues exist in polarity relationship. For example, the positive pole of the kidneys is the shoulder, while the negative pole is the ankles. During massage, tenderness or pain indicates an area where energy is blocked. As with acupuncture, Polarity Therapy has its own loci, where hand manipulation supposedly releases energy flow.

Polarity Therapy is based on Stone's version of dualistic symmetry. To visualize Dr. Stone's theory, imagine the body as a long coil of electromagnetic wires. There are vertical currents running from head to foot, flowing down the right side of the body, then up the back, and up the left side and down the back. Horizontal currents flow east to west; dual, serpentine currents descend from the brain, crossing at different areas of the spine to form energy centers. In Dr. Stone's words, "The location of this energy is in the core of the brain and the spinal cord, where it exists as a highly vibrating, intense etheric essence of a neuter polarity as a molecular energy, this being the key to the entire structure and function of the body."[13]

When the body's energy flow is inhibited, Polarity Therapy teaches that circulation decreases, resulting in pain, tension, and emotional difficulties. The patient is encouraged to "go with nature" rather than running from pain. Polarity Therapy practitioners carefully explain that "the techniques are not magical, psychic, or medical, nor are they tied to any particular religious belief."[14]

Such protestations aside, Polarity Therapy is distinctly Eastern. Dr. Stone has informed his students,

> The emoting done by the patient while you hold one of the polarity reflexes is the karmic result of previous actions lodged here as discordant energy factors and condensed crystallization. Tell the patient that it is literally paying for sins committed when one undergoes the treatment for the release of energy blocks accumulated, like unfulfilled obligations and debts.[15]

The basic training course for Polarity Therapy dwells considerably on metaphysical concepts. The energy therapists presume to balance what is called prana, the energy of the soul that originates in "the Spiritual Realms." Instructors teach how to "read" the body, noting the shape of the patient, to discern what energy imbalances are present. Students are advised to program the "Soul Energy" properly to appropriately influence the mind. Eventually, posturing exercises are taught, along with elimination techniques for the bowels, urine, sweat, breath, and emotions.

NATUROPATHY

The patient had little, red spots on his ankles. At the local clinic, he was given a blood pressure test and precious little of the doctor's time. All the physician could say was, "You're a little hyper, aren't you?"

The patient then consulted a naturopathic doctor (N.D.). The diagnosis? Schamberg's disease. The N.D. recommended that the patient soak a cloth with witch hazel and apply it to the afflicted area fifteen minutes daily. The herb's astringent properties were supposed to strengthen the hemorrhaging capillaries. It worked.[16]

As with Homeopathy, many proponents of Naturopathy don't have anything to do with the New Age Movement. Naturopathy is used by New Agers but is not inherently New Age.

Across the country, Naturopathy is fast becoming a choice for the ill, especially those who have read glowing reports in various New Age journals. One reason for this popularity is the attitude of conventional physicians, who are trained for crisis intervention but have little regard for preventive medicine. On the other hand, medical doctors still view naturopathy as quackery and an insult to scientific medicine.

The term *naturopathy* was coined in 1895 by John H. Scheel, but the main proponent of the practice was a German named Benedict Lust, an osteopath, M.D., and naturopath. He primarily promoted hygienics and hydrotherapy. Lust wrote, "We plead for the renouncing of poisons from the coffee, white flour, glucose, lard, and like venom of the American table."[17]

In 1919, Lust founded the American Naturopathic Association. His concepts remained popular until 1937, when sulfa drugs were used to fight infections. American fascination with miracle drugs and crisis medicine left naturopathy out of favor. Some states declared its practices a misdemeanor. Diploma mills and bogus naturopathic schools further tarnished the art's reputation. Much has changed since Naturopathy fell into disrepute. Today, seven states and the District of Columbia have legislative authority to examine and license naturopaths.[18]

The New Age Movement's return to less technologically sophisticated health remedies spurred new interest in Naturopathy. Predictably, Aquarian (or New Age) naturopaths employ an eclectic variety of disciplines, which can include homeopathy, hypnotherapy, acupuncture, and iridology. Though some naturopaths order blood or urine tests, most naturopaths disdain interventionism, preferring nonintrusive, preventive methods of dietary and herbal remedies. To quote one advocate, "Naturopathy is a method of curing disease by releasing inner vitality and allowing the body to heal itself."[19]

MISCELLANEOUS THERAPIES

Rolfing: Sometimes known as "structural integration," rolfing is a method of physical manipulation invented in the 1930s by a biochemist named Ida Rolf. By using hands and elbows, the practitioner maneuvers connective tissues to achieve "synchronicity" of the entire person—physical, emotional, psychological, and psychic.

Rolf therapists are trained at the Institute of Structural Integration in Boulder, Colorado. They are instructed in ten treatments designed to move the fasciae and reintegrate the head, chest, hips, and legs in a series of ten one-hour sessions. The patient is promised a more erect and supple body. Spiritually, rolfers believe that by removing distortions the body has acquired through aging, the subject may experience spontaneous flashes of intuitive insight and psychic phenomena. Some patients complain of intensive pain, which practitioners say is necessary to unleash the inner transformation.

Chromotherapy: Color therapy has been used by psychics to view auras. Theosophists use it as a method of spiritual diagnosis. Some say it originated with Egyptian sun worship. In modern times, the idea has been popularized by Rosicrucians and spiritualists. Designers, doctors, and psychotherapists acknowledge that colors may indeed affect psychological (if not physiological) health. Some colors definitely are soothing, while others seem to invigorate. But color therapists carry these principles further to suggest that certain colors emit rays that seers and clairvoyants see spiritually to determine the condition of the body and soul. In addition to treating patients by discerning their response to certain colors, therapists may request the subject to hold an object of a specified color to alleviate an organic disorder.

Orgonomy: Developed by psychoanalyst William Reich, orgonomy proposes that all psychological disorders stem from blocked "orgone" energy. Reich taught that this energy was the biological form of a universal energy responsible for everything from the movement of the stars to sexual orgasms. He built what was called an orgone box, a cabinet made of layered steel wool and other materials, which he said would collect orgone energy and transmit it to the patients sitting inside. The federal Food and Drug Administration and other authorities eventually jailed him for distributing the device. Various New Age techniques have been adapted from Reich's ideas, including Alexander Lowen's concept of "bioenergetics." Reich also taught that an invasion of UFOs was polluting earth's atmosphere. Reich's fascination with orgasmic energy has been resurrected by some New Age behavioral psychologists.

Herbology: In a world of health care dominated by harsh chemical drugs with serious side effects, some are returning to the idea that medicines from the earth are the best way to health and healing. Herbologists believe their prescriptions better support the body's natural immunization system and are preferable to drugs for the body to assimilate and use. Some herbs can treat several disorders, or the same herb can be used in combination with other herbs. Common uses are as decongestants (ephedra), laxatives (cascara sagrada and senna leaf), and digestive aids (papaya, ginger, and chamomile).

Ayurveda: Widely practiced in India for five thousand years, Ayurveda is believed by many New Agers to be the first and most accurate form of holistic healing. The term *Ayurveda* comes from Sanskrit, meaning "science of life." Based on classical Hinduism, Ayurveda teaches that the individual existence of each life is indivisible from the "macrocosmic manifestation." Health and disease are considered in the broader context of the relationship between individual souls and the cosmic spirit.

According to Ayurveda, each person has four instincts: religion, finances, procreation, and freedom. Balanced health must fulfill all four. Once that is achieved through diet, yoga, and adherence to Hindu philosophy, self-healing balances the body's energies and retards the onslaught of illness. Ayurveda is often combined with Hindu tantric sexual philosophies to achieve ultimate union with truth. As acupuncture seeks to balance yin and yang, Ayurveda aspires to a symmetry between the Hindu god Lord Shiva (yin) and the goddess Shakti (yang).

STRAIGHT ANSWERS

Q: *Can macrobiotics be considered strictly a method of food preparation, separate from its globalistic associations?*

A: Technically, yes. Practically, no. Most people become involved with a macrobiotic diet because of its philosophical approach to life, not for nutritional reasons. They tend to accept the larger approach to macrobiotics, which adopts a pantheistic world view. This outlook is intrinsically federalistic because it denigrates individualism in favor of planetary oneness. Thus, the way one eats tends to influence the way one thinks.

Q: *Can one eat macrobiotically without encountering any spiritual danger?*

A: Yes, but at great risk. Macrobiotics is steeped in Oriental metaphysical ideas. Directives concerning macrobiotic cooking abound with testimonies about abatement of fears and phobias and the adoption of a more positive outlook on life. Such transformation ignores God's grace, received by repentance of sinful behavior. Instead, macrobiotics promotes almost miraculous well-being by achieving evolutionary spiritual consciousness. Further, the dualistic approach toward life and nature contradicts biblical principles of mankind's relationship to God and His environment. Those who eat macrobiotically often adopt a mystical worldview.

Q: *Have cases of serious disease been resolved by a macrobiotic diet?*

A: Documented testimony claims that properly balancing the yin and yang (acidity and alkalinity) of foods has brought cancer into remission and rejuvenated health. In a celebrated case, Dr. Anthony Sattilaro, president of Methodist Hospital in Philadelphia, claimed to be cured of prostatic cancer that had metastasized in the brain. Such results are probably due to improved eating habits rather than harmony with biocosmic forces. The diet of most Americans is so abysmal that any use of organic vegetables and more sensible consumption of food is likely to produce health benefits.

Q: *If macrobiotics is helpful physically, why not adopt its nutritional practices?*

A: There is great danger that its attendant philosophy will also be accepted. The book *Macrobiotics: An Invitation to Health and Happiness* declares, "It is based on the realization that only you are the master of yourself—not bacteria, doctors, scientists, ministers, philosophers, or dieticians."[20] Those who wish to obtain the health benefits of macrobiotics must avoid accompanying non-Christian philosophical indoctrination.

Q: *Does anything in the homeopathic definition of health invalidate it as a form of therapy?*

A: Homeopaths believe physical health is accompanied by mental health. They conclude, therefore, that organic disorders manifest emotional disturbances. While partially true, the exacting way homeopaths categorize such illnesses leads them to claim cures for conditions that demand spiritual healing. For example, heart ailments (physical dysfunctions) reportedly produce destructive delirium (emotional illness). Such an approach is too rigid in its direct connection between the physical and the emotional. It ignores certain mental-spiritual sicknesses that only the Lord can resolve, such as depression resulting from guilt due to sin.

Q: *Isn't the homeopathic treatment of a single source of illness medically sound?*

A: Not necessarily, especially if the homeopath is committed to New Age ideas. Suppose the patient suffers from a headache, stomachache, and depression. Homeopaths commonly use a single medicine because the person is presumed to have one disease, an underlying susceptibility. This is based on the occult idea that well-being is a state of unitary harmony with a balanced cosmos. Homeopaths may ignore the actual viral intrusion that precipitated the disease and cause the condition to worsen by failing to treat it.

Q: *Is homeopathy scientific, anti-Christian, or occult?*

A: It is definitely not scientific. The process of diluting by potentization is so extreme (sometimes as much as one thousand times) that it is unlikely any significant amount of the original substance remains. There is no proof that an electromagnetic discharge is released by the shaking procedure. Originally, homeopathy proposed an idea approximating the Christian idea of illness, that sin in fallen man causes spiritual estrangement from God, which triggers susceptibility to disease at the core of his being. New Age homeopathy has slightly altered this concept to suggest that the core of illness results not from a person's being sinfully diseased, but rather from his alienation from his true self (i.e., the god within). The belief in a universal life energy force from which health automatically springs is common to New Agers who espouse homeopathy. Some believe it is the vibrational frequency of the dosage to which the patient is responding.

Q: *Why are so many Christians attracted to homeopathy?*

A: Its idea that all illness has a single, fundamental source squares nicely with the biblical stance that all humanity's dysfunctions have a single derivation, sin. In addition, many Christians are skeptical of the medical establishment because of its humanistic approach to behavior and its overdependence on mood-altering drugs. Because of the doubtful effect of homeopathy's diluted dosages, however, Christians must wonder if the effectiveness of homeopathy is due to a psychometric (placebo) cure, a magical response in which homeopathic medicine serves the role of an occult talisman.

Q: *Is there a scientific basis for reflexology and iridology?*

A: No. Anatomically, the theories are unproved. They operate on the basis of a schematic or homunculus approach, which considers certain portions of the human anatomy as miniatures of the whole body (the sole of the foot, eye iris, ear structure). Reflexologists sense tension or heat in the bottom of the foot, indicating dysfunction in the parallel portion of the body. Iridologists measure the texture, pigmentation, and density of the iris, which supposedly links to its corresponding tissue represented by this reflex. In short, each organ or tissue has a corresponding locus within the iris or foot that undergoes simultaneous change in conjunction with the affected organ. The long history of this theory began with pagan shamanistic (witchcraft) healing methods but has no verifiable basis in modern medicine. Ophthalmologists, certified eye doctors, never use iridology as a diagnostic tool, and reflexology has never been acceptable treatment by the mainstream medical community, including podiatrists.

Q: *Isn't alleviation of suffering and an apparent cure more important that quibbling over the New Age orientation of certain forms of healing therapy?*

A: The result of involvement with the occult must never be overridden by other concerns. Those who engage in New Age medical methods often get more than they bargained for. Some could unwittingly swallow occult teachings while undergoing its therapy and subsequently lose spiritual direction in their lives. For example, the cancer patient treated with macrobiotics might gradually accept its underlying philosophy of dualism and come to question the Christian worldview. Others fall prey to occult oppression because the healer placed them in a vulnerable position by unconsciously inviting the assistance of spirit entities.

Q: *What do proponents of practices like Polarity Therapy mean when referring to an energy flow in the body?*

A: Einstein's theory of relativity, the interchangability of energy and matter, is applied to the biochemistry of the body. With a dash of Eastern mysticism, New Agers conclude that all thought, matter, and existence is a manifestation of universal energy, the One from which all emanates. In essence, energy becomes God, and science and religion meet metaphysically. When a therapist claims to be manipulating energy, he asserts that man is an extension of the divine (energy) and is being restored to his oneness with universal energy—that is, reunited with God to achieve health and well-being.

Q: *Are New Age healers being honest when they say no specific religious commitment is needed to practice their therapies?*

A: Though they seek to be eclectic, their therapies are founded essentially on mystical models. For example, Dr. Randolph Stone, who popularized Polarity Therapy, proudly proclaims that anyone can use his manipulative techniques regardless of what his personal faith may be. But a close study of his background reveals an extensive involvement in occult practices. He investigated the powers of the pyramids in Egypt. Stone also credits the powers of gems and has carefully examined Indian yogis and their spiritual teachings.[21]

Q: *What are the essential differences between traditional Western medical practices and New Age techniques?*

A: Many. Fundamentally, New Age practices avoid treating specific ailments. Instead, they work with undefined energies under the assumption that once the body is properly aligned with the forces of nature, it will automatically heal itself. This presumes that mankind's internal disposition is pure and divinely motivated toward health and happiness, not directed by physical and spiritual decay.

Q: *Since naturopaths emphasize diet and nutrition, aren't their medical methods superior to the expensive, drug-oriented treatments of traditional medical doctors?*

A: Naturopaths may be helpful under certain circumstances, but there are dangers. The disease may not have been detected in time for using naturopathic methods and could require immediate crisis intervention with antibiotics or surgery. Many naturopaths are unqualified to make complex diagnoses and thus render erroneous verdicts. Emphasizing diet and nutrition is good, but such advice must employ a complex knowledge of physiology, biochemistry, and pathology. Many naturopaths do not possess such information. They could recommend therapies of questionable value with possible occult connections. Because many naturopaths are firmly aligned with New Age ideology, only careful scrutiny of the naturopath's credentials and personal beliefs can minimize potential physical and spiritual dangers.

Q: *Since rolfing only involves manipulation of connective tissues and skeletal structure, are there any spiritual dangers?*

A: As New Age practitioners acknowledge, a little understood connection exists between the spirit and the body. Yoga adepts recognize this and have designed their calisthenic maneuvers to augment spiritual sensitivities to produce psychic phenomena. Dr. Rolf's work evolved from years of studying yoga. Her philosophical basis for manipulation stemmed from the idea that the energy field of the body must be aligned with the earth's gravitational and energy fields. Just as Hindu yogis seek to properly align their chakras (psychic spiritual energy centers located along the spine), rolfing aims to properly sympathize the body with external, macrocosmic energy forces.

Q: *If certain colors can affect one emotionally and physically, what's wrong with consulting a color therapist?*

A: The so-called gift of discerning the effect of colors usually rests with psychics or spiritists. The actual diagnosis is done by divination, a biblically forbidden practice. The color therapist may recommend use of astrology, mantras, and various forms of psychic phenomena. Some even suggest dietary considerations based on the colors of certain vegetables, according to zodiac associations.

Q: *Since herbs are often associated with witchcraft and the occult, does herbology pose a spiritual threat?*

A: Though natural remedies should never replace synthetic drugs used in conjunction with modern medical technology, herbs can effectively treat minor illnesses such as colds, gastrointestinal difficulties, and influenza. But caution is advised when being treated by a New Age herbologist. Many New Agers borrow the idea of the ancients that herbs have personalities and spiritual patterns of energy. Shamans believed herbs were literal combatants in a war with the evil nature of illness. If the herbologist is merely concerned with the scientific description

96

of a plant, no spiritual harm exists. But if the practitioner sub-scribes to the occult ideology of herbs, the treatment could result in demonic oppression.

Q: *Is the Indian practice of Ayurveda dangerous for Christians because of its association with Hinduism?*

A: Absolutely. It is sometimes used in conjunction with Tantra (the science of union with God through magical sexual inter-course, using occult ceremonies and black magic rituals to achieve orgasm) which compounds its peril. Ayurveda is a metaphysical approach to healing that has little practical scien-tific benefit, but it can be a supernatural means of linking the human patient with demonic spirits.

WHO'S WHO AND WHAT'S WHAT

Ayurveda: Five-thousand-year-old Hindu life science, consid-ered the mother of all healing arts, using yoga, diet, Tantrism, and Vedantic philosophy.

Herbology: Use of plants as natural healing substances to promote health and cure minor illnesses.

Homeopathy: A natural way of stimulating the body's heal-ing ability by using the theory of like cures like, which treats the patient with the same substance that sickened him.

Imagery: Producing physical well-being by thought forma-tion, which envisions the body healing itself without interven-tion of drugs or surgery.

Macrobiotics: Metaphysical dietary system of eating and healing using whole grains, vegetables, and fish, and avoiding meat and processed foods.

Naturopathy: Nonintrusive form of medical care using herbs instead of drugs, generally practiced by chiropractors and oste-opaths as an alternative to allopathic medicine.

Polarity Therapy: Bioenergetic healing therapy teaching that illness results from blockage of energy at certain places in the body, a hindrance that can be removed by strategic laying-on of hands.

Prana: Hindu Sanskrit word for "breath," considered the vital force of life, which emanates from the impersonal energy that is Brahman (God).

Reflexology: Belief that the sole of the foot contains reflex points that correspond to all internal organs and bodily functions, and that manipulation of these points relieves disease and illness.

Rolfing: Deep massage technique designed to restructure the body so it more properly aligns with gravity and the energies of earth.

Zone Therapy: Philosophical basis for such practices as reflexology and iridology, which supposes that certain zones of the body can exhibit symptoms of disease in other, unrelated portions of the body.

IN MY OPINION

It is strange that Christians are so prone to accepting therapies science disdains and New Agers embrace. Practices such as macrobiotics and homeopathy adopt the idea that health is a state of equilibrium with the universal energy of the cosmos. Man is believed to be of divine essence, thus his pure nucleus effects perfect health if unhindered by blockages of disease. In contrast, the Bible teaches that man possesses an evil heart and a sinfully fallen nature, not infinite wisdom and divine perfection.

Undoubtedly, our bodies tell us something when we are ill. Symptoms are a warning system designed by God to alert our immunological response. But it is dangerous to insist, as New Agers do, that a cosmic intelligence uses disease as a learning experience for mankind. Disease is an enemy, which may have physiological or supernatural origins. In the latter case,

Christ healed those who were "oppressed by the devil."[22] Though manifestations of internal dysfunction may herald greater dangers to our bodies, there is no benevolent higher consciousness inflicting misery to correct errors of past incarnations.

While Christians have reason to be wary of science, which so often opposes faith, true science is the accurate examination of observable phenomena. New Age medical methods consistently fail the test of such investigations. For example, studies of the central nervous system have yet to produce reasonable explanations for iridology and reflexology. Still, well-meaning Christians sometimes respond vehemently whenever cautions are expressed concerning these practices. Their argument usually goes like this: "So-and-so is a Christian and has been treating me for years with iridology and reflexology. How dare you question his use of the practice and suggest he is part of New Age medical methods?"

Because one part of the body connects to another does not indicate that a sympathetic system of healing therapy is valid or that physical well-being can be monitored by looking at a single segment of the physique (eye or foot). New Age medical methods often function with circular logic, avoiding scrutiny by controlled study. Instead, they seek the validation of occult sources. As a case in point, Dr. Bernard Jensen, a foremost American proponent of iridology, in his textbook *Iridology: Science and Practice in the Healing Arts*,[23] credits for inspiration such New Age sources as *Isis Unveiled*, by medium and founder of Theosophy H. P. Blavatsky, and *The Aquarian Conspiracy*, by New Age idealist Marilyn Furgeson.

Satan, the author of all suffering, knows people want quick answers and uncomplicated cures. New Age explanations offer immediate resolutions and seemingly practical conclusions. But the therapy usually requires an ongoing relationship with the healer, drawing the patient ever deeper into a web of New Age thinking. Other occult-holistic therapies are gradually introduced, further victimizing the sufferer. The body may indeed be relieved of its misery, but at the cost of eternal torment.

The web of occultism is carefully woven by beliefs in energies and undefined forces. Terms like *prana* and *chi* are seldom explained. Generalized references to life forces are employed, but philosophical assumptions about such energies are circumspectly guarded. Thus, the Westerner with a nominal Christian background may never suspect he is being lured into the trap of occultism, where self is exalted as divine.

The pantheistic presumptions of New Age medical methods are meticulously silenced by teachers of energy therapies. Patients are told this primordial energy pervades the fabric of all life—human, animal, and plant. This singleness of reality makes all of creation part of God, the error elucidated in Romans 1, which describes man as culminating in depravity and indecency.[24]

Chapter 5

TRANCING IN THE LIGHT

Straight Answers on New Age Trance Channeling

She sat naked on a Peruvian mountaintop, bared her breasts on stage during a live AIDS benefit performance, and starred in her own TV mini-series about her extradimensional escapades. Now she is "dancing in the light"—that's the title of her occult guidebook to the spiritual cosmos. With all the world as her stage, Shirley MacLaine bathes with magic crystals at each corner of her tub and chants Hindu mantras while visualizing a white light flowing through her bloodstream.

As a dancer, she incorporates her mystical worldview. Of the way she has melded occultism and dancing, Shirley says in *Dancing in the Light,* "Esoteric, holistic mysticism might be words that sound unpragmatic, but when translated into physical terms, the practitioner understands that he or she is simply learning how to use invisible energies to their best advantage."[1] But her ideologies are not her own. They came to her by spiritual revelation from channeled entities. Shirley MacLaine is trancing in the light.

MacLaine may be the queen of spaced-out Californians, but she also leads a vanguard committed to New Age concepts of entity communication. A special *USA Today* poll revealed that 14 percent of Americans believe in trance mediums.[2] And a new generation of psychic channelers is capitalizing on that fact.

Arthur Ford did it for Bishop Pike, and the witch of Endor did it for King Saul. Today, channeling can be seen on nationwide television and preserved on video and audio cassette. One proponent describes it as a harmless way of "simply detaching your limited sense of self and relaxing into a more natural experience of who you are."[3]

While spirit mediums like Edgar Cayce primarily emphasized the future, today's channelers are generally concerned with the present. Furthermore, Cayce diagnosed illnesses, but New Age trance channelers enter altered or semiconscious states to share a vision that everyone in the world can be happy, healthy, and enlightened. Consider these words from the most popular spirit entities:

"I am waiting at the edge of your reality to love you when you are ready to be loved" (Lazaris, channeled entity of Jach Pursel).[4]

"You will reincarnate whether or not you believe that you will" (Seth, channeled entity of Jane Roberts).[5]

"I am a sovereign entity who lived a long time ago upon earth. In that life I did not die. I ascended" (Ramtha, channeled entity of J. Z. Knight)[6]

"Give yourselves permission at this very moment to touch the world of spirit" (Emanuel, channeled by Pat Rodegast).[7]

Trance channeling is the latest of psychic chic. Once spirits spoke only in darkened seance rooms. Current corporate entities hold workshops, write books, and appear on radio and TV shows. In Los Angeles, several trance channelers have their own radio talk shows. The missive they offer is a smorgasbord of occultism, which includes extraterrestrials, out-of-the-body experiences, psychic phenomena, and speculation regarding past lives.

Trance channeling communicates information through a human being from a source on another spiritual level. Public attitudes toward the practice have varied throughout history. During Old Testament times, the act was known as spiritism and was punishable by death. In other ancient cultures, oracles were considered a mouthpiece of the gods. Since the advent of rationalism, mediumship has generally been considered a con game. One New Age proponent calls it "a crucial experience for human beings in all cultures and times, even though we do not yet understand its origins or mechanisms."[8]

Such eccentricities raise remarkably few eyebrows. Shirley MacLaine, who has been known to run with the elite of entertainment, says none of her close acquaintances have deserted her. Obviously, channeling has successfully bridged the public relations gap. The sensation has brought together the mysticism of the 1960s, the rejection of materialism of the 1970s, and the human potential quest of the 1980s.

Trance channeling is part of a larger philosophy within the movement. It supposes that development of extradimensional forms of "consciousness communication" will resurrect man's memory of his "perfected essence." Consciousness communication will provide access to unlimited intelligence and remove one's "unevolved hindrances." It is nothing less than the awakening of god consciousness within the human family.

Many New Agers refer to our day as the Aquarian era—a time when a mass visitation of angels and Ascended Masters is occurring. Incidental intervention of higher beings in the past has become an invasion of elevated energies. Our brothers in the beyond want only to lead us to unlimited freedom and joy. If we heed the call, we can avoid annihilation and experience the "playground of existence," guided by the "life-force" of the universe.

Communicating with other intelligences isn't just a job for the celebrity channelers of the world. Many in the movement seek to achieve their own trance states through meditation and self-hypnosis. Their ultimate aim is to tune in to the "life-energy force." Once they believe they have done this, many New Agers abandon channeling since they then dwell in a constant state of pure divine awareness. As with any skill, initiates seeking mediumship are reminded that practice makes perfect, and those assisting would-be trance channelers provide detailed instructions on how to achieve the state.

Relaxation, focusing, and concentration techniques are encouraged, with specific directives on how to welcome one's spirit guide. After arduous exercise, the goal is to "end the concept of the self as a physical entity . . . as you begin your graduations and initiations into the higher dimensions."[9]

LAZARIS AND JACH PURSEL

Sharon Gless of TV's "Cagney and Lacey" consults Lazaris, a "spark of consciousness." Gless thanked the spirit when she won an Emmy award, declaring from the podium, "Lazaris—it is magic." Lazaris is channeled by Jach Pursel, a California businessman, who has turned his entity into a money-making machine. It costs $275 to partake of the wisdom of Lazaris during a weekend seminar. Up to 1,800 attend such sessions, resulting in a weekend average of nearly $200,000 per public transcendental discourse.

Lazaris has a two-year waiting list for private consultations at $93 an hour. Less persistent people can reach out and touch Lazaris by phone for $35 per half hour (billed to MasterCard or Visa). There are audio tapes at $20 per set and videos for $60 each. But wait! There's more: Pursel's own brand of New Age jewelry and visionary paintings, providing a gross take of $5 million a year.[10] Gless gleefully comments about Lazaris, "He tries to teach us to take our power back, to create our own reality, and to have fun."[11]

Lazaris even has his own book: *The Sacred Journey: You and Your Higher Self*. With the assistance of guided mental excursions, Lazaris explains how to use meditation to facilitate contacting one's Higher Self. On audio tapes, Lazaris explains the use of crystals in prior civilizations, such as Atlantis and Egypt. The entity also tells listeners about other spirit guides ("Unseen Friends") surrounding humanity.

RAMTHA AND J. Z. KNIGHT

J. Z. Knight is one of the best-known channelers. Originally a cable television industry executive living in Roswell, New Mexico, Knight now calls Yelm, Washington, home. Scores of followers are flocking to this farming community of 1,400 people fifty-five miles south of Seattle, because they believe the messages of Knight's spirit guide, Ramtha. The 35,000-year-old male entity says that the Northwest is the safest place to avoid future earthquakes, tidal waves, and atmospheric pollution.

Knight first met Ramtha in her kitchen, not exactly a place with profound spiritual auras. The year was 1977, and Knight was experimenting with crystal pyramids. Ramtha claimed to be a warrior who had conquered the lost city of Atlantis. Today, followers of Knight-Ramtha pay $400 each to attend her-his seminars. Weekend retreats are offered at the rate of $1,500. During the sessions, Ramtha declares there is no right or wrong, just individual reality. "God is everywhere," the ancient conqueror insists.

Typically, Knight induces a semiconscious state, shakes, and goes limp. Re-animating as Ramtha, she walks through the audience, speaking in a low, rhythmic voice. The transformation is so complete that Knight says she must listen later to a recording to discover what she uttered while under Ramtha's influence. And not everything is encouraging. Sounding like the Ralph Nader of the spirit world, Ramtha prophesies disaster on every hand: California will tumble into the ocean, Florida will sink, and acid rain will poison New England's water supply. Why don't such dire predictions repel reasonable minds? Cult critics say apocalyptic forecasts actually solidify the trance channeler's image as a savior, so that followers are kept off balance by constant manipulation of reality.

Knight has a following among Hollywood's elite, including "Dynasty's" Linda Evans. Reportedly, Evans plans to move out of Los Angeles because Knight told her a killer earthquake will strike the area. One published account claims Evans has already bought a $1.5 million home about a thirty-minute drive from Knight's residence.

But not everyone is convinced of Knight's authenticity. Shirley MacLaine used to recommend Knight but no longer trusts her. Pam McNeeley, who broke away from Ramtha's teachings, says, "I remember an incident when Knight impersonated Ramtha without going into a trance. We thought she did a better job of doing Ramtha than Ramtha. In fact, we couldn't tell the difference."[12]

It is also significant that Ramtha offers investment counseling. He is espe-

cially prone to recommend investing in Arabian race horses, which inciden-
tally, Knight breeds, sells, and races.

OTHER ENTITIES AND MEDIUMS

Other entities offer a somewhat brighter assessment of life on earth,
though their messages are tainted with the same occult premises. The editor of *Metapsychology* magazine, Tam Mossman, channels James. Tapes
with the entity feature his speaking "live" from Ottawa and Hawaii. In some
cases, extraterrestrials speak through trance channelers. *The Starseed
Transmissions*, published communications from other galaxies, are supposedly messages from an interplanetary source. South of Denver in Colorado
Springs, Colorado, Barbara Rollinson-Huss claims to be a channel of information from dolphins and has also served as the conduit for an Oriental
spirit with a Chinese-American accent.

Jane Roberts and Seth

Seth, spirit guide of the late Jane Roberts, declared that mankind can
create its own reality through the power of the mind. Roberts wrote twenty
books promoting Seth's theme that everyone has "counterparts," people
living now and people who lived at other times. These counterparts are
portions of the living individual and form the totality of what Seth said is the
"greater self." Jane Roberts died in 1984, but Seth's message lives on:
"There is not just one dimension in which nonphysical consciousness resides. . . . You must die many times before you enter this particular plane of
existence. . . . There is no need to fear death."[13]

Laura Camaron-Fraser and Jonah

In Seattle, the Reverend Laura Camaron-Fraser, the first woman Episcopalian priest in the Pacific Northwest, was forced to leave her church because she said a spirit named Jonah speaks through her. Fraser argues that
trance channeling is how the Holy Spirit speaks to people today, just as He
spoke to those who wrote the Bible. "We have to see the Bible as a channeled work. The prophets in the Old Testament were channelers," Fraser
says.[14]

Penny Torres and Mafu

Penny Torres, a California housewife, channels Mafu, a member of the
"brotherhood of light." Mafu comes from the seventh dimension and was

last incarnated in first-century Pompeii. Actress Joyce DeWitt, formerly of "Three's Company," spent three years away from the crowds, studying out-of-the-body experiences and investigating channeling. It was DeWitt who first brought Torres and Mafu (who sounds a lot like Ramtha) to the public's attention.

Kevin Ryerson, John, and Tom McPherson

Kevin Ryerson, who is featured prominently in Shirley MacLaine's books, channels two entities: John (who lived in the Essene community at the time of Christ) and Tom McPherson (a mischievous Irish spirit). A student of parapsychology and psychic phenomena since his early twenties, Ryerson currently works with Dr. William Kautz of the Center for Applied Intuition. His interest in channeling began in the sixth grade, when he investigated the Edgar Cayce readings.

Ryerson uses a two-hour counseling format, the first hour to decide on the questions, the second to bring forth channeled responses. He claims 75 percent accuracy for channeled material, including historical information and predictions. The cost: $250 for a private appointment. In Ryerson's own words, "Channeling is a tool for us to look at our spiritual dimension. It's a natural part of ourselves . . . [and] includes our past lives."[15]

Channelers have their critics. *Time* magazine observed that trance channelers attract those disillusioned with organized religion. Practitioners of the phenomenon were described by *Time* as "snake oil salesmen." Reginald Alev, executive director of the Occult Awareness Network of Chicago, put it more bluntly: "Trance channeling reminds me of a ventriloquist act with one partner missing."[16]

Some cult experts warn that channelers represent dangerous leaders who could steer people seriously astray. Susan Rothbaum, director of a California organization that counsels people involved in cult groups, says, "The guru starts with a simple message of openness and love. Then it becomes complicated, paranoid, and fearful."[17] Carl Raschke, professor of religious studies at the University of Denver, declares, "It's a form of mass hypnosis that is leading to mass acceptance of the irrational."[18]

Trance channeling is a curiosity whose popular stock has risen and fallen throughout history. It has been particularly popular among those who have suffered personal bereavement. Its acceptance has increased during times of war and national tragedy, when the public is gripped with uncertainty. But its message never changes. There is no death, man is God, and knowledge of one's true inner divinity brings salvation and power.

STRAIGHT ANSWERS

Q: *If Shirley MacLaine's books are best-sellers, should they be accepted as credible?*

A: Her readers include both New Age advocates and the curious. They uncritically accept as truth what a celebrity says. But journalistic authenticity and spiritual trustworthiness should meet more exacting standards. MacLaine's publishers should be embarrassed that such shallow musings have sold so well. At least they could have listed her books under the fiction category.

Q: *Why do so many Americans believe what channelers and their entities say?*

A: A vacuum of spiritual direction and authoritative guidance exists in our culture. Traditional religious institutions such as the church and the Bible have been questioned as sources of truth. Many are hungry for supernatural verification that life after death exists and that the most mundane occurrences in life have meaning. Spirits and their mediums seem to verify the survivability of the soul and confirm that each day's events have ultimate significance.

Q: *By what means do people seek to become spirit channels?*

A: Many begin with ouija boards, crystal balls, and a variety of occult paraphernalia used by spirit mediums. Some experience automatic handwriting, where an entity writes messages by possessing the psychomotor functions of the medium. Others simply hear voices in their minds or receive thought impulses that are interpreted into words. The ultimate stage of mediumship is total possession. The subject enters a trance state of oblivion, and the personality of the entity is manifested.

Q: *How does the New Age Movement explain the origin of channeled entities?*

A: Some entities are said to be souls formerly living on earth who have not completed their karmic cycle and are awaiting another incarnation. Other entities were spiritual masters who translated themselves into another spiritual realm and are currently disembodied. Certain entities claim to be etheric energy forms of higher consciousness. Some actually say they are Jesus, Buddha, Krishna, or a notable spiritual leader of the past. Certain entities claim they are splintered portions of a multi-faceted universal soul. All consistently deny final accountability for sin at God's judgment seat. All insist life is an ascending acquisition of spiritual knowledge that omits any eventuality of a literal heaven and hell.

Q: *Is it harmful to consult a channel out of curiosity?*

A: God forbids such communication for two reasons (see Deut. 18:9–14). First, it decimates trust in God by substituting an alien source of supernatural information. No matter how skeptical one may be at first, the power of suggestion could eventually overwhelm the most ardent critic, especially if a few circumstances proposed by the channel come to pass. Second, such occult acts enhance accessibility to one's spirit, portending the possibility of demonic possession. God demanded King Saul's life in judgment for his having consulted a medium. Unless one considers the Almighty to be capricious and jealous, it must be assumed that Saul's penalty is a timeless example for all who would seek the intervention of spirits as a means of counsel.

Q: *Do the messages of mediums differ, or is the content basically the same?*

A: Trance-channeled entities may differ slightly in their method of elocution and identification of origin, but the substance of their messages is uncannily similar. Christ may be mentioned, but never as the sole means of mankind's salvation. The Bible may be quoted, but usually out of context to validate an occult theory, such as the god-within doctrine. God is always referred to ambiguously, robbing him of compassionately arbitrating the affairs of men by grace. There is no acknowledgment of a final judgment at which the moral context of a person's actions will be measured. Pantheism, reincarnation in some form, an absence of objective ethical criteria, and the sinlessness of humanity are the most common themes. The way to truth is intuitively within, and the way to life after death comes through development of one's higher consciousness.

Q: *If I am offended by the spiritist commercial exploitation of trance channelers, what can I do to protest?*

A: Media exploitation of the New Age Movement, such as MacLaine's TV mini-series "Out on a Limb," must be economically viable. Protesting your displeasure to commercial sponsorship is the best way to alert those who pay the bills for such productions.

Q: *Why aren't more people alarmed at the obvious commercialization of well-publicized channelers?*

A: Paul told the Corinthians that Satan blinds the eyes of those who refuse to believe God and his Word.[19] How else could one explain the public's naiveté, which readily criticizes the financial dealings of electronic evangelists but conveniently overlooks the shameless scam of personal wealth-building involved with trance channeling? America's success syndrome seems to reward accumulation of material goods, no matter how unscrupulously they are obtained.

Q: *Is there anything in J. Z. Knight's background that led her to spiritism?*

A: Reportedly, Knight once professed a born-again Christian commitment. On at least one occasion, during a prayer session, she was overcome by what was described as a manifestation of demonic control. Apparently unliberated from this supernatural incursion, she became involved in occult practices shortly thereafter.

Q: *Who is Ramtha, and why is he so popular?*

A: He claims to be a 35,000-year-old, discarnate entity from the lost continent of Atlantis, a favorite historical reference point for occultists of all ilk. It is impossible to authenticate such a claim. If the Bible can be believed, Ramtha is actually a fallen angel, one of those who rebelled with Lucifer against God and now await the Lord's eternal punishment.[20]

Q: *Why would someone like Merv Griffin allow an exploitive form of spiritualism like trance channeling on his TV show?*

A: Ratings and viewers. The competition for public attention is so great in the broadcast media that some television producers go to any lengths to get a following. The live appearance of a 35,000-year-old being is dramatic, certain to hold the concentration of any audience.

Q: *Why are some Hollywood stars so gullible, allowing their names and reputations to be exploited on behalf of channelers?*

A: Though the press gives entertainment personalities an aura of confidence and infallibility, the truth is that many celebrities are insecure and easily swayed. Their lives are absorbed in being famous, and many neglect spiritual values. This void is easily filled with ethereal answers so long as some pragmatic, momentary resolutions are forthcoming.

Q: *How can the public ignore biblical warnings about witchcraft practices of trance mediums?*

A: The Bible is simply not considered authoritative by most in our society. Rationalists and skeptics have convinced the masses that the Word of God is fraught with error and is only a metaphorical document about ancient peoples, with no contemporary meaning in our age of AIDS and nuclear war. Old Testament injunctions against witchcraft are dismissed as paranoia from biblical writers, who were opposed to exploring inner spiritual consciousness. Others see the Scriptures' condemnation of occultism as an unreasonable response of a nomadic culture that was surrounded by repugnant pagan practices.

Q: *Who are the most likely prospects for accepting the messages of channelers and their spirit guides?*

A: The most gullible aren't the poorly educated and culturally unsophisticated. The price tag alone leaves out many in the lower class. Surveys of audiences at a Lazaris seminar or a MacLaine higher consciousness course would find the majority to be upwardly mobile. Perhaps this is true because such individuals have disregarded important spiritual values in their pursuit of success.

WHO'S WHO AND WHAT'S WHAT

Automatic Handwriting-Painting: The phenomenon of spirit control in which the subject's psychomotor functions are superimposed by the will of the entity, who supernaturally moves the person's hands to write or paint.

Cayce, Edgar: The so-called sleeping prophet who, while resting, entered trance states in which he foretold future events, philosophized about such occult subjects as reincarnation, and purported to give cures for various ills.

Ectoplasm: A sticky, milky-white substance out of which poltergeists and discarnate entities are said to materialize for the purposes of visible manifestation.

Esoteric: Referring to that which is secret, usually an allusion to teachings or sacred documents, as well as ceremonies and rituals, not available to the uninitiated.

Evans, Linda: Actress who plays Crystal on TV's "Dynasty"; she is the most visible champion of Ramtha because of her commitment to leave Hollywood for the safety of the Washington state area, which Ramtha says will be a harbor from environmental cataclysms.

Gless, Sharon: Actress who plays Cagney on the TV crime show "Cagney and Lacey" and has endorsed the trance channeled entity Lazaris.

Knight, J. Z.: Blonde, middle-aged housewife who claims to be the channel for the entity Ramtha, but whose stable of expensive cars and Arabian horses has raised charges of personal aggrandizement at the expense of exploited followers.

Lazaris: Entity channeled through California businessman Jach Pursel.

Mafu: Discarnate being speaking through the medium Penny Torres.

Mantras: Words or phrases taken from the Hindu Sanskrit scriptures, supposedly possessing supernatural powers when repetitively quoted in a chant.

Pursel, Jach: See *Lazaris*.

Ramtha: See *J. Z. Knight*.

Roberts, Jane: Best-selling author and channel for the spirit Seth, known for her book *Seth Speaks*.

Ryerson, Kevin: Channel consulted by Shirley MacLaine; played himself in the TV production "Out on a Limb."

Seth: See *Jane Roberts*.

Torres, Penny: See *Mafu*.

Trance Channeling: The phenomenon of a spirit's speaking through the mouth of a medium and often subjecting the channel to oblivion so that the channel's neurosensory faculties and psychomotor functions are completely possessed (an occurrence often mimicked by charlatans and fake channelers).

IN MY OPINION

Trance channeling isn't new. It's identical to the old-fashioned medium-trance phenomenon, which ancient shamans practiced. History's most dramatic recent resurgence took place during the 1840s. Margaret and Kate Fox said they heard mysterious rapping in their Hydesville, New York, home. The sisters claimed they were communicating with a discarnate entity called Mr. Splitfoot, a spirit who said he was a peddler who had been murdered in the house years earlier.

The so-called Rochester rapping was endorsed by newspaperman Horace Greeley and a variety of notables, including James Fenimore Cooper, Sir Arthur Conan Doyle, Elizabeth Barrett Browning, Daniel Webster, and William Cullen Bryant. (If the *National Enquirer* had been around, what great headlines they would have had!) A wave of interest in spiritualism swept America. It expanded to include automatic painting and automatic handwriting, as well as materializations of so-called ectoplasm, the stuff out of which spirits supposedly are made. Forty years later, one of the Fox sisters admitted the tapping resulted from some ingenious toe-joint popping on her part, though that confession was later recanted.

One reason trance channeling is so popular today is that death dominates our society—pestilence, pollution, the threat of nuclear war, and a variety of imminent conflagrations. In the midst of all this, channeled entities offer the promise of life after death without the ethical or virtuous cost attached to Christianity. As Ramtha put it on the "Merv Griffin Show," "Christ is within you. You are God."

And who determines the validity of such conclusions? The author of a book on channeling says, "Channeled advice is to be followed only if it rings true to you. . . . Do only those things that feel joyful or right to you."[21]

When a spokesman for trance channeler J. Z. Knight was accosted with accusations that Knight is a fraud, the defender declared, "There's no question she's for real. She's been on the Merv Griffin Show."

Truth requires a more convincing imprimatur than an endorsement by a talk show host. Absolute truth is found in the

God of the Bible. The Scripture declares that trance channeling is a work of deceptive demons, conduct continually condemned in God's Word.[22] MacLaine and her minions need to be reminded of the severity with which the true and living God views such conduct. In the Old Testament, trance channelers didn't get a mini-series on TV. They got capital punishment, a fate worse than low ratings!

Chapter 6

EXTRASENSORY DECEPTION

Straight Answers on New Age Psychic Phenomena

The message is the same. Whether you consult Nostradamus, Ruth Montgomery, or any of the assorted spirit guides, the central idea of the New Age Movement is fairly consistent. Planet earth is undergoing fundamental changes that will profoundly affect the cosmos and the spiritual consciousness of humanity. Some say a quantum leap in elevated brain power will result in an upward alteration in mankind's vibrational rate. Those who worship the globe as a goddess say a shift of earth's poles will occur in the year 2000, displacing present geopolitical alignments and geographical references.

How do New Agers know? The psychics tell them so. Jose Arguelles, the Harmonic Convergence psychic who marshaled the masses in August 1987, claims the Mayan calendar points the way to a New Golden Age. According to Arguelles, the promised land is here, the Millennium is now. In Arguelles' words, "The mystery of the unknown, which has always beckoned us by the light it contained in its question, will expand us into levels of being and knowing undreamed of by the strife-worn ego of the old mental house."[1]

Those like Arguelles say they are not the only ones with expanded forces of the consciousness. Others have the power. It's part of the human heritage. For example, you have a hunch and it pays off with emotional or financial success. You think the phone is going to ring, and it does. You go to the mailbox, and the letter you dreamed of the night before has arrived. You meet someone and know you have met him before. It doesn't involve the five senses, but the message comes through loudly and clearly.

Some say it's a special gift. Others claim it's standard, though underdeveloped, equipment of the mind and soul. Edgar Cayce said, "These [psychic powers] are latent in each and every individual, as has been given. It may be developed by application."[2]

The American Society of Psychical Research may not know where it comes from, but they certainly investigate psychic phenomena assiduously. Among their curiosities are telepathy, clairvoyance, precognition, hallucinations, dreams, psychometry, cognition, psychokinesis, poltergeists, ESP, and all other aspects of the paranormal. In 1882, the original version of the Society for Psychical Research was established in London. Those who joined were primarily men who had lost faith in religion but were averse to the prevailing view of the time, scientific materialism. The Society's stated aim is to "examine without prejudice in a scientific spirit those faculties of man, real or supposed, which appear to be inexplicable on a generally recognized hypothesis."

Psychic occurrences' being taken so seriously is a relatively new chapter in the history of humanity. For centuries, such speculation was considered the work of demons or eccentrics. Then, in the late seventeenth and early eighteenth centuries, traditional religious perspectives were subjected to the scrutiny of such secular philosophers as Hume and Voltaire. The nineteenth-century hypnotist Mesmer experimented with healing and astral projection. Spiritualism surged in popularity during Mesmer's time.

Today's psychic inquests occur not in the musty halls of academia, but on the highways of contemporary life. It even has an acronym, PSI, referring to that branch of the psychological sciences dealing with psychic ability and its phenomena. Singer Della Reese says, "When I want to be especially creative, I don't try to do anything. I just open myself up and let go. I think we all get communications we don't understand." The late William Lear, whose inventions included the Lear jet, agreed: "In designing an airplane, I use an awful lot of intelligence from other sources. I have to visualize something, and if I visualize it, then I can anticipate it so keenly that I can actually feel I'm doing it."[3]

The retired board chairman of Phillips Petroleum claims that parapsychological phenomena have assisted him in oil discoveries. William Keller declares, "Oil fields have been found on hunches through precognitive dreams and by people who don't know anything about geology."[4]

Psychic phenomena are definitely out of the closet. But many wish to once again inhibit this supposed sixth sense. Some are fundamentalist Christians who say such things are the work of the devil. But illusionists and practicing prestidigitators are equally antagonistic. Magician James Randi encouraged two of his protégés to infiltrate an experiment at Washington University's McConnell's Laboratory of Psychical Research. Randi claims that for four years researchers accepted trickery as proof of psychic powers.[5]

The faithful are undaunted. They claim to communicate telepathically with extraterrestrials, seek out-of-the-body experiences, aspire to know past lives, and dabble in clairvoyance. They are convinced that we can know the past, divine the future, receive information intuitively, send thoughts across.

distances, transcend space and time to recall incarnations, soul-travel beyond physical limits, and identify the unknown by the inexplicable powers
of the mind. For them, the New Age isn't a special event of this epoch. It is
the expression of a transformative, creative spirit unleashing the power of
the gods, locked and latent in the divine human soul.

PARAPSYCHOLOGY

As an Apollo 14 astronaut, he walked on the moon. Today, Edgar Mitchell
heads the Institute of Noetic Sciences (see Chap. 12), founded in 1973 and
dedicated to the exploration of inner space. The term *noetic* was derived
from the phrase "noetic quality" used by Harvard psychologist and philosopher William James, describing "mystical states of insight into depths of
truth unplumbed by discursive intellect."[6] Mitchell's machinations represent the spectrum of interest in PSI phenomena. The Institute examines
near-death experiences, Tibetan meditation, clairvoyant remote viewing,
remote healing, and mind-body links.

Generally, extrasensory occurrences are divided by categories. Extrasensory perception (ESP) is a catch-all term that alludes to various kinds of
paranormal curiosities. Clairvoyance involves receiving information from
an object or event. Telepathy refers to the transference of thoughts, mind to
mind, or being aware of the mental state of another person. Cognition
means being conscious of events in the past (postcognitive), present (cognitive), or future (precognitive).

Parapsychology owes its popularity to a Swedish contemporary of Voltaire, Emanuel Swedenborg, who combined his scientific background with
occult speculation and founded his own religion, Swedenborgianism. Modern parapsychology owes its impetus to J. B. Rhine, a biologist whose primary work was conducted at Duke University. Rhine began as a
preministerial student but later declared, "I gave up the ministry when I
found in psychology that there was no scientific basis for the existence of
the will. Without free will, the ministry seems futile."[7] Today, Rhine's associates investigate card guessing, dice throwing, and other standard methods
of testing ESP.

In addition to exploring extrasensory perception, investigators like Rhine
also survey psychokinesis (PK), the exertion of influence on an outside
physical object, event, or situation. The source of PK defies explanation,
since there is no direct use of muscles, physical energy, or instruments.
Psychokinesis is popularly displayed by such theatrical tricks as spoon
bending, table tipping, and levitation.

What's behind it all? Some researchers look to Freud's contemporary Carl Jung for answers. As an investigator of the occult, Jung sought to explain astrological predictions and assorted divinatory developments, such as the I Ching. He proposed that coincidence links seemingly improbable events, something he called "synchronicity." This theory suggests that simultaneous occurrences of a certain condition can take place with one or more objective phenomena in what Jung called "another order of the universe."

Other explanations abound. One researcher says that when excited, the brain emits a cloud of particles of imaginary mass called "psitrons." Others think electromagnetic or gravitational fields are behind it all. Some subscribe to another of Jung's theories that refers to the "collective unconsciousness," a universal mind that connects all individual minds. Certain researchers acknowledge what they call the "subliminal self," a kind of psychic split personality that accomplishes phenomenal feats. Still others refer to unknown nonphysical entities capable of overcoming space-time restraints. Despite years of research and speculation, the elusive origin of psychic phenomena still lurks behind a big question mark that masks its derivation and intentions.

PSYCHICS

With more than one million teenage pregnancies a year, psychic Anna Harcourt's business is booming. For pregnant young women who fear an abortion, Anna claims she can make babies disappear from wombs. She calls it a "psychic abortion." An expert in black magic, Anna maintains she gives the souls of the unborn offspring to the devil in exchange for her services. In the last twenty years, she claims to have performed more than one hundred such abortions at her North England home.[8]

Most New Age psychics who claim paranormal powers don't perform so malevolently. But their assistance is often unorthodox. A tabloid entitled *Astrology and Psychic News* contains some examples. Professor Amen-Ra says he has the ability to gaze into a person's eyes and predict his future. He wants only a photograph and $16.50 to ply his trade. Psychic E. B. Nathan is a palmist who requests that you photocopy both hands and send the sheet with $16 for what he says is "an honest, accurate prediction." Psychic Krishna Ram-Devi will meditate on your name for the same price and determine if your unhappiness and problems result from a wrong name given by your parents.

Throughout the centuries, psychic masters have been sought by the lowly and royalty alike. Capitalizing on superstition, fear, and grief, they have mixed charlatanism and entertainment to beguile the undiscerning. A recent poll by the University of Chicago showed that 67 percent of the public claims psychic experience.[9]

A magazine called *Psychic Guide* has 125,000 subscribers and features interviews with the dead, including Jimmy Hoffa telling his version of his demise. In one issue, *Psychic Guide* recounts a party ex-Beatle John Lennon supposedly had in the spirit world. From the great beyond, Lennon declared, "Carole Lombard was there, and I took to her. We were capable of having sex over there."[10]

On the more serious side, Uri Geller has fascinated millions with his purported ability to bend spoons. The United States Navy has employed psychics to track Soviet ships, and, according to *Omni* magazine, in 1981 the United States Air Force seriously considered developing a "psychic shield" for its missiles.

The bizarre side of psychics seems to interest people the most. In Columbus, Ohio, newspapers reported the story of a fourteen-year-old girl living in a house with a garbage disposal and microwave that went into solo operation, along with a shower that started running unattended. News magazines featured photographs of a telephone levitating in the air, supposedly suspended by a poltergeist. Finally, a group of skeptics representing the Committee for the Scientific Investigation of Claims of the Paranormal checked out the situation. They discovered a surprisingly unsophisticated scam perpetrated by a clever, attention-seeking adolescent.[11]

Psychics come, and psychics go. So do their prophecies. Their success rate displays a minimal amount of accuracy except to the undiscerning, who rationalize failed predictions. The overactive imaginations of psychics leave followers cringing in fear of what might happen, and depressed and disillusioned when nothing does.

STRAIGHT ANSWERS

Q: *Why aren't New Agers disillusioned with the capricious predictions of psychics?*

A: This is partially due to the public's uncritical acceptance of the paranormal. A recent Gallup poll conducted among students aged sixteen to eighteen indicated widespread belief in the supernatural or parapsychological. Sixty-five percent said they believe in angels, 51 percent in astrology, 62 percent in ESP, 8 percent in clairvoyance, 24 percent in witchcraft, and 21 percent in ghosts.

Q: *Could latent paranormal powers of the soul be cultivated if they were dedicated to the Lord?*

A: An important characteristic of such phenomena is the admitted lack of control over how and when the information is received. Accuracy and consistency are rare. Such randomness indicates the influence of a force outside human faculties.

Q: *Can psychic phenomena be scientifically examined without involving occultism?*

A: It's possible but improbable because of the lack of biblical guidelines within the scientific community. Unfortunately, many scientists ascribe to either atheism or New Age ideals of mysticism. In an issue of *The Humanist* magazine, it was revealed that two-thirds of all scientific researchers believe in ESP. Most scientists no longer argue about the validity of such phenomena. Instead, the current quest is to measure such forces and determine how they can be duplicated. How ironic that the best modern minds would fall prey to supernaturalism after expunging their cosmological views of all reference to Christian thought!

Q: *What explanations do parapsychology researchers set forth?*

A: J. B. Rhine posits a theory called "projection hypothesis," which assumes that an agency of the mind can function independently of the physical body. This agency supposedly has the capacity to project and contact an object beyond the organism it occupies. This is a scientific rationalization for what occultists call astral projection. Rhine strives to explain the phenomena of witchcraft without acknowledging existence of the supernatural forces propelling parapsychology.

Q: *Are there hidden dangers behind seemingly harmless psychic phenomena?*

A: In Colossians 2:18, the apostle Paul warns against bragging about mystical experiences and extrasensory communication. Psychics who boast of their abilities and offer their services to the public are described by Paul as being preoccupied with "idle notions."[12] Presumed psychic powers usually solicit spiritual pride and result in vain glorification of the carnal mind, as well as possible demonic influence. For the Christian, the power of Christ working through the believer is important, not some inexplicable force manifested arbitrarily.

Q: *Why aren't psychics held more accountable for their incredible predictions?*

A: From claiming to augment luck to improving libido, psychics stretch the imagination to prove their powers. Few followers evaluate the performance of psychics objectively, because people want to believe such powers are real and that benevolent fate controls their existence. To refute psychic claims is to deny a larger order and meaning in life. Those who refuse God his rightful place in their affairs substitute another principle of goodness and omnipotence, ignoring the logic that insists certain psychics are frauds.

Q: *How are such feats as Uri Geller's spoon bending done?*

A: Debunkers who have investigated Geller's act suspect the spoons are made of nitinol, an alloy so sensitive to heat that the touch of a finger can make it curl. Several professional magicians have duplicated the trick by sleight-of-hand. According to magician Henry Gordon, the psychic secretly bends the spoon on the side of a table, a belt buckle, or a chair. Then he lets it slowly emerge between the thumb and forefinger, appearing to twist as it comes forth. In the absence of either explanation, one cannot discount supernatural demonic intervention to coerce the unwary into believing such powers

125

prove the mind's power over matter. Consequently, some seek these powers and eventually pursue New Age consciousness-raising techniques.

Q: *How seriously are psychics taken?*

A: In France, the police asked Eleanor Rey, a noted psychic, to view the video of a bank robbery. Hours later, the culprits were under arrest because Rey claimed her ESP revealed their hiding place.[13] The president of ABC-TV once hired a psychic to predict which shows would succeed on the network. An investigative reporter in Washington claims the Defense Department spent $6 million to research ESP and mental telepathy. The reporter claims the Navy hired a Madam Zodiac for $400 to look at top-secret photographs and predict movement of Soviet submarines off the East Coast.

WHO'S WHO AND WHAT'S WHAT

Arguelles, Jose: Author of *The Mayan Factor: Path Beyond Technology,* a New Age book predicting certain cosmic events, ushering in an era of "sophisticated technology based on the matching of solar and psychic frequencies"[14] (see Chap. 11).

Clairvoyance: Receiving information from an object or event with nonsensory means.

ESP: Short for "extrasensory perception," the ability to perceive beyond the capability of the five natural senses.

Institute of Noetic Sciences: A tax-exempt, nonprofit foundation started in 1973 to broaden knowledge of the potentials of mind and consciousness by exploring exceptional abilities, health and healing, and societal transformation (see Chap. 12).

Mesmer, Anton: Nineteenth-century German physician who experimented with mind control techniques resembling hypnotism, first known as "Mesmerism."

Montgomery, Ruth: Psychic, former *Washington Post* columnist, and author of such books as *A Search for Truth, Here and Hereafter, A World Beyond, Aliens Among Us,* and *Herald of the New Age.*

Nostradamus: Sixteenth-century occult mystic who wrote ten volumes of prophecy called *Centuries,* supposedly predicting the world's future in minute detail (see Chap. 7).

Parapsychology: The branch of the psychological sciences dealing with psychic abilities, researching mental and physical effects of nonmaterial causes.

Poltergeist: German for "friendly or mischievous ghost."

Precognition: Knowledge of an event or circumstance prior to occurrence.

PSI: Abbreviation for "psychic phenomenon," providing a shortened, all-encompassing designation for extrasensory curiosities.

Psychokinesis: The movement of material objects by mental or psychic powers.

Psychometry: Receiving paranormal information through contact with an object, such as a clairvoyant's seeking the whereabouts of a lost person by holding his ring.

Remote Viewing/Healing: Discerning telepathically or transmitting healing across distances without the psychic's being in direct physical contact with person, object, or circumstance.

Society for Psychical Research: Organization devoted to parapsychological research and the scholarly collection of related information concerning the paranormal (American division founded in 1885).

Swedenborg, Emanuel: Eighteenth-century son of a Lutheran minister; expounded supposed symbolic meanings of Scripture and developed such mediumistic abilities as astral projection and automatic handwriting and founded his own cult religion.

Telepathy: Awareness of the thoughts or mental state of another person, or transmitting thoughts to another person.

IN MY OPINION

From the earliest recorded times, nonmaterial agencies and inexplicable forces have been credited with performing incredible feats. Some of those accomplishments were attributed to ghosts, demons, or mythological beings. In the last half of the nineteenth century, the spiritualist movement supported the idea that the departed precipitate such phenomena.

Christians must do more than speculate about the origin of such powers. When the paranormal occurs, the Bible mandates an explanation of the source. How? First, the Scriptures must be searched to see if such occurrences are forbidden. Second, the psychic gift must be subjected to the authority of Christ and compelled to cease if not from him. Finally, its purpose must be analyzed to see if it truly exalts Christ. Such standards go far beyond scientific precepts of evaluation, because God's principles transcend the material and incorporate the supernatural, where demons and devils ply their wares.

Those who believe in psychic phenomena frequently dismiss any idea that these things could be of the devil, since some psychics appear to do good. But Matthew 7:22–23 warns us that on Judgment Day, some will say they did great things, even in the name of Christ. The response of the Lord will be: "I never knew you; depart from me." Remember, any supernatural occurrence has but two possible sources, God or the devil (or Satan's demons).

Some psychic feats are explicable. Those who say they can start stopped watches simply play the averages. One systematic study shows that 55 percent of stopped watches can be reactivated by the warmth of the human hand, which causes metal parts to expand and loosens internal mechanisms. Even so, some psychic powers are undoubtedly supernatural.

The lure of psychic abilities is rooted in Satan's appeal to Adam and Eve: "You will be like God."[15] The devil wants to convince New Age citizens that they have boundless, untapped powers. Whether these psychic abilities are called biocurrents, brainwaves, or biocosmic forces, Satan's demons externalize their psychic manifestation until they can take up residence within the person who thinks he possesses natural powers. Before assuming some psychic phenomenon is of God or man's mind, heed the words of 1 Thessalonians 5:21: "Test all things; hold fast what is good." Jesus displayed the supernatural and did deeds resembling psychic feats. But Acts 10:38 tells us how: "God was with Him." The same isn't true for psychics.

Chapter 7

NEW AGE ORACLES

Straight Answers on New Age Divinatory Devices

They were awarded a Nobel Prize for a breakthrough in particle physics. But the scientific investigations of Che Ning Yeng and Tsung-dao Lee were guided more by the hand of fate than the impulse of an inquiring mind. "Is there going to be a breakthrough in the next two years?" they asked. "Good fortune lies ahead. Persevere further," came the reply. The question wasn't posed to a committee of academic peers, but to a handful of yarrow sticks. Yeng and Lee had consulted the ancient Chinese divinatory device I Ching, the *Book of Changes*. This combination of hard science with soft irrationalism is typical of the New Age Movement's infiltration of Western thought.[1]

Psychic predictions and prophetic devices such as the I Ching, Tarot cards, astrology, palmistry, runes, dowsing, and biorhythms have become symbols of certitude in a restless age. In spite of the capriciousness of such artifices, many who have rejected organized religion have turned to exotic occult instruments to direct their lives and offer advice about their futures.

To those interested in divination, intuition is the pathway to understanding life. In the New Age, each person is believed to be part of a hologram. Each mind is a segment of this "collective unconscious." Divination is a means of tapping this universal bank of knowledge concerning the past, present, and future. Occult fortune telling is a window opening to the self and the universal consciousness beyond. The key, say New Agers, is to determine which system of divination will most quickly and clearly align one's higher self with the best available channel of esoteric information.

I CHING

Occultism has gone high tech. New York City's Horizons East offers a personalized, computerized analysis of your destiny based on the I Ching. If you send $20 with the time, date, and place of your birth, you receive an appraisal of your lifetime destiny and a year-by-year forecast of the next two years—all this without having to burn incense and bow three times before the silk-wrapped *Book of Changes* (I Ching).

The I Ching originated during China's Han Dynasty and was intended to be a book of collective wisdom. Eventually, however, its sixty-four sections came to be idolatrously revered. Confucius is said to have studied the book so carefully that the thongs binding the tablets on which his copy was inscribed wore out three times from constant use. What fascinated Confucius was a doctrine teaching that the womb of the universe is a limitless, imperceptible void, the T'ai Chi. All material objects have being and individuality due to a particular combination of negative and positive forces, the yin and yang. The I Ching hexagrams supposedly avoid mechanical answers in favor of promoting greater self-understanding so that one can interpret his own future.

Originally, the I Ching used yarrow stalks. Forty-nine stalks were thrown into two random heaps. These were then counted by threes and fives. Today, the most popular method is the tossing of coins. Three identical coins of any denomination are tossed six times. As the coins are laid according to the way they land, heads or tails, two trigrams form a hexagram. Each of the sixty-four possible hexagrams is believed to correspond to psychic principles. The *Book of Changes* is then consulted for the interpretation. Most practitioners of the I Ching acknowledge that the intuition of one's own spirit is the ultimate factor that governs this form of divination's interpretations.

By dislodging the active role of the conscious mind, the I Ching is supposed to reveal true, unconscious tendencies. One advocate has described the *Book of Changes* as "fundamental glyphs of the spiritual and psychological journey."[2] Though the origin of the I Ching was Chinese, its prediction on principles of yin and yang is considered universal. It is also supposed to be a kind of spiritual training exercise to perfect one's ability to perceive accurately the essence of life.

TAROT CARDS

A popular divinatory device at psychic fairs and New Age gatherings is the set of Tarot cards, consisting of the minor arcane and the major arcane with twenty-two cards, a card numbered 0, and the Fool. The four suits are designated wands, cups, swords, and pentacles, symbolizing the four elements of fire, water, air, and earth. Some historians say this system of occultism came from Chaldea by way of Alexandria and was used worldwide by occultists to communicate. (The name Tarot comes from *taro-rota*, meaning "the will of the law, and the law of the will.") First used by a Frenchman in the eighteenth century, the term "tarot" has preserved its Francophile pronunciation, hence the silent final "t."

The cards are said to be symbolic representations of reality. By reading them, one's unconscious powers are awakened. When this happens, the inner forces of fate can be controlled. The color, shape, and symbolic forms on the cards are to be studied intuitively. Some Tarot guides provide meditations while concentrating on the cards.

TASSEOGRAPHY

The fortune-telling practice of tea leaf reading has enjoyed a resurgence with the New Age Movement. No longer relegated to gypsy tents at county fairs, this clairvoyant art attracts yuppies and serious business people. The leaves are said to be a medium through which the reader's psychic abilities are stimulated to uncover hidden truths.

The usual method is to have the client invert an empty cup and turn it around three times. Then the reader places it on the saucer, tapping the bottom three times with the left index finger. In a light trance, the reader picks up the cup and turns it over to survey the lay of the leaves from all angles. Astrological considerations can be pondered, since occult lore holds that the bowl of the cup corresponds to the dome of the sky and the leaves are like the stars in their configurations.

CHIROMANCY

Palmistry is an equally popular New Age technique that predicts physical events, prognosticates financial success, and prophesies the possibility of dire circumstances. A recent issue of an in-flight magazine published by a major airline declared, "Relax your old prejudices and suspicions. Allow a practicing palmist to tell you what's in your hand."

Those adept at the art scan the dominant hand for the life line, indicating major physical events; the head line, revealing mental capabilities; and the heart line, illustrating events connected with emotional qualities of the individual. Additional consideration is given to the success line, the health line, and the mounts, that portion of each hand where calluses are located near the finger joints. These mounts are named after planets, including Jupiter, Saturn, and Mercury, and are said to reveal the qualities of leadership, reserve, artistic competence, and persuasiveness.

The color of one's hand lines also indicates certain qualities. Pale lines denote poor health. Red lines show an active temperament. If the lines are yellowish, one's nature is said to be proud. When questioned about the prophetic abilities of palmistry, proponents caution that the practitioner of chiromancy can only issue warnings. It is the subject who must decide whether the predicted tendencies will be overcome.

NOSTRADAMUS

A popular source of prophecy is the writings of Nostradamus, a sixtccnth-century French medical doctor and avid occultist. His book *Centuries* consisted of a hundred verses composed in quatrains. Much of what he wrote seems a meaningless jumble, but some conclude his esoteric script predicted the rise of Hitler and other historical events, as well as still-future things. Most recently, Californians were alarmed by a video docu-drama concerning Nostradamus that suggested a major earthquake was due near the San Andreas fault—not exactly "earth-shattering" news.

Nostradamus was born of Jewish descent on December 14, 1503. He was raised on the classic languages and attained a doctor's degree, though his reputation as a physician went beyond anatomical boundaries. Nostradamus delved into alchemy, magic, and the occult to publish his *Centuries* volumes, which dealt with events from his time to the end of the world, predicted to come in 3797. He took the word *centuries* to refer to the 100 four-line verses in which his prose was styled.

For those worried about nuclear war, there is this advice: "In the year 1999 and 7 months, there will come from heaven the great king of terror, to raise again the great king of the Mongols, before and after Mars shall reign at will."[3] Hitler himself was fascinated with *Centuries*. Others thought the French term "hister" in one of the quatrains was an anagram for Hitler. Goebbels's wife supervised the German printing of Nostradamus's writings because she believed they prophesied a victorious Third Reich. These predictions were often dropped in pamphlet form from Nazi aircraft.

A reference to three brothers and the Antichrist's annihilating one of them led some in the 1960s to believe Nostradamus predicted the assassination of the Kennedys. Other followers of *Centuries* say he foretold air travel, the military use of aircraft, the space race, electricity, submarines, and even a bombing of New York City.

Critics of Nostradamus claim that even a cursory analysis of his prophecies reveals the quatrains were meant to apply to his time. They were particularly directed to the nobility of his age. Nostradamus apparently wrote in an obscure form of French that was mixed with his own unique linguistic construction. Consequently, his supposed predictions were virtually indecipherable to his contemporaries, let alone understandable centuries later.

Most who read his *Centuries* fail to realize that each version has been heavily editorialized with the translator's own views.

WATER WITCHING

The caves of the Atlas Mountains in North Africa contain wall drawings of a dowser at work 8,000 years ago. The first modern authentication of finding water with a forked stick appeared in medieval Germany. But water witching isn't the only use of this occult craft. In the seventeenth century, William Lilly, an English astrologer, used what he called mosaical rods to discover buried treasure. Ritual magic textbooks of that era published elaborate instructions for preparation and use of divining rods. Today, the New Age Movement considers dowsing rods just one more component in the arsenal of articles available to the student pursuing nonrational means of obtaining information.

The American Society of Dowsers says everyone is born with the ability. Members search for lost articles, archaeological sites, missing persons, and downed aircraft, and they also track criminals and identify malfunctions in home appliances. One dowser says he witches for electrical shorts when his normal skills as an electrician don't suffice. Another dowser consults his pendulum to find out if girls in the office secretly love him.

The image of a dowser, forked hazel rod in hand, plodding over ground that conceals water is fading fast. Today, skilled dowsers stand at a field's edge and determine by remote conjuration the exact location of water. Other water witchers zero in on their targets using only a map of the location. Adept dowsers say they can witch for water from across the street or over the ocean with equal success.

The general technique is to hold a Y-shaped rod in one's hands. When the object or substance being sought is near, the end of the Y twitches downward. Dowsers say a sensation of tightness surges throughout their bodies, and a tingling in their arms precedes the rod's movement. What causes it?

Various theories have been postulated. One suggests that small magnetic field gradient changes (or electromagnetic radiations) stimulate sensors in the adrenal and pituitary glands. Stimuli are then transmitted to the brain, which commands the arms to twist. The minute movement is magnified by the length of the rod, which is a mechanical parametric amplifier. This theory claims that since the attracting field patterns are contingent upon their generator sources, dowsers can program their brains to respond to any kind of stimuli, including water, oil, pipes, or lost objects.

The spectrum of current uses of dowsing ranges from major oil companies to the U.S. armed services. During the Vietnam conflict, American Marines sometimes used bent coat hangers to detect mines, booby traps, and Viet Cong tunnels. An advocate in New Zealand claims to breed horses by reliance on a pendulum to compile breeding charts. In France, over a hundred medical dowsers are officially recognized as a professional group by the ministry of labor. Some New Agers dowse with crystals to locate disease. The crystal hangs from a string while a series of questions is asked. Pendular response guides the healer.

ASTROLOGY

Ms. Nevada Hudson, owner of a temporary employment agency, commutes to work like most other people in her Dallas suburb. But when Nevada arrives at the office, similarities end. Instead of visiting the coffee machine, she heads for her computer to punch in the numbers of her natal chart. In about forty-five seconds, a series of numbers and signs appears on the screen, giving Ms. Hudson all the predictive assistance she requests to guide her day. An Aries, Ms. Hudson is an astrologer who faithfully follows her horoscope.[4]

According to the Gallup polls, 50 million Americans believe their destinies are determined by the movements of celestial bodies. Though astrology has been around for centuries, the New Age Movement has propelled its popularity. In 1970, the American Federation of Astrologers in Tempe, Arizona, had only 1,500 members. Today it claims 5,000.[5]

New Agers have diversified the use of astrology. Some specialize in personal and corporate zodiac charts. Others give guidance on the stock market and recommendations on horse-track betting. Still others help select perfumes, diagnose disease, advise on choosing a pet, and meddle in the affairs of love and romance, telling customers who to love, mate, and bed, and not necessarily in that order. There are astrological greeting cards and perfumes, the latter a line of twelve zodiacal scents, including "Warm Leo," "Balanced Libra," and "Active Aries." Regarded at various times in history as a science or the bluff of buffoonery, astrology today is an active aspect of New Age regalia.

BIORHYTHMS

If you worked for the Wycoff Company of Pocatello, you'd never have a problem knowing when a bad day was in store. The Idaho package express firm provides its sixty drivers with biorhythm charts, advising extra caution on so-called critical days. At one time, AT&T computers in New York were programmed to compare biorhythm charts. A Swiss medical clinic schedules operations according to the charts and claims to have reduced postoperative complications by 30 percent.[6]

For nearly a decade, biorhythms have been lauded as an effective tool for revealing human potential. The concept goes back to a German nose-and-throat specialist named Wilhelm Fliess, a contemporary of Freud. Through his involvement with mystical speculation and numerology, Fliess became convinced that the number twenty-three contained physical significance. The number twenty-eight was designated to correspond with emotional cycles. He then added a thirty-three-day cycle pertaining to the intellect.

Starting the day a person is born, each of the twenty-three-, twenty-eight-, and thirty-three-day periods is plotted. When depicted on a graph, the modulating cycles are indicated as curves above and below a horizontal line at the center of each complete cycle. If the curve is above the line, high energy is expected. The person should be full of vitality in that area of his life. Creativity and cheerfulness can be expected. After passing the midpoint of the cycle, the line curves downward, signifying a recharging period. At this time, the person will likely be tired, moody, and unable to concentrate.

A critical day is revealed when the midpoint of the curve crosses the line, a transition day demanding attention. If two of these twenty-three-, twenty-eight-, or thirty-three-day cycles should cross at the same midpoint, it is known as a "double-critical" day. Watch out! If all three cycles cross at the same midpoint, a "triple-critical" day is at hand, and extreme caution should be exercised.

As popularized by the New Age Movement, biorhythms have attracted an unusual group of advocates. Consulting firms employ them. Special biorhythm calculators are available from New Age mail order houses. Sports enthusiasts and gamblers all have reasons to predict their winning days. It's claimed that about 5,000 Japanese firms believe in the efficacy of biorhythms. Defenders and detractors square off with equal aplomb. Dr. Colin Pittendrigh of Stanford University says, "I consider the biorhythm theory an utter, total, unadulterated fraud. I consider anyone who offers to explain my life in terms of twenty-three-, twenty-eight-, and thirty-three-day cycles a numerical nut."

The author of a book on biorhythms says a large percentage of commercial and private airplane crashes is attributable to human error on a pilot's "critical" days; thus, many crashes presumably could be avoided if pilots refrained from flying on such days. A researcher at the University of Minnesota Chronobiology Laboratory dismisses biorhythms as a "silly numerological scheme that contradicts everything we know about real biorhythms with their dozens of variables."[7]

Advocates say proof of biorhythms' predictive power exists in the history of famous people. On down or critical days, Ted Kennedy experienced his misadventure at Chappaquiddick; Marilyn Monroe and Judy Garland poisoned themselves; Arthur Bremer attempted to kill Governor George Wallace; and Sirhan Sirhan assassinated Robert Kennedy.

Researchers acknowledge the body does have chronobiological rhythms, including an inner clock that regulates sleep, another that calculates appetite, and a hormonal regulator that affects menstruation, hair growth, and fertility. The real rhythms of the body are circadian (twenty-four-hour cycles regulating sleep); ultradian (100-minute cycles influencing appetite and sex); circamensual (monthly cycles of hormones); and circannual (yearly clocks governing hair growth and menstruation). Scientists insist these somewhat predictable cycles are a far cry from the claims of biorhythm believers, who assert their ability to forestall death, destruction, heartache, and inefficiency.

AURAS

"Don't look for Sherwin Williams colors. Look past the person. Look for evanescent colors." That's the advice of one psychic who claims he can detect health, sickness, anger, and enthusiasm by the brightly glowing emanations surrounding a person's body.

Said to be a manifestation of one's higher self, auras are a field of multi-hued colors surrounding one's body, radiating from a few inches to several feet in every direction. The dominant color at any point in time is said to indicate the emotional, physical, and spiritual condition of the subject. Dark red shows anger, black indicates stress, and blue means a state of peacefulness. A smaller aura displays tension, while a more widely dispersed one demonstrates a relaxed condition.

Auras are said to exist in three zones. The first extends no more than a half inch from the body. This is the "etheric double" of one's physique. From that band, the inner aura extends an additional three inches. The outer aura expands a foot or more. Psychics generally contend that anyone can read these auras if he is attuned to them.

One New Age teacher claims to use aura reading regularly in the classroom to ascertain the capabilities of his students. Once, he witnessed a swirling, overly-active aura and discovered the student was pregnant and worried that she wouldn't be able to finish school. The teacher was able to direct her to helpful counseling, which he says exemplifies how learning to read auras would create a more aware, compassionate world.

Because New Agers often concentrate on the healing aspects of occult indulgences, the use of auras for relieving problems is stressed. In conjunction with guided imagery, a patient may be told to visualize a healing blue light surrounding the afflicted area.

DREAMWORK

Who wrote *Dr. Jekyll and Mr. Hyde?* Robert Louis Stevenson? Wrong. The correct answer is the "brownies."

The brownies? That's what Stevenson called them. They were "little people" who appeared to him in dreams. Whenever he was running low on money and needed to write, he would sleep, dream, then ask the little people to spin stories for him. Edgar Allan Poe apparently also relied on dreams. The master of the macabre drew heavily on his nightmares to write chilling poems.

Jung, Freud, and the prophet Daniel would be amazed to witness how dreams are used today to guide human behavior. (All three were involved with dream interpretation.) The New Age concept of dreamwork divorces dreams from a psychoanalytical and biblical framework. Dreams supposedly are honest indications of immediate predicaments. More assertive New Agers believe dreams link the subconscious with the Universal Mind. What one dreams is said to be a unified connection to the global and cosmic forces of clairvoyance. Dream guidance is suggested as a means of achieving future goals. According to one dreamwork advocate, "Dreams are among God's original blessings for those who are visionary enough to attune their innate wisdom to Divine Direction."[8]

New Agers have adopted various forms of dream therapy, because they believe nocturnal fantasies are directly linked with the superconscious, one's higher spiritual self. They insist that supernatural revelation is not limited to religious teachers and sacred books, but that direct contact with "truth" is possible while asleep, when our cognitive inhibitions are at rest. Insisting that even the Bible uses dreams as a medium of revelation, they encourage direct communication with whatever being may appear in dreams, assuming the innate goodness and spiritual validity of any information received during slumber.

New Agers say that dreams reflect an unconscious response to waking reality. New Age dream analysts seek ways to translate that unconscious point of view into terms the conscious mind can comprehend. Dreams are a bridge between two states of mind, two ways of experiencing reality. They

141

are also considered a precognitive key to warning against certain actions. In addition, some New Agers insist that dreamwork can actually change reality. By controlling dreams, one can manipulate real life.

RUNES

"Should I take that job? Am I ready for marriage? Will this venture make me rich? When in doubt, reach for your runes."

Runes? That's what the promotional brochure says. Previously, runes were known only to those interested in Scandinavian mythology. With the advent of the New Age Movement, however, runes have become a major form of occult divination. Viking legend claims its supreme god, Odin, sacrificed an eye in his consuming passion to win the sacred knowledge runes contained.

Runes were originally characters of an alphabet used in an ancient form of Germanic writing. Consisting of twenty-four characters and typified by angular shapes, the earliest runes were credited with miraculous powers. They were thought to possess the ability to tell the future and were considered sacred talismans. It was common for those during the Viking epoch (about A.D. 800) to inscribe weapons and jewelry with runic symbols. To make the magic more potent, the inscription was frequently carved on the back of the object so the spell would work in secret.

Today, New Age bookstores and metaphysical shops sell these small clay or stone replicas as a means of interpreting dreams, attaining self-knowledge, and as oracles of the past and future. They are promoted as nothing less than a "personal adviser" contributing a dimension of "self-awareness."

Usage is simple. The rune stones (each inscribed with a letter from the Viking alphabet) are held or laid in front of the one seeking an answer. Gradually, a resolution is supposed to emerge from the core of the "listening heart." But where does the answer really come from? According to one advocate, runes will "put you in touch with your own inner guidance, with the part of you that knows everything you need to know for your life now."[9]

STRAIGHT ANSWERS

Q: *Can the I Ching actually foretell the future, or is casting yarrow sticks merely arbitrary?*

A: Divinatory devices that involve the erratic forces of chance generally reveal only what is intuitively assumed. There is always a possibility, however, that evil, supernatural forces could manipulate the results to validate a preselected plan and lead the seeker spiritually astray. Even so, evil supernatural forces are neither omniscient nor omnipotent, having absolute control over the future.

Q: *Do Tarot cards reveal objective insights about reality, or does their interpretation depend on the reader's responses?*

A: The Tarot is one of the least precise forms of occult divination. In fact, there are no standardized pictures appearing on the cards. Some adherents make up their own diagrammed figures and attach their own meanings to these designations. In addition, there are several methods of shuffling and laying the cards. Such arbitrariness ensures inaccuracy in determining crucial information. Consequently, Tarot cards are only a psychic point of contact between the reader and the subject.

Q: *Does an unseen force guide the manner in which tea leaves come to rest in a cup to provide a view of the future?*

A: Gravity determines how the leaves land. The variables of interpretation concerning the lay of the leaves are so erratic that almost any configuration could indicate something. For example, a triangular form supposedly indicates jealousy or rivalry. The tea-leaf reader would normally proceed to ask clever questions that the unsuspecting client would innocently answer, giving sufficient information to draw common-sense conclusions. If few leaves are left, it means direct action needs to be taken. An array of leaves without a pattern indicates confusion. Both are suitably ambiguous deductions to satisfy the patron that psychically derived data has been acquired.

Q: *Is the palm of one's hand a mirror of his past life and future plans?*

A: The creases and patterns in one's hand exhibit vocational use more than reflections of the soul. The relationship of palmistry to astrological guidance further shows its whimsical nature. In most cases, the palmist is probably studying the customer's body language and listening carefully to answers of prudently worded quatrains. Thus, the indications of the fate line or the heart line are more likely an evaluation of the conversation than of the hand.

Q: *Did Nostradamus see the future, or do his advocates only retro- spectively read into his predictions something he couldn't have known?*

A: The colorful and highly metaphorical language employed by Nostradamus insures a variety of translations. Anyone profess- ing biblical allegiance cannot accept the predictions of his questions. To believe Nostradamus is to deny the scriptural premise that only the Lord knows the future because "the se- cret things belong to the Lord our God."[10]

Q: *Is there a natural scientific explanation for dowsing?*

A: Various theories have been suggested, such as molecular mag- netism, the converging of some undefined biocosmic force, and electromagnetic attraction. One theory proposes that ground water is positively charged and the dowser is nega- tively charged, converting the sap-filled dowsing rod into a conductor. Another hypothesis suggests the dowser receives undetectable extrasensory impulses, but there is no way to measure minute muscular movements that dowsers claim are subconsciously generated. Actually, there is no way to verify any of the explanations for water witching. In fact, many scien- tific reports show that dowsing never achieves any better than chance results, which cannot be predicted reliably in any sin- gle situation.

Q: *Can the stars and other planets affect our lives on earth?*

A: The gravitational pull of the moon on the tides, the energy-generating power of sunlight, and photosynthesis are scientifically measurable ways in which heavenly bodies affect life on earth. Other kinds of radiant and gravitational effects may be possible, but that is far removed from concluding that decisions regarding life and love can be influenced by Jupiter and Mars. The current zodiac charts were constructed prior to Copernicus, when an erroneous geocentric view of the cosmos dominated thought. Since the horoscope characteristics were assigned centuries ago, a gradual, slight shift on the earth's axis has resulted in the shift of an entire astrological house. Modern astrologers have never updated their blueprint of the heavens to include this alteration. Also, each religious branch of astrology assigns different characteristics to each house, so that a horoscope cast by a Buddhist in Bangkok will say something much different from the horoscope of a Hindu in Calcutta.

Q: *Do the natural biorhythmic cycles of the mind and body have any predictive value?*

A: The science of chronobiology recognizes the body does have biological rhythms that follow somewhat predictable, though variable, patterns. Blood pressure, respiration, temperature, pulse rate, blood sugar, hormones, and hemoglobin levels all conform to moderately definable configurations. One doctor who has studied chronobiology concluded that by charting rhythms of cell division in healthy and cancerous tissue, it may be possible to determine the most appropriate time to conduct chemotherapy. But assuming that human behavior can be controlled and anticipated by studying the body's internal rhythms leaves the arena of science and enters the realm of occultism.

Q: *Is there a varicolored aura surrounding the human body that can be seen and psychically analyzed?*

A: Science has yet to confirm that anything such as an aura exists. Kirlian photography has reproduced color emanations from fingertips, but some scientists insist this involves nothing more than the ionization of the air from warmth of the hand and is not internal radiation from man's soul, as claimed by New Agers. The phenomenon could be hallucinatory or spiritistic. In the latter case, it could be a demonic occurrence visible only to the eye of the beholder, who is experiencing satanic manipulation of his senses.

Q: *Can dreams be a gateway to the soul, revealing our true nature?*

A: Psychologists say dreams reflect our inner thought life and may mirror repressed anxieties or inhibited desires. That deduction hardly assigns a predictive quality to dreams. It is true that in the Old Testament God sometimes revealed His will through dreams. But we observe no continuing occurrence of this practice in the New Testament, because the guidance of Holy Scripture and the presence of the Spirit of truth abides with us to give continuing counsel day and night. When God did use dreams it was under His direction and at His prerogative. Such dreams could not be solicited, controlled, or interpreted without the Lord's guidance. Those who believe dreams provide access to psychic powers and are a means of guiding the future venture into the territory of divination, which God has forbidden. According to Scripture, interpretation of dreams belongs to the Lord. Nebuchadnezzar's occult soothsayers could not reveal his dreams, but Daniel declared, "There is a God in heaven who reveals secrets."[11]

Q: *Can runes predict, or are their prognostications merely capricious?*

A: Runes are yet another means of exposing one's spirit to evil vulnerabilities and subjecting human inquisitiveness to fatalistic forces. No power of perception exists in a piece of rock. The only information comes from the imagination of the seeker or the imposition of information by demons.

WHO'S WHO AND WHAT'S WHAT

Astrology: The ancient art of the occult Chaldeans; it supposes that the planets and other heavenly bodies have power over the decisions and destinies of men on earth, depending on the planets' alignments and arbitrarily assigned characteristics.

Auras: Color emanations surrounding the human body that reveal the condition of the body, soul, and spirit, depending on the visionary analysis of the psychic viewing the aura.

Biorhythms: An occult explanation for the rhythmical recurrence of physical and psychological tendencies, presuming existence of a precise regularity that can be used to chart human behavior.

Book of Changes: A 3,000-year-old book of Chinese wisdom, consisting of sixty-four sections, each introduced by a hexagram, and said to reveal the secrets of the universe and the path to a blameless, peaceful existence on earth.

Centuries: See *Nostradamus*.

Chiromancy: See *Palmistry*.

Dowsing: Use of a hazel rod or other Y-shaped device that responds with attraction to a predetermined substance hidden underground, detectable by one who possesses the gift or has cultivated so-called water witching expertise.

Dream Therapy: The theory that future events can be determined by dream analysis since these nocturnal visions reveal the goals and desires of one's higher spiritual self.

I Ching: See *Book of Changes*.

Nostradamus: (1503-1555) A French physician and occultist whose esoteric poetry many believe foretold events of modern history.

Palmistry: The assumption that the shape, size, and creases of a person's hand reflect past experiences and foreshadow coming events.

Runes: Stones inscribed with letters of the ancient Scandinavian alphabet, believed to have been used by the Vikings for predictive purposes and revived today for fortune telling.

Tarot Cards: Playing cards with specially inscribed figures and emblems (such as the moon, sun, devil, and Egyptian god Isis) that are said to reveal the cosmic purpose of the universe and the future of each individual's life.

Tasseography: See *Tea-Leaf Reading.*

Tea-Leaf Reading: An imprecise method of divination suggesting that the patterns formed by tea leaves left in the bottom of a cup reveal hidden truths about the subject in question.

Water Witching: See *Dowsing.*

IN MY OPINION

Since civilization began, people have looked for ways to predict the future and uncover the purposes of the past. Some sought the significance of a single event, such as lighting a fire (capnomancy). Others studied causimomancy, the fate of objects thrown into the fire. Still others surveyed the entrails of animals or contemplated the bumps on the head (phrenology) or the moles on a face (moleosophy).

If they could know the future, people felt they could act on the information to better their circumstances or outwit the gods. Even today, nearly a million Frenchmen have paid $20 each for a computerized translation of Nostradamus's *Centuries,* 400 years after it was written. Christian critics are not alone in warning that such searches are futile and dangerous. Commenting on astrology and similar pseudosciences, a university professor of astronomy remarked, "It's dangerous to cling to this superstition because it abdicates responsibilities for your actions and your own destiny. That's a very dangerous illusion to live by."[12]

Often forgotten is the poor track record demonstrated by psychics and diviners. Jeane Dixon, who has parlayed her prognostications into millions of dollars, once said Jacqueline

Kennedy would not remarry. Apparently her zodiac charts never consulted a Greek ship owner named Onassis. If psychics and fortune tellers have anything in common, it is a studied ambiguity that circumvents exacting scrutiny.

In this uncertain age, people are searching for patterns of security by which to live. They want to know what fatalistic forces guide the movements of men, the decisions of governments, and the destinies of civilizations. And they are willing to accept less than total accuracy. God is not. Deuteronomy 18:22 warns, "When a prophet speaks in the name of the Lord, if the thing does not happen . . . that is the thing which the Lord has not spoken." So stern was God's view of psychic error that capital punishment was instituted for any self-proclaimed prophet whose prophecies did not come true.

Not all occult divination is inaccurate. Sometimes the law of averages prevails and a psychic prediction lucks out. In other instances, common sense succeeds and intuition triumphs to give the appearance of a portent. Sometimes, evil forces conspire to predict a course of action, then summarily fulfill it with seeming accuracy. But even when the information is unerring, God's principles cannot be ignored. In Acts 16, a damsel with a spirit of divination followed the apostle Paul for several days, declaring that Paul was sent from God. But the apostle would not accept the praise and endorsement of a demon despite its apparent reliability. Deuteronomy 13 warns that even when a prophecy comes to pass, the prediction is not to be revered if the prognosticator is an idolater.

Why does the Bible have such exacting standards for evaluating prognostication? Psychic determinism and fatalistic chance lure people away from trusting God, whose mercy guides the affairs of humanity. In the process, volitional accountability is ignored. There is always someone or something else to blame: "My biorhythms weren't right" or "My horoscope chart said I could do it." If Eve had been a New Ager, imagine how much more creative her excuse might have been!

Chapter 8

THE GRATEFUL DEAD

Straight Answers on New Age
Consciousness

Kathryn Lanza, a thirty-three-year-old Los Angeles legal secretary, knows what will happen when she dies. A hole will be cut in her skull, her brains will be removed, and the cavity will be filled with resins. Her internal organs, except her heart, will be extracted and placed in jars, and her body will be stuffed with herbs and submerged for two weeks in a preserving solution. She'll be coated with myrrh, scented with frankincense, and wrapped in silk and linen. Her bodily remains will then be placed in a noncorrosive metal sarcophagus lined with blue velvet. Kathryn Lanza will be mummified like the ancient pharaohs.[1]

In Salt Lake City, Utah, Summan Bonum Amen-Ra founded a New Age cult dedicated to understanding the spiritual forces he believes governed ancient Atlantis and Egypt. Summan lifted rituals from the ancient *Tibetan Book of the Dead* to derive a mummification process that ranges from a no-frills $7,000 job to a $500,000 extravaganza that includes a sarcophagus encrusted with gold leaf and jewels. One of the fifty customers who have signed up declares, "I want to be at peace when I die. I am no longer scared of death."[2]

Immortality is a mainstay of futuristic New Age thought. Unlike the scientific rationalists who have dominated the American mindset since the 1950s, New Agers are convinced there is life after death in one form or another. That's why cremation, cryonics, and even mummification attract an increasing number of customers who believe disposition of the body profoundly affects its immortal destination.

There are differing ideas determining which form of burial one should choose. Historically, cremation has been selected by those who believe the spirit should be released from the body for its next incarnation. Cryonics may be embraced by those who want their bodies re-animated at some later date. Mummification is picked as a way to prepare the body for its journey to the world of the afterlife where it progresses through various spiritual planes.

Cryonics is an increasingly popular, though expensive, means of insuring an orderly transition to the next life—or a possible return to this one. For

153

only $125,000, one's dead body can be frozen with the hope it will be revived after science has learned to reverse death or repair damaged cells.

Cryonics involves putting the dead patient on a heart and lung machine to maintain a heartbeat and keep blood circulating. Ice is gradually applied around the body to lower the body temperature, while various chemicals are injected. Then the patient is taken to a laboratory where the blood is replaced with a balanced salt solution, which in turn is displaced later with a glycerol solution to minimize tissue damage. Finally, it's off to the warehouse, where the body is tucked into a cooling chest that resembles a coffin. The corpse is covered with dry ice until it reaches a temperature of -320 degrees Fahrenheit, after which it is covered with a foil material and put into a bag.

For those incapable of affording mummification or cryonics, the philosophy of reincarnation suffices. Shirley MacLaine's publishers report that since the release of her first New Age tome, *Out on a Limb,* they have been flooded with letters from readers claiming they knew MacLaine in a past life. One of them wrote, "Shirley is a gutsy gal, who is giving me the courage to say I was a Catholic nun in the eleventh century."[3]

In *Out on a Limb,* MacLaine insists that in her many past lives she was, among other things, an aristocrat beheaded during the French Revolution, and a prostitute. Hence, she says, her warm regard for contemporary ladies of the night, and, her critics conclude, her own morally controversial lifestyle. "This book is a quest for myself, a long journey . . . firmly exposed to dimensions of time and space that I would describe as the occult," she declares.[4] MacLaine also quotes Carl Jung as having said, "What happens after death is so unspeakably glorious that our imagination and our feelings do not suffice to form even an approximate conception of it."[5]

How did MacLaine reach her conclusions about immortality? She explored a variety of occult disciplines, including contacting an entity through a trance medium. One of her New Age spiritual mentors informed her, "When we die, only our bodies die. Our souls simply leave them and take up residence in the astral form. It's all necessary for the development of the soul."[6]

The New Age Movement has effectively transformed mankind's most fundamental question from "Who am I?" into "Who was I?" Consequently, various groups espousing reincarnation are enjoying a resurgent interest in their teachings. These organizations include The Association for Research and Enlightenment (Edgar Cayce's group), the Urantia Foundation, the Theosophical Society, and Unity School of Christianity. Their growing memberships are reflected in a recent study indicating that 60 percent of Americans consider reincarnation a reasonable probability.

MYSTICISM AND ENLIGHTENMENT

Exotic views of immortality are only part of the New Age mindset. Theories of enlightenment and mystical insights are abundant. *California Business* magazine asked state business leaders a series of questions regarding spiritual phenomena and discovered that 69 percent of Californians questioned said they were guided by a spiritual force, even though 30 percent said they never attended religious services. Interestingly, more than 50 percent claimed their spiritual insights had come from various New Age consciousness-raising techniques.

The mystical search of the New Age Movement is a quest for "consciousness." Science, behaviorism, metaphysics, psychology, and religion have been combined to navigate uncharted realms of human potential. The key to New Age mysticism is discovering that reality depends upon the viewer's perspective. Since mankind is on an evolutionary course toward developing greater "potentiality," even the self can be recreated by an altered viewpoint.

Enlightenment in assorted New Age models has become big business. And the search for these insights no longer requires years of arduous discipline in remote sanctuaries. The word is out that enlightenment is for everyone, quickly and reasonably priced. Various psycho-technologies and consciousness-altering devices claim to induce transformative states. Some use hypnotic regression. Others offer out-of-the-body experiences by listening to taped astral sounds. Still other techniques embrace flotation tanks, hyperventilation, and frenetic dancing.

The end product has several names. In Zen, it is *satori*. In yoga, *samadhi*. In Hinduism, *nirvana*. In Sufism, *fana*. Some call it the "supreme consciousness." Others speak of "liberation" or "self-realization." To some it is the "mystic rose" or the "eternal flame." But whatever the intimation, for New Agers it is a holy grail, the end of their spiritual search in this life. Becoming one with the pantheistic cosmos is their goal. In the words of one New Age guru, Da Free John, "It is so direct, so obvious . . . [that] when you come to the point of acknowledging the Divine Identity and Condition of Manifested Existence, then you are enlightened."[7] If such doublespeak endorsing one's own ego as god doesn't make sense to the rationalist, the response is predictable: It works, therefore it must be right.

STRAIGHT ANSWERS

Q: *Is there anything wrong with replacing the traditional funeral and burial ceremony with an alternate means of disposing of the deceased?*

A: The particular technique may not of itself be objectionable, but the philosophy behind body disposal is crucial. New Agers want to deny Christian warnings regarding the horrors of hell and to avoid acknowledgment of an eternal judgment. Consequently, they pursue funeral arrangements that reflect their philosophy, such as cremation, which suggests the spirit is freed by destroying the body. In contrast, Christian burial testifies to faith in the biblical doctrine regarding the resurrection of the body.

Q: *Why are Shirley MacLaine's books and spiritual conclusions so uncritically accepted?*

A: To New Agers, truth is self-validating, based on experience. Therefore, no matter how incredible and nonobjective MacLaine's meanderings may be, her "truth" is considered to be truth for her. She also claims supernatural verification in the form of messages from entities of a higher spiritual consciousness.

Q: *Is it true that Christ taught reincarnation?*

A: Though reincarnation was a popular theory among some sects of mystical Jews at the time of Christ, not a single Scripture exists to endorse this proposition. Some reincarnationists cite John 8:58 ("Before Abraham was, I AM.") as evidence. But if Christ had suggested he was Abraham reincarnated, he would have been dismissed as a lunatic by his legalistic Jewish audiences. In fact, the Jewish leaders sought to kill Christ for blasphemy because they knew his statement was an assertion of his eternal deity (see v. 59; 10:30–33).

Q: *Doesn't the Bible teach that John the Baptist was a reincarnation of the prophet Elijah?*

A: Reincarnationists have claimed that Matthew 11:14 says John the Baptist was Elijah come again. But Luke 1:17 clearly explains that John came in "the spirit and power," the *style*, of Elijah's ministry.

Q: *Why are some traditional churches losing members to New Age cults?*

A: Sterile theology cannot compete with the supernatural dynamics and profound experiences claimed by New Agers. Their religion is one of immediacy, providing apparent empirical evidence for their beliefs. Liberal theologians, who have "demythologized" the Bible by downgrading the miraculous accounts of Scripture, leave those seeking validation for their lives vulnerable to New Age claims of sensory certification.[8]

Q: *If the accounts of past lives told by reincarnationists aren't true, why are they so convincingly accurate?*

A: Those with low self-esteem readily invent stories of marvelous past existences when they were persons of power, beauty, and nobility. These accounts are often conjured from the subconscious mind, which contains an incalculable record of sights and sounds, along with thousands of bits of long-forgotten information. Unrecalled movies, TV programs, photographs, songs, and literature may congeal into the "recollection" of an esteemed past life. Also, the influence of demons could concoct a past life scenario and hallucinogenically implant its fiction.

Q: *If New Age enlightenment is occult, is there any kind of proper spiritual insight one should seek?*

A: The apostle John declared that Jesus is "the true Light which gives light to every man."[9] For the Christian, spiritual perspicacity is centered in a person, Christ, not an experience. In truth, the enlightenment of New Age mysticism is actually the darkness of the devil, who has transformed himself into "an angel of light."[10]

WHO'S WHO AND WHAT'S WHAT

Association for Research and Enlightenment: See *Edgar Cayce.*

Atlantis: A mythical civilization buried in the sea after a volcanic explosion and earthquake, believed to be the center of an ancient occult people adept in psychic powers and possessing the secrets of higher consciousness sought by New Agers.

Cayce, Edgar: A twentieth-century psychic who entered countless trances, giving nearly 9,000 "readings" that proposed cures for the body and mind.

Cremation: The practice of burning the dead body, historically founded on the Eastern mystical concept that unless the body is destroyed at death, it will become a prison for the soul and prevent future transmigrations.

Cryonics: The science of freezing the body upon death for future thawing and rejuvenation once a cure is found for what caused its demise.

Enlightenment: A state of awareness (sometimes called "nirvana," "cosmic consciousness," or "transcendental bliss") that assumes all of existence is interwoven and man is innately god with untapped potential.

Flotation tanks: Cylinders containing a saline solution in which people lie, floating on the water's surface to create an illusion of cosmic awareness to achieve spiritual enlightenment (see Chap. 12).

Hyperventilation: Based on the Hindu theory that biocosmic power is in the breath and that by rapid breathing, one may transcend to a state of spiritual awareness.

Immortality: Immunity from any kind of death or decay that comes from having eternal, divine life; in Christianity, that immortality is received from God as his gracious gift.

Jung, Carl: A disciple of Sigmund Freud who entertained various forms of occultism, including the idea that the ultimate reality of existence and the source of all truth lies in a "collective unconsciousness" into which spiritually developed beings can tap.

MacLaine, Shirley: Academy Award-winning actress whose personal problems led her to investigate psychic phenomena from trance channeling to astral projection, resulting in a series of best-selling books (see Chap. 12).

Mummification: The ancient Egyptian means of preserving the physical body after death to facilitate its journey into the next life.

Mysticism: The experience of acquiring union or direct communion with ultimate reality, usually defined as the god within.

Out on a Limb: A book by Shirley MacLaine, published in 1983, recounting her experiences in South America that supposedly validate her previous occult encounters.

Reincarnation: The idea that existence is a series of endless cycles of returning to inhabit another body after death, depending on one's good and bad deeds in this life (as opposed to transmigration, which teaches that a person may return to the body of either a human, animal, or inanimate object).

Theosophical Society: A highly developed system of occultism based on mystery religions and Hindu philosophy, founded on the writings of Helena Petrovna Blavatsky, a nineteenth-century Russian mystic.

***Tibetan* Book of the Dead:** Scriptures of Tibetan Buddhism based on esoteric experiences concerning the nature of the soul and the stages to be encountered during death.

Unity School of Christianity: An eclectic cult based on the teachings of Charles and Myrtle Fillmore, late nineteenth-century spiritualists, who adapted the teachings of Christian Science and concluded that Jesus was merely a great teacher who acquired a "Christ-consciousness" we can all attain.

Urantia Foundation: Promotes psychic revelations and a cosmological view of the universe based on the 2,097-page *Urantia Book,* supposedly dictated by extraterrestrial beings (see Chap.10).

IN MY OPINION

Plato maintained nothing could destroy the soul. Aristotle said only reason was eternal. The Epicureans declared there is no consciousness after death, so one may as well eat, drink, and be merry. Today, equally adamant ideologies compete. Materialists insist man is a machine in a mechanized world, and since science cannot prove the dubious possibility of the soul's continued existence, immortality is unverifiable. Universalists say all will be saved, so no one should care what happens after death. Actor Glenn Ford says he was once eaten by lions as a Christian martyr, and macho-man Sylvester Stallone claims he was previously a Guatemalan monkey.

For the Christian, the hereafter holds certitude because mortality will be "swallowed up by life."[11] Those who trust in the Bible seek neither a highway to hell paved with endless orgies nor a paradise of sensuous delights. God's promise is sufficient: "Eye has not seen, nor ear heard, nor have entered into the heart of man the things which God has prepared for those who love him."[12]

Reincarnation is a serious consideration for some. Don't our souls need purifying? Why not let our existence continue until a state of perfection is finally reached and the soul can merge back into its source? Couldn't mental stress in this life be alleviated if the traumas of previous existences were identified? If a parent realizes a child had a history before conception, wouldn't that enhance respect for the newborn as an individual with a distinct chronology? Wouldn't everyone have an opportunity to finish every worthy goal left uncompleted at death?

Reincarnation insists there are countless opportunities for reformation. Christianity emphasizes the finished work of redemption achieved by Christ on the cross. Furthermore, reincarnation inhibits any choice of the will to determine a life of obedience to God's plan. Hidden in the implied merits of reincarnation is a selfishness that concedes no virtue in sacrificing for the welfare of others, since their lot in life is retribution for past sins. Reincarnation may seem reasonable until compared to a forgiving God who offers undeserved grace and mercy.

Unlike reincarnation, Christianity is not based on relativistic impressions of reality. It is founded on the teachings of Jesus and the doctrines of the apostles. It is what Jesus actually said and what his disciples really wrote that objectively guides the true follower of Christ. And no intermediaries are acceptable—not Buddha or Krishna, not angels, ascended masters, or channeled entities. Only Christ is the ultimate authority, because "all things were created through him and for him."[13] And the only enlightenment needed is to know him and "the hope of his calling, what are the riches of the glory of his inheritance in the saints."[14]

Today's explorers of truth are fond of contorting through postured positions and meditating to achieve deepened transcendental thought. As one New Age seeker said, "Enlightenment is the core truth of all religions. It is the essence of life. It is the discovery of the ultimate answer."[15] The search for ultimate reality instigated Jewish leaders to confront Christ in John 5. They demanded to know the authority by which he healed and forgave sins. Christ could have lured them down the road of spiritual introspection, but he did not. He might have told them to contemplate the cosmos, but he deferred. Instead, he offered himself and his teachings, declaring, "He who hears my word and believes in him who sent me has everlasting life, and shall not come into judgment."[16]

Zen masters are fond of confounding their disciples with irrational behavior to help them break out of conditioned cultural states. They pose insoluble riddles or ask unanswerable questions. As one stated, "Enlightenment is beyond words and concepts. It cannot be grasped by intellect or any aspect of our rational, mental being."[17]

In contrast, Jesus never told his initiates to play mind

games. He didn't instruct them to pursue an undifferentiated self that would dissolve their egos. Plainly and simply, he said, "I am the light of the world. He who follows me shall not walk in darkness."[18] New Agers may discover a form of enlightenment and a fleeting sense of well-being, but the darkness of their light cannot forgive sin.

Chapter 9

IT'S ALL IN THE SELLING

Straight Answers on New Age Media Manipulation

It's an axiom of modern life. Nothing and no one gets anywhere without advertising. Consumer products require it. Celebrities crave it. Movements demand it. Advertising is the stuff by which contemporary religious and social sects live or die. The New Age Movement has had its share of promotion, some deliberate, most incidental.

The press has been anything but silent. The *New York Times Sunday Magazine, Time, Newsweek, People,* and assorted periodicals have covered in detail the Movement and its eccentricities. New Agers say press coverage has been a campaign of ridicule. They accuse journalists of emphasizing flakiness, poor scholarship, narcissism, and delusions of grandeur while ignoring more serious aspects of New Age ideology such as futurism, social engineering, anthropology, and behaviorism.

Newspapers and magazines have had a heyday covering New Age events and phenomena. Headlines have ranged from "Moronic Convergence" to "New Age: The End of the World—Again." New Age proponents say the press is interested in conflict and confrontation because they make catchy headlines. Since their cause appeals for peace and world harmony, New Age Movement incidents supposedly become targets for insult.

But the Movement has done quite well on its own, bombarding bookstores with an incredible array of music, books, and audio and video tapes. In fact, rather than being the brunt of abuse, the Movement has seduced the public with a slick crusade, glossing over its freakishness and highlighting its proposed benefits. While New Agers accuse the press of vilifying their motives and methods, some argue that the Movement has manipulated the media to advertise in complimentary terms its vision for the future.

It certainly hasn't lacked exposure. New Age books appear in the racks of America's airports and supermarkets. Ballantine Books is contracting to reprint books on New Age subjects that previously were released only by specialized dealers. According to *Publisher's Weekly,* a thousand New Age bookstores can be found throughout the United States, and thirty new ones spring up each month. Fifty-two publishers have formed the New Age Publishing Alliance to promote the Movement's books. Their motto: "A consciousness whose time has come."[1]

The networking capabilities of the New Age Movement have expanded proportionately to technological advances. Laser printers and word processing software are increasingly employed. Exchange networks of floppy disks have been established to propagate the latest New Age rage. Computers have proved especially helpful in performing the complex mathematical calculations necessary for astrological computations.

A high percentage of New Age published product is being bought by women. Movement leaders acknowledge that a female spirituality movement is growing rapidly. Many New Age women are discovering an interest in female fertility religions, which they claim historically preceded male-deity religion. Female spirituality advocates claim one universal goddess religion was supreme before patriarchal creeds dominated civilization. Consequently, many New Age writers aim their books at the female consumer.

The perspective of New Age literature has shifted in recent years. Metaphysical bookstores previously carried volumes about occult phenomena. Today, New Age bookshelves contain an increasing number of experiential volumes. Writers such as Shirley MacLaine are telling readers how to personally apply occult concepts. This workbook approach has brought New Age ideas from abstract realms into practical approaches. Along with such pragmatism, product appearance has been upgraded. Metaphysical books are no longer inexpensively produced with plain covers. Book retailers like Waldenbooks and B. Dalton have encouraged quality by demanding better layout design and more evocative covers.

These advances have introduced formerly esoteric materials into the publishing mainstream. Consequently, the occult is going public. Housewives are attempting channeling. Ordinary consumers are purchasing tomes on the Tarot. America's mundane mindset is turning on to the secrets of divination, including astral projection and creative visualization. Fads are developing. Yesterday it was pyramids. Today, crystals. Tomorrow? Check out the bookshelf.

NEW AGE MUSIC

Nothing has done more to promote mainstream movement acceptance than New Age music, already a $100 million a year business.[2] Derisively referred to by some as yuppie elevator music, its aesthetic appeal attracts those who want to set emotional moods for mind trips. John Sebastian, a major radio consultant, left his $400,000 a year job promoting rock 'n' roll to program New Age music for client stations. Sebastian says, "New Age music creates an ambience, an atmosphere, almost an oasis. It is music for people who are intelligent and sophisticated."

Instrumental artists are flooding the market with relaxing sounds bearing titles like "Cosmic Energy" and "Sister-Sea." The soft and dreamy vibrations attempt to create musical moods consistent with the philosophy of New Age consciousness. Andrea Vollenweider, a Swiss harpist specializing in New Age music, says of the genre, "With this music, you can build a bridge between the conscious and the subconscious . . . to excite our spirituality."

Records, cassettes, and CDs are often retailed through such nontraditional outlets as health food stores, metaphysical bookshops, and meditation centers. Some say it's more yuppie than transcendental because of its appeal to the upwardly mobile segment of society. Some have dubbed it Aquarian Musak because of its blandness. Whatever the appellation, it has penetrated a significant portion of the FM audience.

Early roots of New Age music can be found in progressive instrumental music first released in the 1970s. More recently, however, its development accelerated through accompanying metaphysical concepts of New Age philosophy. In New Age music, intent is more important than form. It may be acoustic, electronic, or both. It can contain elements of classical patterns or exude free-form ambient explorations. True New Age music, as distinguished from the more commercial variety, is composed to affect the listener's consciousness.

The labels producing New Age music claim it will sweep radio programming off its feet. The most devoted adherents say it conditions people to accept New Age thought. English-born rock musician Eddy Jobson, who used to perform with the group Roxy Music, says it is a "soundtrack for the movie of the mind."[3] Referring to the globalistic slant of New Age music, a composer describes it as "music that springs from a world culture." Another radio consultant declares, "It merely continues where the Pink Floyd album 'Dark Side of the Moon' left off."

Steven Bergman, who promotes New Age music, says, "Most of us benefit from love music that calms us, nurtures us, and inspires us. It plays a fundamental role in the transition to a new age. We want to spread this vibrant energy form as far as we can."[4]

The New Age Catalog refers to the genre as music that "reflects our times and encourages the integration of the inner and outer being, offering an audio portrait of world peace."[5] The *Catalog* also suggests, "On one level, New Age music is really a return to roots, an existential exegesis to the primordial power of sound."[6]

Whatever it is, people are listening. The premier New Age music station, KTWV in Los Angeles, referred to as "The Wave," debuted in the ratings book with a respectable share of the city's audience. In fact, its format is the third-most-listened-to genre in the twenty-five-to-fifty-four age group. Not all are BMW types, either. Some drive eighteen-wheelers and listen to "The Wave" for its soothing effect. It's also known as "the Breeze," "hip AC," "the Key," and "the Oasis."

New Age music artists include such previously prominent musicians as the Paul Winter Consort, Paul Horn, Patrick O'Hearn, and new groups like Full Circle. Windham Hill, the largest New Age label, has been joined by established companies like Columbia, RCA, and MCA. Windham Hill started in 1976 when Will Ackerman and Anne Robinson pooled $300 to press 300 copies of a mellow guitar solo entitled "In Search of the Turtle's Navel." Today, it is a $30 million-a-year label offering vocal, electronic, and children's music ranging from jazz to rock and including music videos.

Windham Hill's big breakthrough came in 1980 when George Winston's solo piano album "Autumn" sold more than a million copies. Many inventive New Age artists get their start by being included on the popular "Windham Hill Samplers" releases. True to their New Age roots, the label has also produced nonmusical commodities such as the "Tibetan Tantric Choir," Tibetan prayer chants based on the supposed magic of spiritual sexual energy. And if the success of New Age music needed any imprimatur, the recording industry has added an appropriate category to its yearly Grammy awards.

Though not all New Age musical proponents agree on how to define and create their craft, they do concur that these harmonies must be tension-relieving and spiritually inspiring. Above all, New Age musicians seek to attune the listener to a celestial dimension. They believe this is possible, since music is not a conceptual form of communication but an intuitive message to the mind. Many New Age musicians now propose intensive multimedia experiences to create a vibrational gateway to higher levels of consciousness.

With more megabucks available to New Age artists, some are concerned the music is distancing itself from its philosophical roots. Purists insist their goal is to continue promoting their inner vision of encouraging higher grades of consciousness. They believe, contrary to the findings of non-New Age scientists, that most music appeals to the analytical left brain, which has hypnotized society into intellectual modes. Instrumental New Age music is designed to engage the intuitive right brain, evoking imagination and altered states of consciousness. In the words of Suzanne Doucet, a recording artist, New Age music's purpose is to "create serenity in a world of aural pollution, as well as to help fill a global need for inner peace, harmony, and understanding."[7]

NEW AGE PERIODICALS

The Movement should not complain that it has gotten a raw deal from the press. Any misconceptions can be readily corrected by a variety of New Age periodicals. The most potent testimony to the Movement's scope is the tangible proof that a consuming public for New Age products exists in the form of magazine purchasers. All you need to know about the New Age can be readily deciphered by a visit to your local newsstand. In addition to the magazines available there, you can also subscribe to such publications as *Metapsychology: The Journal of Disincarnate Intelligence* (a quarterly journal published by a former editor at Prentice-Hall) or the bimonthly *Spirit Speaks*, which deals with such topics as healing, karma, sex, and life in the spirit world.

The *New Age Journal,* most prominent of all New Age publications, has grown from a circulation of 15,000 to 150,000 in just four years. The name of the journal was instrumental in designating the Movement's name, New Age. Articles range from a discussion of near-death experiences to dialogues concerning Zen, extraterrestrials, and humanistic psychoanalysis. At $2.95 per issue, The *New Age Journal* purports to be the consummate dispatch "exploring the new frontiers of human potential." Reading the ads is an education in New Age product development and consumer interest. They promote assorted New Age symposiums, video and audio self-hypnosis tools, quartz crystals, rune stones, natural food products, yoga aids, cosmetic and body care products, isolation boxes, subliminal tapes for babies, and posters. Regular magazine departments include book and music reviews, a newsbrief section on the latest New Age social trends, intimate perspectives on well-known New Age personalities, and a holistic segment entitled "Body/Mind."

East West describes itself as "The Journal of Natural Health and Living." Its scope, however, goes far beyond concerns for the body to explore New Age realms of the spirit. A section called "Compass" provides a digest of the latest in New Age developments. Other divisions include Natural Healing, Whole Foods, feature articles, gardening, cooking, and a potpourri of New

Age advice on well-being for the body, mind, and spirit. The ads provide a conglomeration of what there is to buy for effective living in the New Age. Those with sufficient interest and money can buy books on talking with plants, handmade crystal jewelry, healing herbs, miscellaneous therapies (Reiki, self-chiropractic), Buddhist meditation supplies, ceremonial toe rings, massage videos, amulet pouches, and vitamin supplements.

Formerly known as *Psychic, New Realities* has moved from an emphasis on the paranormal to mainstream New Age thought. Its masthead declares it promotes "Oneness of Self, Mind, and Body." Its editorial board includes Willis Harman (head of Edgar Mitchell's Institute of Noetic Sciences) and Judith Skutch (original publisher of *A Course in Miracles*). New Age technologies and techniques are heavily advertised. Published bimonthly, *New Realities* articles endorse trance channeling, plant communication, and shamanism.

Yoga Journal focuses more specifically on Eastern mysticism with a comprehensive guide to yoga techniques, including Iyengar Yoga Institute, the works of Sri Swami Sivananda, 3-H-O Yoga, Integral Yoga, Feldenkrais, and yoga lessons with your choice of Mimmie Louis, Yogi Shalom, Allan Bateman, Georgina Clarke, Sant Thakar Singh, or Lilias Folan. Product advertisements offer yoga instruction audio cassettes, metaphysical posters, yoga sweat suits, bench props, mats, chi pants, peace bells, and sexual yoga instruction.

John Denver's *Windstar Journal* expounds the outlook of his Aspen, Colorado, Windstar Foundation (see Chap. 12). Windstar's philosophy is, "Each of us is part of and responsible for the quality of life on Planet Earth." To that Denver adds, "A new world is being constantly created every day as a product of our being."[8] This slick, four-color publication explores New Age art, environmental concerns, and Soviet-American coexistence. An annual Aspen Windstar conference features New Age luminaries. A clever Adopt-a-Leader subscription program aims the glossy magazine at the influential, including mayors, senators, teachers, ministers, governors, and business people.

NEW AGE BOOKS

No longer relegated to the "occult" or "metaphysical" shelves in obscure bookstores, New Age books are reviewed in serious literary journals and are prominently displayed. They fall into three basic categories: widely read popular titles, classic volumes providing general impetus for the movement, and esoteric manuals usually known only to insiders of the movement. All are part of the media manipulation whereby New Age thought is being introduced into popular culture. This section, however, will focus on the writings of Shirley MacLaine, who has become the most prominent and popular spokesperson for New Age ideology.

Her books are a repository of New Age concepts and the means by which millions have been introduced to the movement. The order in which they were written is *Out on a Limb, Dancing in the Light,* and *It's All in the Playing.* Each book will be analyzed for its presentation of New Age notions. An examination of the trustworthiness and accuracy of MacLaine's views will be found in the "Straight Answers" section that follows.

Dancing in the Light

Beginning with MacLaine's fiftieth birthday party, attended by hundreds of celebrities, she gradually introduces the reader to her continuing exploration of New Age realities. Unlike the seeker in *Out on a Limb,* MacLaine is firmly committed to her metaphysical lifestyle, which includes chanting Hindu mantras and bathing with quartz crystals. The birthday was important because a spiritual guide had informed her that the energy one inherits at birth is emitted again on one's natal anniversary.

A health crisis in her mother's life urged MacLaine to converse with her parents about New Age ideology. She learned that her parents accepted her reincarnation beliefs. MacLaine told her father and mother, "When you leave the body [die] and become just souls again . . . there won't be this separation of cities like there is now. When you're on the other side and out of your body, you can talk to me all the time and I'll hear it because I really understand how that stuff works now."[9]

As a preacher, MacLaine fills the book with her new-found philosophy: "The higher unlimited superconsciousness can better be defined as one's eternal unlimited soul—the soul that is the real 'you.' The soul that has been through incarnation after incarnation and knows all there is to know about you because it is you. It knows and resonates to God because it is part of God."[10]

Encouraging her readers to meditate with affirmations, she recommends the word *Aum,* which she says is Hindi for "I am." According to MacLaine, Aum sets up a vibrational frequency in the body, aligning one with his higher self, the God-source. "You can use 'I am God' or 'I am that I am' as Christ often did,"[11] she suggests. And if her readers find that a little hard to accept, there is an additional bit of advice for those who have suffered abuse, including rape and murder. "There are no victims," MacLaine says. "There is only self-perception and self-realization."[12]

MacLaine describes her encounter with trance channeler J. Z. Knight, who serves as the medium for Ramtha. In an encounter with Ramtha, MacLaine discovers this ancient spirit from the Atlantean period was her brother during that incarnation. Ramtha advises her on the necessity of vitamins and exercise. He predicts personal events in her life and, according to MacLaine, even foretold the incredible success of her role in "Terms of Endearment."

The passionate soul of the book lies in her account of a torrid affair with a young Russian filmmaker, whom she calls Vassy. Both believed they had been lovers in previous lifetimes. (Once they were Greek oracles.) They had even exchanged sexual roles in certain past lives when MacLaine was a man and Vassy was her female lover. In spite of her involvement in conduct traditionally considered immoral, MacLaine explains she and Vassy were only re-experiencing the memory of an episode in another life. In MacLaine's words, "How could one argue good and evil where sexual fantasies that hurt no one were concerned?"[13]

MacLaine and Vassy had continuing conflicts regarding the nature of good and evil until an encounter with medium Kevin Ryerson and his spirit entity, John. The entity declared that Satan was merely a term denoting the struggle of one's lower consciousness seeking to regain the knowledge of one's inner divinity.

Since Vassy was a filmmaker, another entity declared that such films as *2001: A Space Odyssey* and *Star Wars* were successful milestones that introduced metaphysical art forms. The entity entreated, "The artists [filmmakers] got the attention of the people, and then the public was ready for more subtle messages. Yes, much of the public reacted to 'the Force' as an activity of God."[14]

The book concludes with MacLaine's account of visiting a New Mexico woman named Chris Griscom, who administers past-life recall treatments via acupuncture. Chris claimed spiritual guides helped to direct her regarding needle placement. A silver needle was placed in the center of MacLaine's forehead, location of the so-called third eye of psychic awareness. While undergoing the treatment, MacLaine saw her mother as an Egyptian queen, a starving African, and a Roman athlete. She witnessed Atlantis and its citizens, who communicated telepathically, and saw herself as a Buddhist monk.

MacLaine's metaphysical journeys climaxed when she encountered a seven-foot-tall Oriental being that identified itself as her "higher unlimited self." The entity declared, "I am your unlimited soul that guides and teaches you through each incarnation."[15] The being told her she could communicate with trees. MacLaine claims she successfully used telepathy to ask a tree to quit swaying in the wind. Then the higher self enjoined, "Until mankind realizes there is no good and no evil, there will be no peace."[16]

It's All in the Playing

The subject of trance channeling begins the book, with MacLaine's taking great pains to endorse and explain the phenomenon. She insists that the medium is not "possessed," only "overshadowed." As MacLaine explains, "The medium puts his own 'self' consciousness into a trance state and gives permission for the spiritual entity to overshadow him, imbuing him with the energy that accesses the larynx, the hands, the face, the body, and so on."[17]

MacLaine uses the case of trance channeler, Jach Pursel, and his entity, Lazaris, as a case in point. Lazaris explained that ABC-TV's reluctance to do her miniseries based on *Out on a Limb* was because she feared public judgment. MacLaine's appreciation for the information received from Pursel and others is so great that she defends their soliciting and acquiring large sums of money. After all, for MacLaine the test of a medium's validity is, in her words, "how I felt about their advice and projections of the future."[18]

Plans for the television production included discussions about whether multiple cameras should be used during trance channeling sessions in case the medium didn't stay unconscious long enough. Some on the set expected UFO visitations because "it would be a marvelous demonstration of the collective karma" of each member of the team.[19] If they did appear, MacLaine informed all involved why they would come: the basic lesson brought by UFOs is that "each human being was a god . . . capable of doing and learning and understanding all that is."[20] In any case, according to a channeled entity, the entire miniseries production team had been together before as Egyptians under the reign of Akhenaton.

MacLaine leaves little to the imagination when it comes to her metaphysical conclusions. AIDS, she claims, is increasing in "direct order to the homophobia" in society. It is a "social consciousness disease." Those suffering its debilitating dread of death should be encouraged to learn that AIDS is a kind of godsend to help mankind understand that "all disease is a question of human consciousness."[21]

When it came time for filming *Out on a Limb,* the entities of Kevin Ryerson wanted billing and credit. His Irish spirit insisted the billing read, "Tom McPherson, appearing as Tom McPherson." John wanted to be called "John, son of Zebedee," an indication the entity claimed to be the beloved apostle who wrote the Revelation.[22]

Sprinkled throughout the book are liberal doses of MacLaine's New Age philosophy. Evil, she believes, is a point of view, not a moral reality. Some readers couldn't be blamed for being shocked at her conclusion that stealing, abortion, terrorism, and even murder are not inherently wrong. As MacLaine says, "If a person kills simply out of hatred or greed, he perceives his motives as his need—others make the judgment that his act is 'evil.'"[23]

Not content to contact the supernatural through other entities, MacLaine developed the art of self-channeling, speaking with an entity known as her "higher self." Puzzled that she couldn't find reincarnation in the Bible, she consulted the higher self, who directed her to Matthew 16:13, where Jesus inquired of His disciples who people were saying he was. Their reply in verse 14, "Some say John the Baptist, some Elijah, and others Jeremiah or one of the prophets," convinced MacLaine that Scripture endorses reincarnation. She concluded that the Bible taught John the Baptist had lived as Elijah in a previous incarnation. MacLaine writes that the Bible is "a metaphysical document . . . referring to the Kingdom of Heaven existing within each of us and a New Age of recognition coming that would attest to it."[24]

The book claims that MacLaine's personal spirit guide is none other than Mary, the mother of Jesus. That revelation prompts a monologue on the goddess aspect of the God-force. After centuries of masculine domination, MacLaine says the New Age will endorse feminine supremacy. She writes, "The male domination and female submission as a way of life had brought us to the brink of ruin."[25] Now all that would change with the influence of "the New Age energy with roots deep in the very ancient worship of the mother-image, the Goddess aspect of the God-force."[26]

Filming *Out on a Limb* in the Peruvian Andes was significant because, according to MacLaine, the Andes represent the feminine vibration on earth and the Himalayas the masculine. So, she concludes, "the feminine vibration was what was finally coming into its own to balance the planet's preparation for the New Age."[27]

A visit to her Galisteo, New Mexico, psychic acupuncturist revealed increasingly bizarre revelations about her past lives. MacLaine had been both a grandfather in one incarnation and his grandson in another. Tina Turner appeared during one past life. The conclusion of such visualizations? MacLaine writes,

> I had created a role for myself this time around whereby I would be at the forefront of the New Age spiritual movement, heralding the giant truth that an individual is her own best teacher and that no other idol or false image should be worshipped or adored because the God we are all seeking lies inside one's self, not outside.[28]

The book concludes with a dissertation that amounts to a primer on New Age theology. Traditional religion is rejected, along with its supposition of "an exterior, unknowable God" offering humanity a "mythological garden of paradisiacal afterlife."[29] In its place is the truth, "God is light."[30] But to MacLaine, "the light is not outside of us. We are the light."[31] For those seeking spiritual truth, MacLaine suggests, "The ultimate enlightenment was to touch the Christ consciousness."[32] Adopting a supremely metaphysical stance, she concludes the book by declaring, "Until now, we had identified with reality as though it existed only objectively, outside ourselves. We are responsible for creating everything . . . we and the God-force are one and the same."[33]

Out on a Limb

In her early forties, the Academy Award-winning actress claims she suddenly set off on a spiritual quest, sparked by a clandestine love affair with a prominent married British politician. From Stockholm to Hawaii to the mountaintops of Peru, this book chronicles her search for spontaneous reality. Disillusioned by the uselessness of power politics to effect world change and the divisiveness of religious faiths, she began networking with various New Age leaders.

In her teens, MacLaine rejected conventional Christianity because of its teachings about hell and its rigid authoritarianism. Now she was ready for reincarnation, because her New Age mentor convinced her Jesus taught "the soul's quest was to rise higher and higher until we are free."[34] Eventually, she came to believe that the Christian church had thrown out teachings about reincarnation that were replaced by the concepts of heaven and hell. Instead of atonement's being a redemptive act of God's grace, MacLaine came to believe in its Science of Mind definition: at-one-ment, harmony with the "Karmic Law of Justice."

Her ensuing search led her to the readings of Edgar Cayce and encounters with spirit entities, beginning with Ambres, who spoke through a Swedish man named Sture Johanssen. MacLaine also relates her discussions concerning reincarnation with actor Peter Sellers and tells of sensing his spirit come to her the moment he died. Then she met trance channeler Kevin Ryerson, who convinced her Jesus had traveled to India, studied the teachings of Buddha, and became an adept yogi.

Ryerson also introduced her to the concept of *Akashic Records,* the collective consciousness of mankind stored as ethereal energy. His entity, John, told MacLaine, "Your soul is a metaphor for God."[35] John also informed MacLaine that since all souls are androgynous, she had previously lived twice as a male and once as a female. According to John, Jesus was celibate, and his male and femaleness (yin and yang) were perfectly balanced frequencies.

The concept of soulmates, the idea that extraterrestrials are currently on earth, and the exploration of out-of-the-body experiences rounded out her New Age investigations. MacLaine proceeded to visit New Age spiritual communities like Findhorn. Her mystical meanderings led her to conclude, "More and more people were turning to the dimension of the spirit . . . a process of humanity catching up with itself, an acceleration of spiritual discovery."[36]

STRAIGHT ANSWERS

Q: *Is there anything spiritually dangerous about New Age music composers?*

A: It is generally recognized that New Age musicians indulge in various forms of occult meditation and cosmic awareness philosophies. Some of them freely admit using trance channeling as a source of inspiration. Consequently, a biblical perspective would define some of the music as satanically inspired. Just as an intangible blessing from the Lord rests on a Christian musician dedicated to Christ, some New Age music could threaten spiritual oppression through an "anointing" of evil forces if listened to for extended periods.

Q: *Can New Age musicians contact the spirit world?*

A: One New Age composer referred to channeling assistance from "co-operative, co-creative wave lengths and dimension." That same composer described his music as a "psychospiritual technology" providing "emotional, psychological and spiritual nourishment," resulting in "peace, joy, and bliss and the opportunity for all of us to rediscover in ourselves our highest nature."[37] The benefits claimed by New Age music are precisely the same advantages offered by the Word of God. Thus, some forms of New Age music, by certain composers, would be biblically labeled as demon-inspired, proposing counterfeit benefits to lead people away from the Lord.

Q: *Is there a purpose behind New Age music that provides a metaphysical mission for the listener?*

A: Not all mellow or nonintrusive music is spiritually dangerous and shouldn't be labeled "New Age." Genuine New Age music is written to alter personal reality and expose one to his supposed inner divine nature. In this sense, it is a kind of musical yoga. Serious New Age composers actually believe they can vibrate the body's psychic energy centers to awaken and transform the spiritual awareness of the human spirit. They also hope to alter the listener's consciousness to induce a state of "globalistic realization." All these goals are contrary to Holy Scripture, and those listening to New Age music must guard against accepting the underlying principles and intentions which New Age music cannot, after all, actually achieve.

Q: *Is it advisable to read New Age periodicals?*

A: That depends on the reader's motives and spiritual maturity. Not all articles in such publications are evil or predicated on the occult. Many are merely informational and explore various social phenomena and trends. The undiscerning reader, however, could easily be lead to accept metaphysical thought without knowing it. Philippians 4:8 admonishes us to think on things that are "true . . . [and] of good report." Most New Age periodicals could not meet that standard.

Q: *Is it possible to talk with loved ones after they die?*

A: The Bible teaches that our eternal destination is determined at death.[38] An impassable gulf exists between heaven and hell and between this life and the next.[39] Scripture also forbids the practice of necromancy, seeking to contact the dead by means of a spiritualist medium.[40] It was for this deed that King Saul lost his life.[41] Those who presume to talk with the dead are actually speaking with an evil spirit who impersonates the one sought by spiritualism.

Q: *Is the soul a real part of us, or is it part of God?*

A: Man is a tripartite being consisting of body (physical nature), soul (mind or consciousness, which gives the sense of self), and spirit (the eternal aspect breathed into man by God when life is created). Unlike Platonism and reincarnationism, which teach that souls pre-exist, orthodox Christians believe God creates each soul individually *ex nihilo* (out of nothing). Support for this doctrine is found in Genesis 2:7 and Hebrews 12:9. The soul imparts our sense of identity, but it is different in substance from God, and its nature is apart from Him.

Q: *What kind of spiritual error does Shirley MacLaine commit by chanting "I am that I am"?*

A: This profession was spoken by the Lord to Moses as a confirmation of his divine existence.[42] It is a self-validating statement in which God swears by himself who he is. It is utterly arrogant and blasphemous for any human being to say the same. Of course, MacLaine's belief in self-deification finds no contradiction in espousing the title God has reserved for himself alone.

Q: *Where does MacLaine get the idea that victims are victims only if they think they are?*

A: A common theme in MacLaine's writings, and that of most New Age theorists, is that reality is what you perceive it to be. Thus, the victim of rape or abuse is victimized only to the extent she allows herself to be internally judged in that manner. This viewpoint hinges on the metaphysical hypothesis that there is no objective reality, only mind and thought. Such abstract theories sound philosophically respectable, but those who suffer as victims know the empirical reality is painful. The purpose for the concept of denying reality is to negate the existence of evil and a personal devil. If there is no Satan to tempt people to sin, and no material state of evil in which moral beings exist, then all perceptions of wrongdoing are mental. Adopting this viewpoint enables New Agers to avoid extending human compassion and offering God's grace, since neither is needed in a world without transgression.

Q: *Can entities like Ramtha predict the future?*

A: Scripture plainly states that God is the Alpha and Omega. He alone omnisciently knows the past and the future. Psychics operating under the influence of evil spirits prognosticate what Satan thinks may come to pass or what he may attempt to make happen. Once the prediction is made, the devil clandestinely seeks to alter circumstances so that his soothsaying will appear to be fulfilled. It isn't that he knew what would happen, but he attempts to make it happen as an endorsement of the false prophet. Deuteronomy 18:22 declares that 100 percent accuracy and conformity to Holy Scripture are the only criteria by which any foretelling can be judged.

Q: *How can Shirley MacLaine speak freely of her sexual promiscuity, apparently without feeling guilt, and simultaneously claim to be God?*

A: Two aspects of New Age thought ignore the human conscience regarding biblically defined evil acts. First, reality is what each individual perceives it to be. Consequently, Shirley MacLaine's self-defined reality does not encompass moral guidelines concerning sexuality, as proved by her acceptance of infidelity and homosexuality. Second, New Agers perceive themselves as God. Thus, when an individual has reached the consciousness level of God-realization, he can do no wrong, because to become God is to achieve perfection. The frightening possibilities of that attitude are considerable, portending the possibility that fornication and perversion are excusable. Indeed, any act not deemed by the God-realized person as contrary to his own divine nature would be permissible.

Q: *Is evil an objective reality or a lack of spiritual awareness?*

A: New Agers confuse the cause with the condition. Lacking spiritual awareness causes one to commit evil. Galatians 3:24 tells us that the law of God was to serve as a "tutor." Romans 3:20 teaches that "by the law is the knowledge of sin." God gave the Ten Commandments because mankind needed an objective, external revelation concerning proper conduct in the sight of God. Since New Agers proclaim themselves as God, they must eliminate any concept of an external deity who tells us what is right and wrong. They must also deny the existence of evil, since the objective reality of physical and moral corruption undercuts their notion that man is really God, unable to perish or do wrong.

Q: *Was the entity MacLaine consulted correct in saying George Lucas's "Star Wars" Force is a metaphysical, New Age concept?*

A: Yes. Though entities (demons) often lie, in this case he was bragging. Scripture teaches that good and evil are diametric opposites invested in the personal characters of God and the devil. Occultism and witchcraft teach that good and evil are invested in a neutral, primordial force whose moral quality depends on the motive of the individual. Thus, white witches can claim to use the same power as black witches, except they propose to avoid harm. In the "Star Wars" epics, Darth Vader and Luke Skywalker both use the same Force, but their motives differ. This concept makes good and evil opposite sides of the same spiritual coin, since both derive their energy from the same source. The notion of the Force is derived from pantheism and is contrary to the Christian view.

Q: *Can acupuncture induce the kind of occult images Shirley MacLaine observed?*

A: Acupuncture can induce altered states of consciousness if it is used within a mystical context by a practitioner who is committed to an occult worldview. The images of past incarnations witnessed by MacLaine were demonically induced hallucinations, figments of her mind, not testimonies to past realities. By acquiescing to the psychical application of acupuncture by a spirit medium, MacLaine yielded to evil forces that manipulated her mind according to the expectations for which she underwent the treatment.

Q: *With whom was Shirley MacLaine communicating when she consulted her "higher unlimited self"?*

A: No objective determination can be made. There are two possibilities. Because of her mental disorientation associated with so many occult, psychological eccentricities, she may have simply fantasized a being in her mind, consistent with her prior New Age indoctrination. On the other hand, MacLaine may have encountered an evil spirit masquerading as her deified ego.

Q: *Is there a difference between the terms "possessed" and "overshadowed" when applied to the manifestation of an entity through a medium?*

A: No. The term *overshadowed* is a euphemism coined by spiritualists because it sounds less threatening. The word *possessed* has an unsavory connotation and indicates the medium is a mere vessel for the whims of an external force. Trance channelers would like to believe their entities come only upon bidding and are subject to the medium's volition. The biblical truth is that once an individual has allowed his body and soul to be inhabited by a demon, he surrenders much of his ability to think and act independently.

Q: *Is Shirley MacLaine being spiritually rational when she says her test of a medium's veracity is how she feels about the advice?*

A: Not according to 1 John 4:1–4. The true test of any extra-dimensional information should be its harmony with God's

Word and its testimony concerning the deity of Christ. How one feels about any spiritual occurrence has no objective merit. Such conclusions rest solely on the perceptive abilities and the frail discernment of the individual. That's why Scripture gives us guidelines for investigating messages or messengers who claim to be from God.

Q: *With all the talk about UFO appearances during the filming of "Out on a Limb," weren't MacLaine and her New Age friends embarrassed that none appeared?*

A: Undoubtedly, occult forces would have preferred to precipitate an atmospheric phenomenon to confirm those predictions. Why they didn't is unknown. But those entities and persons speculating about the appearance of UFOs carefully crafted an excuse—lack of harmony and spiritual consciousness among the filming crew. In other words, the reason no UFOs appeared was the negative vibrations from the skeptics.

Q: *What about the entity's idea that AIDS is caused by homophobia and serves as a teaching vehicle to make mankind realize such afflictions result from an improper consciousness?*

A: It's an ironic twist of logic that since male homosexuals are largely responsible for transmitting AIDS, the virulency of this disease should be blamed on heterosexuals, who believe homosexual behavior is morally wrong. According to this assumption, paranoid homophobia instead of perverted practices causes the increasing death rate from AIDS. It's an equally cruel distortion to say that people should suffer and die so society can learn a metaphysical lesson.

Q: *What about the idea that abortion, stealing, and even murder are simply aspects of reality and not inherently evil?*

A: This is an absurd and dangerous aspect of New Age thought. But such presumptions are consistent with the lack of a moral frame of reference to guide personal conduct. Such thinking, carried to its logical conclusion, would allow murderers and rapists to be freed from prison if they could convince the public their "reality" did not define their deeds as evil.

Q: *Is reincarnation taught in Matthew 16:13–16, and does Matthew 11:14 suggest that John the Baptist was Elijah reincarnated, as Shirley MacLaine claims?*

A: Matthew 16 only states what some reincarnationists said, and this is nowhere endorsed by Christ or his disciples. In fact, Peter's confession of faith in 16:16 was to the contrary: "You are the Christ." In Matthew 11:14, Christ refers to the fact that the prophecies about the return of Elijah had been fulfilled in John the Baptist. When John himself was confronted with the question of whether he was Elijah, he answered plainly, "I am not." This contradiction of New Age ideas of reincarnation shows how little New Agers know of the Bible and how cleverly spirit entities twist the Word of God and quote Scripture out of context.

Q: *Is the Bible a metaphysical document?*

A: New Agers are fond of suggesting that the real truths of the Bible are esoteric and can only be understood by deciphering its hidden meaning. This idea was expounded by early Gnosticism and has been repeatedly refuted by orthodoxy. New Agers adopt this approach to Scripture because the Bible condemns so many of their practices and doctrines, such as mediumship, necromancy, clairvoyance, etc. Thus, they must negate these injunctions by suggesting the meaning of Scripture is camouflaged. Jesus instructed us to come as little children to understand his teachings, hardly the qualifications for decoding secret, obscured precepts.

Q: *Why does Shirley MacLaine emphasize feminine dominance and goddess worship theories?*

A: New Age thought is little more than paganized witchcraft dressed in contemporary garments. Most ancient cult practices were based on goddess worship. Eve was perceived as wise instead of evil when she disobeyed God. Her eating the forbidden fruit did not bring sin upon humanity. Instead, Eve's sin supposedly opened the eyes of humanity as the serpent promised, so people could become gods. Pagan veneration has concentrated on sexual ritualism involved with fertility; since women are child-bearers, they have been seen as sacred and of greater worth than men. This fact has traditionally elevated women to spiritual prominence in occult circles. In addition, witchcraft and similar traditions view women as being more psychically tuned. Thus, to usher in the New Age, women will play a primary role.

Q: *What is unique about MacLaine's contention that worship of a god other than one's self is idolatry?*

A: This is a clever twist of reason. It takes the first commandment of God and changes it to mean exactly the opposite. To Shirley MacLaine, each individual is god, and worship must be directed to one's own ego. Consequently, to bow in obeisance to an external deity such as Christ becomes an act of idolatry, since it worships someone other than one's "higher unlimited self."

Q: *Did the Christian church disregard teachings about reincarnation and remove them from the Bible?*

A: Absolutely not! This is a frequently circulated myth for which there is no historical evidence. The majority of early church fathers viewed reincarnation with unqualified hostility. Some have suggested that Origen, an early church theologian, may have espoused metempsychosis (transmigration of the soul), but his belief in the eternal pre-existence of souls only envisioned a single bodily incarnation, not repeated attempts to work out the soul's karmic debt. Besides, Origen admitted that his view did not come from the Bible, and the Council of Chalcedon condemned his work as heresy in A.D. 451. Some reincarnationists say the Council of Nicaea (A.D. 325) squashed all recognition of past lives. But the main purpose of this council was to affirm the divinity of Christ and the Holy Spirit. There is no record of any attempt to deny reincarnation, since the Church had already soundly rejected the idea.

Q: *Why does the idea of androgyny occur repeatedly in MacLaine's books?*

A: There are several reasons. Androgyny's moral ambivalence is consistent with the situational ethics of the movement. New Age ideology has no rigid moral code, so the sins of homosexuality, bisexuality, fornication, and all forms of perversion must be validated. By believing that each person is a composite of equal male and female qualities, this goal is accomplished. Androgyny is compatible with the mystical perception of the cosmological force consisting of equivalent quantities of yin and yang, light and dark, maleness and femaleness. Biblically, the relationship of Christ to his church is spoken of in conjugal terms, the bride (the Church) awaiting the consummation of redemption by the bridegroom (Christ). If all is androgynous, no sexual or theological distinctions exist in the relationship between God and mankind.

Q: *What is the meaning of the "soulmate" concept?*

A: Reincarnation teaches that lovers meant for each other have consummated their relationship in past lives. Thus, they are intended to be lovers in this life as part of their karmic conclusion. The theory of soulmates supposes that everyone is destined for someone else, and each must find that person. If already married, that relationship must be dissolved to enhance the preeminent soulmate connection. Shirley MacLaine could excuse her sexual affair with a married man because her paramour was not married to his proper soulmate, thus not fulfilling his proper role according to fate.

WHO'S WHO AND WHAT'S WHAT

Affirmations: Repetitive phrases embodying a statement of fact or essence, designed to create reality by repetition, such as chanting "I am that I am."

Akasha: A metaphysical theory that all reality exists in humanity's accumulated unconscious thought, a form of spiritual energy.

Androgyny: Possessing the characteristics of both sexes, a New Age belief that underlies the ambivalent reality of all existence.

At-One-Ment: A redefinition of the theological term *atonement* (the redemption of humanity by the blood sacrifice of Christ) to mean "at one with God"—that is, achieving a God-realized state that acknowledges one's inner divinity.

Aum: A syllable taken from the Hindu Sanskrit language and believed to embody the essence of God; if reverently spoken in a mantra-like chant, it supposedly permits the meditator to become one with God.

Christ Consciousness: The belief that the term *Christ* refers to an office instead of the person Jesus of Nazareth, and that Jesus realized his "Christed" oneness with God, as can anyone who attains a similar state of realization.

"Dark Side of the Moon": A popular album by the rock group Pink Floyd featuring spacey sounds and musically adventuresome elements that have inspired some New Age musicians; believed by some to facilitate mind expansion techniques.

East West: Monthly New Age magazine accentuating occult, mystical, and natural healing methods, along with metaphysical nutrition.

Force, The: A concept presented by George Lucas in the "Star Wars" movie epics; based on the Taoist idea of a primordial essence that is both good and evil and may be used for either, depending on one's motive.

Karmic Law of Justice: The idea that one's accumulated good and evil deeds will culminate in a fate commensurate with past spiritual accomplishments.

Metapsychology: Quarterly New Age journal emphasizing trance-channeled information.

Natal Anniversary: The idea that the positions of the planets and other heavenly bodies, as they were located at one's birth, affect that individual on recurring birthdates.

Networking: The New Age concept of linkage of ideas, practices, and metaphysical efforts; combines the endeavors of various aspects of the movement worldwide through written and verbal communication, as well as telepathic communiqués.

New Age Journal: Bimonthly New Age magazine emphasizing human potential aspects of the movement.

New Age Music: A contemporary musical genre, usually instrumental and often acoustic, based on classical and jazz styles; generally played in a free-form or unstructured style for the purpose of altering the listener's consciousness and perception of reality.

Overshadow: When an invisible entity takes over the mind, emotions, will, and sometimes the body of a spirit medium.

Self-Realization: The act of acknowledging that one's self (ego) is identifiable with God and that one's highest inner nature is pure and devoid of all evil.

Spirit Speaks: Bimonthly New Age publication featuring occult phenomena.

Superconsciousness: That aspect of one's soul beyond the rational world of material reality that can achieve God-realization.

Third Eye: An occult concept assuming that a spiritually intuitive center of consciousness exists in the center of the forehead, the so-called seventh chakra of enlightenment in yoga.

2001: A Space Odyssey: An Arthur C. Clarke epic postulating the idea of superior, extraterrestrial intelligences with benevolent intentions for humanity.

Wave, The: Description of a commercial radio programming approach based on a New Age music format, originating in Los Angeles on station KTWV-FM.

Windham Hill: New Age music label started by two college dropouts who wanted to record and distribute solo instrumental music; now the largest New Age music distributor, growing from sales of $150,000 in 1981 to $30 million in 1986.

IN MY OPINION

New Age music is merely recycled soft jazz, the same instrumental mood music that's been around for years. Now it's touted as a way to relax and create moods to expand the mind. Not mentioned are the dangers of accompanying visualization and mental excursions, which could lead to occult ideology. Those who trip out with alpha wave instruments may believe they have left their bodies and endanger their spirits.

Music is music. There is nothing inherently evil in its components of harmony, rhythm, and melody. But for those who seek the assistance of music to leave their bodies and alter their consciousness, the music could indeed be dangerous. New Age motivation isn't to be trusted. Don't dismiss such sounds as banal and more evocative of waterfalls than musical ingenuity. The synthesized symphonies of New Age music can lead directly to the occult. The overt egotism incited by New Age music may not only soothe the mind but also damn the soul.

New Age books are an unusual genre whose credibility is questionable since there is no way to verify objectively much of their information. Some musings are the conjectural assumptions of the authors. Other conclusions are derived from trance-channeled sources. Ruth Montgomery, who has written nine books under the influence of spirits, explains her acceptance of mediumship this way: "I was reared in the Methodist church, and I never heard ministers say anything with such depth. I research everything they tell me before I publish my books. Much of the information is verifiable."[43]

Even if some information in New Age books is accurate, it's a mistake to assume that the verifiability of facts attests to the authenticity of the source. God demands a higher standard for spiritual truth. Historical or cultural accuracy is not the primary consideration. Truth must be gauged by its compatibility with Scripture. Paul warned the Galatians, "Even if we, or an angel from heaven, preach any other gospel to you than what we have preached to you, let him be accursed."[44]

It is common for spirit entities to proclaim their messages and books as superior to the Bible. The discarnate beings behind these communications generally deny the deity of Jesus, denigrate the concept of original sin, and demote the work done by Christ on the cross. They promote the idea of self-validation without outside critical inquiry. For example, *Emanuel's Book,* the recorded transmissions of a popular spirit entity, says, "Accept nothing that does not sound right to you."[45] But that subjective verification depends upon self-analysis and is prone to self-deception. The truth of a religious doctrine should be whether it agrees with revealed Scripture, not how it sounds to the inquirer.

Stripped of their more sensational aspects, published documents of the New Age teach a basic theology: Man is god and sin is nonexistent, since God cannot commit an act offensive to himself. New Age exploration for reality ends in self-deification. In the process, New Agers may profess reverence for Christ and the teachings of Scripture. But stripping New Age ideology of its ingratiating comments about Christianity reveals pantheism, the idea that all is part of God.

The ultimate ideology of the New Age Movement is egoism. New Agers have swallowed the age-old fallacy that truth and spirituality lie within and can be known intuitively. Thus, if man is a god, he is absolved of all wrong conduct, because God can do no wrong. That's why Shirley MacLaine boldly writes of her promiscuity and sexual escapades without blushing. For Christians, the conclusion is quite different. We are not gods in embryo, sparks of the divine. God is involved in our world, but our world is not God. The New Age Movement might better be called the exaltation of self.

Chapter 10

THE SECOND COMING

Straight Answers on New Age
Religious Cults

The chicken or the egg—which came first? More appropriately put for this book, which came first, the cult-sect or the New Age Movement?

No philosophy can exist in a vacuum, without a doctrinaire ideology. As eclectic as the New Age Movement is, and as ambiguous as its goals are, it nevertheless has needed some sort of mooring. Several belief systems have provided that anchor. Some of these organizations existed prior to the movement's explosion (e.g., the Association for Research and Enlightenment). In other instances, the cult has developed in conjunction with New Age Movement expansion (e.g., the Church Universal and Triumphant).

It should be noted that the term *cult* is not being used in a pejorative sense. Certainly some New Age groups are almost universally viewed disapprovingly. Others, although considered exotic, are not as repugnant. Use of the expression *cult* in this portion of the book is based on Webster's designation of a religious body that is "unorthodox" or embodies "devotion to a person or idea."

Despite their dissimilarities, New Age religious cults have a notable resemblance to each other. Most conspicuous is the idea that the subconscious dictates the active choices of life. Understanding its compulsions and achieving its enlightenment are fundamental objectives. New Age cults propose to understand hidden stimuli so that the subconscious can be reprogrammed with a redefined reality. Rather than delineating existence in relationship to an external deity, New Age cults are determined to launch adherents on the path of self-discovery.

The subconscious (often referred to as the higher self) presumably is a loyal guide to truth. To unlock such truths, the seeker must find a system to help him open the door to the path of spiritual innovation. Consequently, New Agers hop from one cult to another, constantly pursuing the ultimate key to getting in touch with their "ground of being."

Reliance upon intuitive confirmation of spirituality is a common denominator in New Age cults, since intuition is believed to be totally accurate. The aesthetic practices of these groups are designed to sharpen one's ability to hear the inner voice of intuition. Adherents are usually told that old ways of believing and programmed patterns of thought must be relinquished before hearing the inner voice. Thus, meditation, fasting, isolation, mantras, yoga, self-hypnosis, and other tools are employed to shut out the active world and enter the intuitive realm of passivity. Unlike traditional religious devotion, which focuses on the assistance of an external deity, New Age cults encourage consulting the inner self and receiving words, images, feelings, and sounds that supposedly are guides of the soul.

The appeal of New Age cults is that they purport to offer what traditional religions have not—a new way of perceiving reality. It is an unconventional way of interpreting our relationship to the universe. Whatever the codification of beliefs found in a particular New Age cult, the purpose is to prove and experience what mystics, shamans, and ancient seekers of the mysteries have always said.

New Age cults do not always represent aberrations of belief outside the mainstream of secular thought. Their affirmation of reincarnation, psychic contact with the dead, and the survivability of the soul is supported by part of the scientific community. No less a source than Candace Pert, chief of brain biochemistry at the National Institutes of Health, has said, "It is conceivable to me that the information stored in the brain could transform itself into some other realm. Matter can neither be created nor destroyed; and perhaps biological information flow cannot just disappear at death and must be transformed into another realm."[1]

With the irrational excess of some cults (such as Rajneesh) and the anti-intellectualism of some New Age practices (such as crystals), the power of New Age ideology could be underestimated. But consider that a National Opinion Research Council survey shows that nearly 50 percent of American adults believe they have been in contact with someone who has died. However one views the eccentricities of New Age sects, their growth signifies the demise of empirical science and the authoritarianism of established faiths. New Age cults offer revelation of the self, the idea that the soul is universal and the repository of ultimate reality.

New Age cults thrive because of their proposal that mankind is undergoing a galactic shift in consciousness that only their adherents will understand. The old ways of believing by means of creeds and ecclesiastical dogma are gone. Time, space, and human consciousness must now be viewed, they say, from a multidimensional level that can be understood only by communicating with the primordial vibration of life. From this verity, no cathedrals will be built to scrape the sky; we need only the worship of the inner self in the sanctuary of the soul. The Second Coming is no longer an anticipated event confined to limitations of time and space. To the New Ager, it is now. Christ has come, and He dwells within all humanity in the consciousness all of us overlook and the Supreme Self we fail to recognize.

A COURSE IN MIRACLES

This huge, three-volume set reinterprets almost every orthodox Christian belief. Such doctrines as the atonement and the crucifixion of Christ are blatantly denied. Known as *A Course in Miracles,* it was dictated to a Columbia University psychologist, Helen Schucman, by an inner voice claiming to be Jesus. "This is a course in miracles," the voice began. "It is a required course. Only the time you take it is voluntary."[2]

Summing up the *Course*'s essence, the voice declared, "Nothing real can be threatened, nothing unreal exists." The entire *Course,* consisting of nearly 1,200 pages, was acquired by a form of automatic handwriting over a period of seven years, between 1965 and 1973. It was eventually published in 1976 by the Foundation for Inner Peace, headed by parapsychological investigators Robert and Judy Skutch. Over 160,000 sets of the *Course* have been sold without the benefit of advertising.[3] The Foundation also offers other books and pamphlets, as well as audio and video cassettes.

Schucman admits the handwriting made her "very uncomfortable." After writing what the voice said, she gave the documents to her close friend Dr. William Thetford, professor of medical psychology at Columbia University's College of Physicians and Surgeons. Schucman, who died in 1981, was a religious skeptic with little regard for spirituality and mysticism. Thetford had been raised in the Christian Science church. He explained his personal theological views in a manner resembling pantheism: "Since all life stems from God and is one and inseparable, certainly the life force that animates animals and plants is the same as the life force that animates us."[4]

Schucman kept notepads handy to take down what the voice dictated. Messages came almost daily, sometimes several times a day. She gave the *Course* instructions to Thetford, who typed a manuscript. First came the 622-page text, then the 478-page *Workbook for Students,* followed by an 88-page *Manual for Teachers.*

Schucman's entity claimed to have an important message for our time, centered in the philosophy that guilt is absolved through forgiving others, not by seeking personal forgiveness from a loving God. The *Course* aims to correct what it says are errors of Christianity that overemphasize suffering, sacrifice, and sacrament. "Every religion . . . has been inspired by God. To believe in the God in everyone is the ultimate religion," the *Course* declares.

Such statements are typical of the *Course's* unconventional approach to theology. Whereas most religions are concerned with the exculpation of sin and communion with God, *A Course in Miracles* boldly proclaims, "It is impossible to think of anything God created that could need forgiveness."[5] Elsewhere, pardon for transgression is referred to as an illusion, a "happy fiction." Ironically, though the *Course* denigrates God's forgiveness, it conversely claims that personal peace is possible when humans forgive others.

As might be expected, Christ is stripped of his divinity. "The name of Jesus is the name of one who was a man but saw the face of Christ in all his brothers and remembered God," the *Course* alleges. For those Christians who find such comments to border on blasphemy, literature from the Foundation that publishes the books pronounces: "the *Course* [lends] itself to teaching, parallel to the ongoing teaching of the Holy Spirit."[6]

Explicitly, the *Course* states its aims as: (1) "the undoing of our belief in the reality of guilt," (2) "emphasizing the importance of Jesus as our gentle teacher," and (3) "correcting the errors of Christianity." The Foundation's statement of purpose certifies: "The corporation has as its specific aims . . . helping those interested to integrate the *Course's* principles into their personal lives, that they may better realize their true identity . . . as children of God."[7]

CHURCH UNIVERSAL AND TRIUMPHANT

The female leader reads from the Bible. Congregants make the sign of the cross. A sermon follows on the subject of healing. The air is thick with incense. Suddenly, the gathered hundreds begin chanting in an eerie tone, "I am the lighted flame." Decreeing, they call it. But to residents of Park County, Montana's, Paradise Valley, it has shades of the Bhagwan and Oregon's Rajneeshpuram, except the place is Royal Teton Ranch and the group is known as the Church Universal and Triumphant (CUT). Its leader is Elizabeth Clare Prophet—Guru Ma, as she is known to her followers.

The group was first headquartered in Colorado Springs, Colorado. From there it relocated to Los Angeles and a 218-acre headquarters known as Camelot. Finally, CUT established a 257-acre retreat near Corwin Springs, Montana. Operations include a major publishing enterprise, vegetable farming, raising livestock, and a church training institution known as Summit University.

Guru Ma is heir to the church started in 1958 by her husband, Mark L. Prophet. Elizabeth Clare had experienced psychic phenomena since childhood. Upon meeting Mark in 1961, she was introduced to his doctrine of serving as a medium for the so-called Ascended Masters of the Great White Brotherhood. The belief system they developed mixed Christian terminology with Eastern mysticism. Devotees of CUT seek to cleanse their karma by surrounding themselves with the Violet Consuming Flame, a state achieved by decreeing. A CUT meeting may find them chanting, "I am that I am," an affirmation of self-deity.

In the hierarchy of departed souls, Christ is known as Sanat Kumura, who supposedly came to earth from Venus. He is joined by other spirits, such as Master Kuthumi, Master Godfre, El Morya, Saint Germain (an eighteenth-century occultist), and Prophet's departed husband. These entities convinced Guru Ma that God did not require the sacrifice of Christ for sin and that his blood atonement was merely a pagan rite. She is particularly concerned about the supposed lost years of Jesus—when, she says, he journeyed to the Himalayas to learn Eastern mysticism.

Not all is well in the Church Universal. A number of former followers of the "Mother of the Universe," as some call her, have brought legal actions, including one who charged her with "intellectual and sexual seduction."[8] Others say they were bilked out of money and were victims of "extortion, fraud, and involuntary servitude."[9] The validity of such charges is as questionable as Prophet's claim to be a reincarnation of the biblical Martha, the only contemporary medium of truth endorsed by the Ascended Masters.

URANTIA

Who is God? Why am I here? What happens after I die?

If those questions concern you, the *Urantia Book* claims to have the answers. God is the Lord of a universe containing numerous inhabited planets, it says. Man's purpose is to discover his pre-existence as a god. After death, developed souls may inherit their own planet over which they can reign as a deity. Among other Urantia rejoinders are these: the real name for earth is Urantia; Adam was sent here from another planet 38,000 years ago; Urantia's first human being was over eight feet tall and appeared as a god to biologically uplift the human race.[10]

The inventory of controversial Urantia doctrines doesn't stop there. Christ was not the creator of all that is, only the originator of our local universe, Urantia. This universe is said to consist of a thousand inhabitable worlds (i.e., solar systems), several super-universes, and a trillion inhabitable planets, one of which is Urantia. The Holy Spirit is actually the Mother Spirit, who was the sexual consort of Jesus Christ.[11] Additional details are available in the 503-page *Concordex of the Urantia Book*, which maintains that the Bible is "a magnificent collection of beautiful devotional, inspired writings, along with various human writings that are far from sacred or inspired."

First published in 1955, the 2,097-page *Urantia Book* was supposedly delivered to a Dr. Bill Sadler by seven spirit beings. These entities claimed to be celestial creatures who communicated by automatic handwriting. They declared the Urantia revelation was "the finest world view of religions available to contemporary man." According to these beings, man's ultimate guide to faith is reliance on what are called "Indwelling Thought Adjusters," presumably parts of divinity who advise people through successions of re-incarnated universes until they attain the presence of the "Paradise Father." A central theme is the hidden years of Christ, from age twelve to his public ministry. During that time, Jesus supposedly learned to develop his psychic powers by being tutored in the East's mysticism.

Many New Age advocates have gravitated to Urantia in search of esoteric explanations for the serious issues of life. Its presupposition that man is evolved from the animal kingdom and destined to be a god fits well into New Age concepts. The longing for arcane information renders these people susceptible to Urantia's bogus offer of the "finest major divine revelation since the coming of Christ to our planet."

LORD MAITREYA

"The Christ is Now Here!"

When that pronouncement emblazoned full-page newspaper ads on April 25, 1982, those unaware of New Age messianic predictions were abruptly introduced to one of the movement's more exotic prophecies. Behind the headline was the belief that an Asian secretly living in London is the Jewish Messiah, the Buddhist Fifth Buddha, the Muslim Imam Mahadi, the Hindu Krishna, and the Christian Jesus—Lord Maitreya. The Second Coming had arrived!

Spokesman for Maitreya is Benjamin Creme, a sixty-five-year-old Scottish artist from London with a lifelong interest in esoteric philosophy. In 1959, Creme claims to have received a telepathic message from his Master Maitreya, the foremost member of a band of departed spiritual masters. Creme learned that the Second Coming, the return of the Christ, was at hand, and Creme was to be the forerunner. In 1975, Creme was told that he was to begin publicly announcing the coming of Maitreya, though no date was specified for the Messiah's expected time of arrival.[12]

Creme professes that Maitreya moved to London in 1977 and started giving him telepathic messages during his public lectures, when Maitreya over-shadowed (possessed) him. By May 1982, more than 140 messages had been received. These were published, along with books and a magazine, *Share International*. Creme began training arduously to prepare himself for the coming task. As he did, the telepathic messages became immediate and continuous. In 1980, Creme came to Los Angeles and formed the Tara Center to spread the teachings of Maitreya. This led to development of a nation-wide network of so-called transmission groups, gatherings of Maitreya's/Creme's disciples who study Creme's tapes and books, seeking to receive their own revelation. Meanwhile, Creme's London group continues to meet regularly, receiving transmitted energies from the Master.

As delivered by Creme, Maitreya's message is simple: the Master comes not as a religious, political, economic, or social leader, yet he intends to solve all the world's problems in these areas and also usher in the New Age with love, peace, and shared wealth. Strife, disease, and labor will be eliminated. A secret initiation process will be implemented, showing everyone how to become a god.[13]

Creme is mindful that his Christian critics see Maitreya as an antichrist. The Scotsman responds that Jesus of Nazareth was a disciple of Maitreya. Jesus was only a temporary Christ who initiated his way to become a Senior Master in Maitreya's hierarchy.[14] In fact, Christ has reincarnated and lives today in Rome, though in whose body Maitreya doesn't say. Furthermore, Maitreya says that Jesus was not Jewish, didn't come from the lineage of David, and was not virgin born. In place of Christian doctrine concerning Jesus Christ is a blend of esotericism, Theosophy (via Alice Bailey and Lucis Trust), Eastern mysticism, and New Age philosophy.

Maitreya's goals sound millenialistic when compared with Christian prophecies. He will remove all guilt and fear. Inexplicably, hearts and minds will be cleansed, and all mankind will be introduced to the ancient mysteries, which will create a pool of spiritual knowledge accessible to all.[15] Cremation will replace burial so diseased bodies will not contaminate the environment. Death will be welcomed as an unfolding of reincarnation's purpose. Globalist New Agers will be happy to learn that the United Nations will be the seat of a world government of federated states.

Undaunted by criticism, Creme insists that Maitreya will reveal himself only when mankind is ready and the world press is willing to herald his coming. Apparently, mankind's dilemmas must worsen until men beg for Maitreya's second coming. Meanwhile, other "Masters of Wisdom" are at work among humanity, awaiting that day. Creme claims that special groups in New York, Geneva, London, Darjeeling, and Tokyo have been in training for years, led by Masters who will propose precise legislation to change our current political, economic, and social structures.

As this book is being written, Maitreya has not revealed himself. Newsletters from Tara Center say that day is soon coming. Creme has hinted that Maitreya, whom he sometimes calls the Avatar, will be witnessed by millions via an international satellite TV broadcast. Creme says Maitreya is still working patiently behind the scenes, preparing world leaders and politicians for his acceptance. Comforting his followers, Creme writes, "The new age will be built by man himself under the guidance of Maitreya and His Group. From within man himself will come the urge for betterment, a testimony to the divinity inherent in us all. That divinity will Maitreya show to be the nature of man, and He the Agent of its manifestation."[16]

According to Creme, Maitreya is meeting with select groups, as many as 500 to 600 simultaneously. Dates of his appearances are given only after the fact, so no verification is available. Meanwhile, Tara Center continues to promote New Age practices such as channeling and the study of "astral energies." Though Maitreya has yet to speak directly with the press, Tara Center does report on his latest predictions via a close associate. Among the messages: the Palestinians will have their own country; President Botha and Desmond Tutu will sit down together to solve South Africa's problems; the Russians and the Americans will destroy all nuclear weapons; if sick individuals practice detachment from their mind, body, and spirit, they will be cured of AIDS, and the dreaded disease will vanish. The most important message of Maitreya is that his "Day of Declaration" will arrive, and all the world will announce his arrival as the Christ.[17]

STRAIGHT ANSWERS

Q: *Are moral and spiritual failures of humanity caused by inattention to the voice of the subconscious?*

A: No. New Agers confuse their reference to the subconscious with biblical indications that man's conscience helps guide moral decisions. The New Age concept of the subconscious and the Christian concept of the conscience are incompatible. The subconscious is the collective repository of personal and sensory experiences. It is an informational "computer bank." But it has no capacity to interpret that data in a morally qualitative sense. It is spiritually neutral and an inappropriate guide to virtuous behavior. The conscience, however, can be morally quantified. When the Christian speaks of conscience, he refers to one of two inner voices, God's moral law and the indwelling Holy Spirit. Romans 2:15 speaks of God's law being written on man's heart, his "conscience also bearing witness" to the moral message of divine directive. Furthermore, it is the assignment of the Holy Spirit, speaking through conscience, to "convict the world of sin, and of righteousness, and of judgment."[18]

Q: *How trustworthy is intuition?*

A: What we commonly call intuition is no more than feeling strongly about something without conscious reasoning. Intuition is derived from an intellectual component, as well as a composite of life's experiences. Its veracity is only as good as the person's powers of judgment and reasoning. Assigning to intuition infallible attributes of deity is idolatry. Replacing the role of a transcendent supreme being with ego is arrogance of the worst sort. It also leaves the evaluation of each action up to the individual instead of an external (biblical) moral code.

Q: *Is secular thought infiltrated with New Age ideals?*

A: A brief consideration of New Age ideology quickly reveals how subtly such concepts have become part of America's sociological and political agenda. It is common today to hear politicians such as Colorado ex-Governor Richard Lamm speak of environmental limitations, the obsolescence of sovereign international boundaries, the infeasibility of war as a means of solving conflicts, and the shift in consciousness toward individual perceptions instead of objective realities. Such concepts have been on the New Age agenda for more than a decade. The fact that such notions have widespread acceptance underscores the success of New Age cultural indoctrination.

Q: *Does the soul represent ultimate reality?*

A: This belief is derived from the notion of self-deification. If the "Higher Self," or soul, is a spark of the divine, it must be the ultimate reality. In contrast, Christianity teaches that God is the ultimate reality, for only he has existed from eternity past. Scripture instructs that only the character of God is immutable. Even the cosmos as we know it will disappear, and only the Word of God will endure forever.[19] To liken the attributes of God to the soul is to indulge in idolatry by exalting man's mind to the status of sacredness.

Q: *Why do some entities claim to be Jesus, such as the spirit that dictated* A Course in Miracles?

A: Such tactics mislead people into believing that Christ still communicates directly by verbal revelation. In Acts 1:11, the angels proclaimed at Christ's ascension, "This same Jesus . . . will so come in like manner as you saw him go into heaven." The second coming of Christ will occur in the same manner as His ascension, not as a message communicated through a trance channeler. Christ made it plain that the Holy Spirit would be sent in his place to indwell his disciples and "guide you into all truth."[20] Nowhere in Scripture are we told to expect either a bodily or oral manifestation of Christ with additional divulgences of truth.

Q: *What is the attraction of such Christianized cults as* A Course in Miracles?

A: Many in the New Age Movement come from a Christian background and cannot totally jettison their beliefs in Christ. Thus, they seek a system that ignores such cardinal doctrines as hell, guilt over sin, and the blood atonement of Christ while maintaining reverence for Jesus the man. *A Course in Miracles,* with its platitudes about love and forgiveness, sounds somewhat Christian while ignoring Satan as a personal source of evil and the need of divine redemption.

Q: *Why is decreeing dangerous?*

A: Many affirmations are blasphemous, such as the "I am that I am" decree whereby one claims for himself the title of God. Those who frequently indulge in decreeing enter trance states in which they involuntarily permit entities to enter them and display spirit possession. Devotees often practice affirmations for extended periods of time, during which they experience the yogic state of disengagement from reality, making them prey for cult indoctrination. Decreeing also increases the disciple's vulnerability to thought transformation, brainwashing, and demonic control.

Q: *Where did the idea of Ascended Masters originate?*

A: Both Hinduism and Buddhism teach that the karmic cycles of reincarnation can be ended by enlightenment. The soul may then merge completely into the godhead and thus enter a state of impersonality. Such souls may also choose to retain their individuality as a means of guiding less spiritually developed souls on earth. Spiritualist trance mediums, who prefer to identify their entities, developed this doctrine to explain why beings on the other side wish to communicate across death's gulf.

Q: *Why do cults like the Church Universal develop retreat centers?*

A: There are several reasons. First, they isolate members from the outside world, thus avoiding any critical inquiry into cult practices. Second, they encourage development of a self-sufficient community, allowing the group to sequester itself from former family members and objective contact with reality. Finally, they provide an opportunity for cultivating the us-versus-them mentality by juxtaposing cult doctrine with other ideologies, increasing devotion to the cause.

Q: *Considering the absurdity of such doctrines as those found in Urantia, why do New Agers so readily accept them?*

A: What may seem preposterous to the uninitiated is logical to

203

proponents of the Aquarian Age. Why? Their involvement means they have accepted mystical concepts of irrationality, so almost nothing seems ludicrous. Logic and verifiability are irrelevant because reality is as they perceive it. They have an insatiable appetite for increasingly outlandish material, so virtually nothing is too shocking or inconceivable. Each new divulgence merely adds to their storehouse of hitherto unknown data. Critical inquiry and objective corroboration are inconsequential in their psychological universe of intuitive spiritual experiences.

Q: *Who can say that the Urantia book is wrong, since God may have provided additional revelations of spiritual knowledge for mankind's benefit?*

A: The Bible views very sternly the communication of spiritual information not sanctioned by the Lord. Deuteronomy 18:20 instituted the death penalty for false prophets. How can they be known? "When a prophet speaks in the name of the Lord, if the thing does not happen or come to pass, that is the thing which the Lord has not spoken," Deuteronomy 18:22 states. The apostle Paul affirmed the accuracy of his teachings by warning that if "an angel from heaven, preach any other gospel to you than what we have preached to you, let him be accursed."[21] God's principle of legal judgment and spiritual jurisprudence is that every truth must be established by two or more witnesses. At Christ's baptism, the Father spoke and the Spirit descended. A supposed revelation like Urantia, which disagrees with apostolic doctrine, has no objectively verifiable corroboration.

Q: *With so many sources of revelation and information, don't New Agers get confused?*

A: Most New Agers seem to accept all esoteric information and additional revelation as an unfolding of progressive truth. No practice or doctrine is considered taboo. Instead, every convention and creed is believed to contain only fragments of the ultimate reality. Therefore, each supplementary portion of spiritual enlightenment continues to reveal the path to higher spiritual consciousness.

Q: *Is there any significance in Benjamin Creme's use of the article "the" when referring to Lord Maitreya as "the" Christ?*

A: Creme has borrowed the esoteric speculation that the term *Christ* refers to an office, not a person. Whereas Scripture teaches that Christ is the specific title of God's son, Jesus of Nazareth, and refers to the "Lord's anointed," Creme believes that Christ is an appointment acquired by enlightenment. Thus, there have been several christs in history (Krishna, Buddha, and other illuminated Masters), and the future may reveal others. For our era, the New Age, Maitreya has supposedly excelled in the hierarchy of departed souls and is bringing God's message to earth.

Q: *What are the central teachings of Lord Maitreya, and how are they consistent with New Age thought?*

A: Maitreya's message is a primer on New Age concepts with two central theses: (1) man is an emerging god who requires new social structures to allow his divinity to flourish; (2) strife, distrustfulness, starvation, inequitable wealth, and death must be eliminated. These goals are referred to as "The Great Plan."[22]

Q: *How can Benjamin Creme avoid the criticism that Maitreya is an antichrist, since his political predictions resemble totalitarianism?*

A: The futuristic politics of the New Age Movement naively place trust in the wisdom of "ascended spiritual masters," which could lead to a totalitarian state. Christians who understand that one-world concepts are rooted in the political agenda of Mystery Babylon, as explained in John's revelation,[23] easily see how Maitreya's vision of an international legislative body could lead to dictatorial, satanic control. New Agers are blind to the fascist implications of their views because they consider each citizen of the New Age an emerging god with altruistic motives.

Q: *What does the theology of the Maitreya movement say concerning Christ?*

A: Jesus isn't ignored. An elaborate explanation has been concocted to replace his mission with that of Maitreya. Jesus is said to be a fourth-degree initiate of the "masters of wisdom." Maitreya actually used him to fulfill his own (Maitreya's) mission by having Jesus come to earth and exhibit the initiation processes of spiritual ascension: birth, baptism, transfiguration, death, and resurrection by the power of Maitreya. After appearing on earth, Christ (not Jesus) reincarnated as Apollonius of Tyana, went to India, and died in Kashmir. For the last 640 years, he has been living in Palestine, incarnated in the body of a Syrian until a later entry into an Italian body. Other incarnations included the biblical Joshua and Isaiah the prophet.[24]

Q: *With so many New Age gurus and spiritual masters claiming to be a christ, how can the true Christ and the antichrist be recognized?*

A: The formula is simple. First John 2:22 tells us, "He is antichrist who denies the Father and the Son." That Scripture indicates spiritual figures like Maitreya are antichrists. Also, consider the following biblical facts. Isaiah 9:7 says Christ must belong to the house of David. Maitreya, on the other hand, is said to be Asian. Micah 5:2 says he would be born in Bethlehem. Maitreya supposedly was born in the Himalayan Mountains. Isaiah 7:14 prophesies that Christ would be born of a virgin. Maitreya was not. In the New Testament alone, over 550 references to the Christ refer specifically to the person of Jesus of Nazareth. As to the idea that there are many Christs, John 3:16 clearly states that Jesus is God's *only* begotten son. Concerning Maitreya's ability to bring peace to Earth and introduce a kingdom age of international harmony, Jesus' words in Matthew 28:18 settle the issue: "All authority has been given to me in heaven and on earth."

WHO'S WHO AND WHAT'S WHAT

A Course in Miracles: A Christianized form of occultism based on documents obtained supernaturally and codified into three large books that proclaim "a universal theology is impossible, but a universal experience is not only possible but necessary."

Ascended Masters: Departed souls who have passed beyond the cycles of reincarnation and now divulge the hidden mysteries of truth by discourses channeled through select human messengers.

Avatar: Hindu doctrine regarding incarnations of the godhead in human flesh that occur when mankind is spiritually confused and needs direction; Krishna, Buddha, Mohammed, and Christ are all considered avatars.

Bhagwan Shree Rajneesh: The so-called Indian sex guru who established a spiritual retreat center in Antelope, Oregon, claiming to be God and precipitating an international scandal around immorality and drugs; eventually deported from the United States, he now lives in his native India.

Church Universal and Triumphant: A spiritistic cult founded more than thirty years ago and enjoying a current membership between 75,000 and 150,000, with assets in the neighborhood of $50 million; teaches that spiritual purification is obtained by decreeing and that you are God.

Cult: A spurious, unorthodox religious body centered on a person or idea that differs quantitatively from the normative religious expressions of a culture; omits or declares opposition to biblical doctrine if a "Christian" cult.

Decrees: Oral affirmations invoking supernatural powers by the authority of the words spoken, similar to chanting a mantra.

Esoteric Philosophy: The study of secret knowledge understood by and revealed to only a select few initiates, who usually attain such information by spirit guides or arcane, sacred books.

207

Lord Maitreya: The supreme member of a spiritual hierarchy who has supposedly incarnated in the body of an Asian New Age messiah and who claims that sharing is the only way to achieve peace on earth.

Share International: Official publication of the Tara Center, expounding the teachings of Lord Maitreya along with various New Age doctrines.

Tara Center: Nonprofit organization founded in 1980 by Benjamin Creme, dedicated to the principle of internationally shared resources and disseminating information about the reappearance of the Christ in the person of Lord Maitreya.

Thought Adjusters: In the cult Urantia, spirit guides that are "undiluted parts of Deity" and communicate with one's higher self.

Transmission: A method of spiritual communication from an extradimensional entity that relays its messages through thought-to-thought transference or other mediumistic conveyances.

Urantia Book: A 2,097-page occult volume, delivered by automatic handwriting from extraterrestrial beings, claiming to deliver the "greatest message ever given to man."

IN MY OPINION

Two cups of hope; two cups of altered consciousness; three tablespoons each of self-awareness, self-improvement, and self-esteem; one heaping teaspoon of peace; one generous pinch of humanism, Eastern mysticism, and occultism; one handful of holism; one scoop of mystical experience. Mix thoroughly together, bake in a warm, friendly environment, fill with your most appealing dreams, garnish generously with positive thoughts and good vibrations.[25]

That's the way Caryl Matrisciana describes New Age beliefs in her book *Gods of the New Age*. Her well-articulated evaluation of New Age concepts illustrates why cults are so successful. Our world starves for the reality and love proffered but seldom delivered by great religions, including Christianity. Thus, the spiritually searching public is easy prey for the message of replacing old sentiments and modes of culture with the theme that mankind can achieve global harmony by tapping into higher consciousness.

Such gullible acceptance of New Age explanations illustrates a poor sense of history and is devoid of an understanding of the New Age's unproved theories. For millennia, New Age ideas have been age old ideologies in the East. The result? Immeasurable poverty, indifference to human misery, and a fatalistic outlook that awaits the justice of karma rather than inviting immediate human compassion.

In India, a deformed beggar sits indefinitely in a gutter. A female child is allowed to die. A holy man streaks his hair with cow manure. And it's all done in the name of mysticism. The explanation? The beggar's bad karma placed him in this position, and helping him could hinder the "Great Cause" of karmic fairness. The child came into a world where females are considered less desirable than boys. The holy man believes all creatures are extensions of God. The cow is the mother of life, thus its excrement is blessed.

It can't happen here? It already has. *A Course in Miracles* denigrates the sanctity of suffering, so why should man mortify himself to benefit another? The Church Universal and Triumphant decrees in mantra-like fashion, encouraging detachment from reality and denial of human need. Benjamin Creme's Transmission Groups await telepathic messages from an unidentified savior, a spiritual leader who preaches a future of shared resources rather than selling goods now, giving the resources to the poor, and following Jesus of Nazareth in self-denial.

New Age cults thrive in the atmosphere of Satan's lie, "You will not surely die."[26] It has taken form in the films of George Lucas (among others), the holistic healing techniques of mystical medicine, and the belief in energy dualities that has invaded the halls of academia. New Age cults are but a stage-stop in the Aquarian quest for man's evolutionary transformation to levels of consciousness beyond evil. What the initiate fails to see is that the holding pen is a pigsty, the devil's destination.

"For many deceivers have gone out into the world who do not confess Jesus Christ as coming in the flesh," Scripture warns.[27] New Age cults offer alternative routes to God. They tender hopes that the earth will be beautified and man's soul purified. They propose a world in which guilt, fear, and selfishness will be things of the past Picean Age, unworthy of the New Age's agenda. While New Age cults may promise godhead, however, they deliver only the same lie sold by Satan in Eden.

Chapter 11

THE BIG PICTURE FROM THE WRONG ANGLE

Straight Answers on New Age Globalism

"Science has made unrestrictive national sovereignty incompatible with human survival. The only possibilities now are world government or death" (Bertrand Russell, writer and philosopher).[1]

"Unless the concept of planetary government is universally accepted, the human race must live with the perpetual threat of nuclear extinction" ("Letters to the Editor," *Time*).[2]

"We have an obligation to expose and attack the world of Bible worship, salvationism, heaven, hell, and all the mythical deities" *(The Humanist).*[3]

"One of these days I'll be so complete I won't be human. I will be a god" (John Denver, singer and composer).[4]

John Denver, Bertrand Russell, a letter writer from Akron, Ohio, and the editors of *The Humanist* have much in common. All have enthroned man at the center of existence, and all have concluded that nationalistic sovereignty and patriotic pride are deadly foes to be extinguished. All ascribe to a form of political and social philosophy known as globalism.

Delineating a term like globalism isn't easy. Definitions vary from one advocacy group to another, depending on whether their primary allegiance is to scholarly interests or one-world unity concepts. But all globalists have found the welcome mat out among New Agers. Despite their differences, globalists hold certain things in common. Ethnocentricity has to go. Believing that one's cultural heritage is superior is a no-no. "Equivalency" is the goal—the idea that all governments, as well as all legal and economic systems, deserve identical international respect.

Among globalistic aspirations are abolition of the traditional family structure, an international court of law to arbitrate worldwide disputes, and a common economic structure. International laws would abolish war, hunger, and poverty. Extreme factions even suggest that children be produced by genetic control, with fertilization and gestation occurring outside the body. Most globalists favor unilateral disarmament.

213

The New Age Movement is a key to achieving these goals. Political practicalities are possible in any society only if a corresponding ideology provides philosophical support. New Age thinking furnishes globalism with an integrated values system drawn from various mystical religious traditions. New Age globalism would replace belief in a transcendent deity with reliance on man's inherent goodness and wisdom. To oversee this arrangement, a more liberally funded United Nations, with greater powers of police enforcement, would be established.

GLOBAL CONSCIOUSNESS

Widespread injustice. Nuclear arsenals and warheads in waiting. Famine of measureless proportions. Mankind on the edge of time. That's the way New Agers see our planet, a world inhabited by a dangerous species called man. What's to be done? The solution is supposedly simple. Achieve a state of inner peace, and reconcile differing political ideologies. Meditate. Smile peacefully. Become one with your adversaries.

A Zen master puts it this way: Imagine yourself as a swimmer in a river. Then imagine yourself as the river. Become the river to understand its perspective. Then imagine yourself as a Soviet. Become the Communist. A new understanding of political consciousness will overcome you. As each citizen of the planet follows, the world will become one.

Organizations abound that seek to achieve these ends. Volunteers for Peace, Inc., sponsor their own peace corps that promotes living and working in foreign countries. Citizens Exchange Council advocates exchanges between Russians and Americans. World Peace University envisions a world where "peace is the way of life, where hunger no longer exists, and where individuals achieve their highest degree of personal fulfillment."[5]

New Age techniques to accomplish world peace range from so-called citizens summitry (promoting international personal diplomacy) to visualization and affirmation methods, which pursue peace by mentally creating a state of harmony. Some New Agers advocate a Peace Tax Fund Bill by which Congress could mandate the taxpayer's right to designate tax contributions for nonmilitary purposes. Much New Age focus is on antinuclear interests, supporting establishment of nuclear-free zones, where atomic weapons, facilities, equipment, and supplies would be banned. Some even suggest that countries renounce the right to be defended by nuclear weapons.

Dr. F. Richard Schneider of the World Peace University says, "Humankind, in kinship with the earth, is embarking on a historic journey that will lead to the highest peaks of consciousness, or the end of survival as we know it. At this very moment, you and I, along with our fellow planetary travelers, hold a common destiny in our hearts and minds."[6]

What is that destiny? Visualize a world in which there is no right or wrong, politically speaking. There is no other side. No enemy. No inevitability of war. The planet is one, and we are one with the planet. This physical reality must become a political reality. And these aspirations can be achieved only when mankind acquires higher consciousness. This will be done by allowing the self-generating powers of love and hope to heal each person's inner self. Then the world will be healed.

GLOBAL EVENTS

At the end of 1986, it was the World of Instant Cooperation (also known as the World Healing Meditation). In the summer of 1987, it was the Harmonic Convergence. These events attempted to draw together humanists, idealists, and globalists under the banner of the New Age. The underlying concept was that 1 percent of the critical mass of the earth's population gathering in harmony to produce a vibratory resonance would introduce a quantum leap forward in the movement toward world peace.

Both events were billed as capable of introducing global unanimity, producing supernatural healings, and inaugurating a "planetary pentecost." A much-heralded "quantum leap" was the next purported stage in the "spiritual evolution toward reaching Godhead." The impetus for the December 31, 1986, World Healing Meditation was a book entitled *Practical Spirituality* by John Randolph Price.

The author told of communicating with an Ascended Awakened One, a spirit entity who called himself Asher. In one encounter, Asher declared: "There will be a uniting of spiritually-minded people on the planet through a particular vibration in the ethers. This fusion of energy will reach a peak on December 31, 1986, and it will remove the threat of global war."[7] Price may have gotten Asher's message, but critics argue retrospectively that Asher must have missed informing the Iraqis, Iranians, Palestinians, and Afghans, plus assorted terrorists.

Asher's message reassured some and frightened others, particularly those not enamored with New Age monologues. What did Asher mean when he warned that "those individuals with lower vibratory rates will be removed during the next two decades?"[8] To Christians, it smacked of New Testament passages referring to the Antichrist. Asher was hardly encouraging when he declared, "Those looking for a savior can find one in the mirror."[9]

The Harmonic Convergence of August 16–17, 1987, was heralded by some New Agers as the largest event of prayer, meditation, and ceremony ever to occur at sacred sites. The call for this gathering went out in 1987 via Jose Arguelles' book, *The Mayan Factor: Path Beyond Technology*. It declared a 5,125-year cycle was ending, and this opportunity would provide a window during which the earth could be cleansed of its fear. August 16–17 was designated to inaugurate the last 25 years of this cycle. Arguelles promised that if at least 144,000 people would gather as channels for positive energies to flood the earth, the intensity of humanity's suffering could be alleviated. (Arguelles says he's in touch with a "star person" named Treadwell of the stellar system Actara, who phones him at home.)

In his book *The Global Brain,* Peter Russell likened the human family on earth to the cells in a body. If one-tenth of one-percent of the cells were astute, the whole body would be awakened, he said. Likewise, the number 144,000 was chosen as the critical mass necessary to illuminate the entire body of beings on earth. (The same number is cited in Revelation 14:3, but in a different context.) To celebrate the Harmonic Convergence, New Agers gathered at sacred sites such as Macchu Picchu in Peru and Stonehenge in England. Participants saw themselves as balancers of the planet's energy, for the first time equalizing the feminine and masculine powers of the planet.

When the day of convergence arrived, non-New Agers witnessed meager crowds and commonplace circumstances. Movement members thought otherwise. From Arizona to Florida, Maui to Maine, they gathered in sweat lodges, campgrounds, and meditation circles to heal the earth. Some said they communicated with UFOs. Others claimed to observe atmospheric phenomena, including rainbows, sweeps of wind, shooting stars, and unusually clear air, indicative of the earth's releasing new purity. On Mount Shasta in northern California, 5,000 pilgrims shivered on the rocky, fir-covered slopes. A National Public Radio satellite carried a three-hour broadcast. In Australia, a guided meditation was held on national television. Critics said it was harmonic boredom. New Agers believed their deepest prayers had been heard and that prevailing peace had been introduced on earth.

GLOBAL HUMANISM

If New Age globalists have a creed, it is probably the tenets of humanism. As a man-centered "religion," humanism has drawn fire from Christian parents concerned about school textbooks, and from television evangelists who see it as the enemy of Americanism and evangelicalism. A publication called *The Humanist* recently stated, "We would be particularly specific and energetic in attacking such quack millennialists as Billy Graham, such embattled reactionaries as Pope Paul VI, because they represent the greatest anti-humanist aggregates in our society."[10]

Responding to assaults on humanism by the religious right, humanists have often allied themselves with atheists, secularists, and civil libertarians. Because of their eclectic social vision, they also have found friends with globalists and all those committed to the idea of planetary unity and custodianship of the earth's monetary and environmental resources.

Prominent New Ager Dr. Robert Muller, former secretary of the United Nations Economic and Social Council, has said, "Humanity is evolving toward a coherent global form best described by a metaphor of the human brain; each person, young or old, able-bodied or handicapped, is an important neuron in the emerging planetary brain that is constituted by the meridian networkings among people."

Such views represent an incredible shift in the thinking of Western civilization. For several centuries, a theocentric worldview has dominated nations of the First World. Now, an anthropocentric perception of society is gaining precedence. The earth itself is seen as a kind of living organism, demanding globalists and New Agers to oppose industrial development and nuclear power.

Traditional concepts of God have no place on the agenda of globalists. Humanist Manifesto II states, "As nontheists, we begin with humans, not God, nature, not deity . . . no deity will save us: We must save ourselves."[11] This fits well into the framework of New Age ideology, since man is perceived as a god who is capable of saving himself. Likewise, the humanist condemns diversity of worship as an impediment to progress. In fact, humanists believe all religions are a disservice to the human species. Since the New Age Movement wants to synthesize all religious doctrines into an eclectic system, old orders of religions would be abolished and replaced with a globalistic set of beliefs acceptable to both humanists and New Agers.

GLOBAL PANTHEISM

Globalists have also advanced the idea of a universal interdependence in which God and nature are fused into one. The groves may no longer be worshiped, but the hills and trees are revered ("resacrilized," as New Agers put it) to the extent that man is no longer a unique moral creature. Today, a merged perception of God's being and man's existence dominates Western thought, closely resembling Hinduism. God is seen as being at one with and pervasive in all matter. Thus, moral objectives are measured by their contribution to cosmological oneness, not personal moral accountability to a transcendent Creator. And if God is not out there looking down on each person's moral conduct, then right is what each part of the one perceives right to be.

Interdependence is a commonly heard term among globalists and New Agers. In fact, globalists have drafted what they call a "Declaration of Interdependence" whose stated purpose is as follows: "To establish a new world order of compassion, peace, justice, and security, it is essential that mankind free itself from the limitations of national prejudice and acknowledge that the forces that unite it are incomparably deeper than those that divide it."[12]

Futurist, architect, and inventor Buckminster Fuller said, "Cosmic evolution is irrevocably intent upon completely transforming differently competing entities into a completely integrated, comprehensively interconsiderate, harmoniously whole."[13]

New Age proponent Benjamin Creme, a founding father of the New Age Movement, publishes through his Tara Foundation a periodical called *Share International*. Claiming to receive directives from a spiritual master known as Maitreya, Creme promotes unselfish allotments of all national resources as the only way to solve starvation (see Chap. 10).

GLOBAL SOCIOLOGY

Globalism's social agenda is guided by several presuppositions that are highly amenable to the New Age Movement. First, the entire earth, including its oceans and biosphere, is seen as the common property of mankind. Because the purity of earth's water and air affect all living creatures, globalists insist that all of nature be placed under international jurisdiction. New Agers readily accept this proposition because of their pantheistic principles. To them, nature is not only interdependent but also cosmologically interrelated because of its one source. If "all is one," as the mystic declares, that proposition can be easily ratified by legislative powers that are internationally binding.

The New Age Movement easily combines metaphysical and political concepts. For example, New Agers speak one moment of the necessity of data flow across borders and ecological interdependence. In the next breath, they refer as easily to planetary self-realization. To the humanistic globalist, there is no God. All that matters is, well, matter. That's all right with the New Ager, since his premises conclude de facto that the planet is God.

The New Age philosophy of holism also underpins this social agenda. If man, nature, Mother Earth, and the entire cosmos are interconnected, national sovereignty would be antithetical. The globalist needs only the rationale of apparent logic to confirm his conclusions. But the New Ager relies on the mystical experience of oneness achieved in altered states of consciousness, plus the messages of trance-channeled entities, both confirming unitary awareness and global interdependence.

The scene of social engineering is the best place to observe the mutuality of globalism and humanism. Among the items on their bilateral agenda are abolishing traditional family structures, minority rights, and universal education. As for women's rights, both tend to see our male-dominated society as stemming from the West's Judeo-Christian heritage. The New Age Movement tends to be more matriarchal. Some contingencies have resurrected ancient ideas of goddess worship, tracing their devotion to such archaic deities as Diana and Aphrodite.

GLOBAL GODDESSES

Fertility cults were common in ancient agrarian societies. People were close to the earth and especially conscious of reproductive cycles in their herds and families. Fruitfulness was crucial to survival, so female-oriented nature religions flourished. Idols of Artemis were depicted with multiple mammaries to nourish life. With such matriarchal emphasis came the belief that women were unusually gifted spiritually. Male dominance as a source of spiritual guidance and creator of the species' future was a relatively new cultural phenomenon that arrived with the supremacy of Christianity in the West.

European society viewed man as the creator and myth maker of civilization. It is men who forge the way into the wilderness of economic competition. Men wage wars and build weapons of mass destruction. It is the virility of men that emblazons the silver screen in the roles of Rambo and the Terminator. And it is men who serve primarily as our priests and pastors.

New Age globalists see this as a cosmic imbalance, the reason for the nuclear precipice on which humanity hangs. They envision a world led by women, with feminine spirituality and wisdom predominating over an elevated consciousness. This synthesis of feminism and spiritual devotion is known as Womanspirit, a resurgence of the "Cosmic Mother" to her rightful place as central in the earth's religion.

Certain feminist New Agers have planned resurrecting the mysteries of goddess worship by erecting temples to the female deities of antiquity.

Other New Agers committed to a matriarchal culture have instituted Wiccan celebrations and rituals to raise the vibrations of Mother Nature and to usher in the New Age of Womanspirit. Occult feminists look for female principles of piety in astrology, Tarot, mythology, and folklore. They see mystical significance in the announcement of Christ's resurrection to two women. Ancient mysteries are searched for hidden perspectives on feminine dominance as the source of social harmony.

GLOBAL PLAN

The globalistic transformation sought by New Agers has a highly visible agenda for those who understand its networking. These New Age theorists propose nothing less than a newly evolved human race that would follow a great master plan (known as The Plan) laid down by higher spiritual masters. These beings have ascended to a new consciousness, an astral plane all mankind is destined to achieve. Marilyn Ferguson explains it this way:

> Migrant beings—souls from a higher order—are born into every generation. They are destined to be triggers of evolution. These rebellious spirits . . . offend the good manners of the day. At an end-of-days period, when the world is to be remade, an even greater number of such chaotic spirits arrive to shake the status quo to its roots . . . these people are only freeing the energy from dying forms. A new breed will emerge—the masters of construction.[14]

Inherent in The Plan are two simple suppositions: All that exists is God, and all mankind is an extension of God. From these assumptions flow the corollary: A cosmic evolutionary leap in consciousness will lead humanity back to the Garden, where psychic forces will restore planetary harmony and peace. But New Age critics are troubled by the means New Agers seek to employ on their way to an Eden of paradise.

Author Dave Hunt, a New Age nemesis, compares Aquarian predictions to the biblical view of a rapture and the following period of tribulation. Hunt warns,

> The Shamballa force is credited with a "tremendous crisis" that will transform consciousness. Is this the Master of Shamballa's diabolically clever way of making it seem that the Great Disappearance [rapture] is just part of The Plan, after all, and is tremendously beneficial to human evolution? It seems inescapable that what [Alice] Bailey and others call "the initiation . . . into the Mysteries of the Ages" the Bible calls receiving a deluding influence to believe the ancient lie.[15]

Best-selling author Texe Marrs concludes, "The conspiratorial impulse is the throbbing vibration, or heartbeat, that universally grips the minds and souls of the New Age believers. It is the spirit of the Antichrist, the philosophy of seducing demons who work every minute of the day to drive The Plan to ultimate success."[16]

Perennial New Age antagonist Constance Cumbey cautions, "It is clear that there has been much working out of The Plan. The tragedy is not that there is a plan for world domination. What they fail to recognize is that The Plan is for capture instead of their souls."[17]

The Plan fails to differentiate between animal and human life, democracy and communism, Christianity and Hinduism. All religions, sovereign boundaries, economics systems, forms of worship, and political ideologies must merge, since all are part of the Source that is perfect in its undivided state.

STRAIGHT ANSWERS

Q: *How does Christianity differ from the monist view that all reality is of one essence?*

A: To the mystic, all of creation is an undivided unity. The Bible presents a cosmos that consists of individual personalities, a diversity of events, and material objects that exist of themselves, apart from God. Though God has a purpose for all existence, his will for each person and circumstance differs, except for the ultimate goal of bringing glory to God. More importantly, God's moral qualities are intrinsic to his character. Human beings are not extensions of his nature but of a differentiated essence, with the capacity of moral volition to choose sin or obedience to the Creator.

Q: *Are there any secret items on the New Ager's agenda when he refers to a world of peace?*

A: Their true goals are not secret, but they're seldom explicit. They often refer to a quantum leap or a paradigm shift. They seek a radical revolution in global consciousness. All of earth's citizens will need to see that each nation's sovereignty is negotiable, that all national self-interests are identical. The key to accomplishing this is a global economy devoid of competitive advantage. Such management of monetary resources can occur only with appropriate policing methods. Christians have every reason to be wary of such suggestions because of the similarities to the antichrist economy in Revelation, where no one will buy or sell without the mark of the beast.[18]

Q: *What practices were historically associated with goddess worship?*

A: Ancient goddess worship cults were incredibly licentious. Temple prostitutes served as an access to the matriarchal mysteries. Sexual fertility was emphasized, and ritual intercourse was an initiatory procedure. In Aphrodite worship, virgins were inducted into the cult by being deflowered with a male statuette bearing an oversized phallus. It is reasonable to assume that New Age goddess worship would eventually demonstrate this same preoccupation with sexuality. In addition, goddess worship is based on appreciation of feminine psychic inclinations. New Age advocates of goddess worship often align themselves with witchcraft and have been known to declare blasphemously, "In the beginning was the goddess."

Q: *What is the globalistic spiritual intent of the New Age Movement?*

A: Scripture tells us the spiritual whore of Mystery Babylon foretold in Revelation 17 will be the ultimate culmination of all spiritual error, led by the beast that ascends from the bottomless pit. With its blasphemous declaration of man as a god and its espousal of occult abominations, New Age spirituality is an excellent candidate to be this false system of worship that is the "Mother of Harlots." The final purpose of the New Age Movement will be to deliver to the devil a deceived generation seduced by false science, indoctrinated by trance channelers, and blinded by The Plan, which calls for peace and world harmony at the sake of people's souls.

Q: *In a world of racial tensions and ideological allegiances,* *wouldn't globalism be better than competitiveness, which leads to war and bloodshed?*

A: The answer would be yes if globalism's laudable goals could be achieved. But eighteenth-century utopianism and twentieth-century socialism, both of similar design, illustrate that human greed dominates all such social experiments. In fact, competitiveness on an economic level can be healthy. Japan transformed its society from a war footing to the most vibrant of world economies by converting the contest for world power into monetary accomplishments. Unfortunately, the only way globalism can stop international rivalry is by enforcing the sharing of resources through police-state powers.

Q: *With so many special interest groups competing for attention and money, wouldn't a unified world order be a preferable way of dealing more expediently with our problems?*

A: Every historical instance of power's being concentrated in the hands of a few for the benefit of the many has resulted in totalitarianism. There is no reason to assume that altruistic New Agers have greater capacity for avoiding such peril. In fact, they are even more dangerous because of their egotistical insistence that those opposing their plans hinder the advancing Age of Aquarius.

Q: *Wouldn't peace be promoted if the world disarmed and international political boundaries were dissolved?*

A: Such suggestions sound like a speech of appeasement by England's prime minister prior to World War II, Neville Chamberlain. Hitler preached the same message, but his hidden goal soon demonstrated that lust for political control far exceeds altruistic desire for world harmony. Permanent disarmament would be unattainable, because some despot would seize the opportunity to arm and destroy the balance of impotency. After 6,000 years of civilizations' carving up territorial perimeters, it would be folly to believe war and bloodshed to acquire territory would be unselfishly surrendered.

Q: *If globalistic events bring people together to concentrate on peace and common goals, doesn't the good outweigh any harm caused?*

A: Behind the agenda of harmony and world peace is a religious itinerary that assumes these goals will be accomplished by mystical means. Consequently, New Age gatherings in the name of peace feature an occult agenda that invites participants to indulge in guided meditation exercise, yogic maneuvers, and various consciousness-altering procedures. Some attendees might be innocently drawn into dangerous spiritual techniques.

Q: *What do New Agers mean by the term "quantum leap in consciousness"?*

A: According to New Age thought, mankind's progress toward harmonious relationships has been slowly evolving. At the dawn of this new Aquarian age, a significant step forward will be taken, allowing humanity to break through to a new spiritual consciousness. Thus, after centuries of a gradual shift in global consciousness, the pace of evolution is now accelerating to usher in the New Age overnight.

Q: *What do New Age globalists mean when they speak of "purging" those who disagree because of "lower vibratory rates"?*

A: This concept has been mentioned by several New Age spokespersons. Understandably, they are ambiguous when explaining their true intentions. Christians who comprehend Bible prophecy know New Agers are consciously or unconsciously referring to the antichrist's goal of destroying any faithful spiritual remnant. The term "lower vibratory rate" is a euphemism for those who refuse to accept the "benevolent" goals of the Aquarian regime. Bible believers can hardly be blamed for assuming that New Agers are actually referring to a time of persecution and martyrdom for the followers of Christ, who refuse to accept the occultism of Mystery Babylon.[19]

Q: *Is there a difference between the terms* humanities *and* human-ism?

A: The term *humanities* refers to academic studies associated with mankind's highest achievements in art, literature, and communication. Defined as such, the term has no negative connotations. It must be distinguished, however, from the word *humanism,* an ideological belief that man is the highest creature on evolution's ladder and the supreme source of moral and aesthetic ideals. Though humanism does not explicitly deny God, as does atheism, its tenets pragmatically rule out divine intervention in the affairs of mankind.

Q: *How can humanism be dangerous if some people claim to be both Christians and humanists?*

A: Those who claim to be Christian humanists are either ignorant of the true humanist agenda, as stated in such documents as the "Humanist Manifesto," or they are being theologically double-minded. No one can honestly lay claim to trusting the grace of Christ and simultaneously profess a philosophy that denies God's providence.

Q: *Why do humanists, globalists, and New Agers get along so well philosophically?*

A: They share certain common beliefs such as the inherent goodness of man, the necessity of abandoning nationalistic identities, the belief that peace is achievable through human effort, and the assumption that nuclear annihilation is inevitable unless enforced global interdependence is established.

Q: *Isn't it commendable that humanists defend the rights of others?*

A: Consider the rights they defend—abortion, euthanasia, and homosexuality. They tolerate and endorse behavior the Bible condemns as sinful and an affront to the Lord. Humanists can hardly be commended for insulting the moral law of God.

Q: *If it is a dangerous document, why have important people signed the "Declaration of Interdependence"?*

A: Many people are naive about globalism's true intentions. Some of the problems globalists address are serious concerns, such as pollution, poverty, distribution of wealth, and the specter of nuclear war. Documents such as the Declaration are carefully worded to avoid mentioning the true designs of the elitists who guide such plans. Consequently, uninformed individuals may unwittingly endorse theories they would otherwise avoid.

Q: *Since it seems that world economies and culture are increasingly intertwined, what's wrong with the idea of interdependence?*

A: Interdependence destroys the healthy economic competition upon which the advances of mankind have been based. Our current quality of health care, common conveniences, and food surpluses result from global rivalry that has spurred international inventiveness and productiveness. Removing that incentive would destroy the desire to generate wealth, which fuels productivity. Failed communist economies are excellent examples of what happens when a noncompetitive marketplace exists.

Q: *If God has given humanity dominion over the earth, isn't a concern for the environment compatible with Christianity?*

A: Christians should be in the forefront of environmental concerns because of the biblical principle of stewardship over the resources of earth. The biblical ethic of man being given dominion over creation is an act of trust, not folly. The Christian who understands the sacredness of this stewardship over the environment is even more interested in safeguarding our natural resources. But what New Age globalists propose is quite different. They seek "resacralization" of the environment and refer to the "enchantment" of the environmental ethic. These are religious concepts compatible with a pantheistic approach to environmentalism. New Agers often adopt a concept similar to aboriginals, who believe earth is our mother, imbued with a sense of sacredness. In effect, the soil and vegetation become gods to be revered. This sin is referred to in Romans 1 when it speaks of unregenerate pagans who "worshiped and served the creature rather than the Creator" and thus "exchanged the truth of God for the lie."[20]

WHO'S WHO AND WHAT'S WHAT

Aphrodite: Ancient pagan goddess depicted with dozens of breasts denoting fertility, revered by neopagan New Agers as Mother Goddess of the Earth.

Anthropocentricity: The belief that man is the center of the universe, the highest rung on evolution's ascending ladder, and therefore the final arbiter of all conduct and morals.

Artemis: Ancient female goddess of Mesopotamia and Eurasia, depicted as a fertility symbol.

Asher: Spirit guide of John Randolph Price and source of information for his books.

Creme, Benjamin: Considered a father of the New Age Movement and a present guiding force through his trance-channeled sessions when he is "overshadowed" by the spirit of Lord Maitreya, an Ascended Master who has returned to earth to teach humanity the importance of global sharing (see Chap. 10).

Diana: Greek fertility goddess, also known in other eras as Aphrodite, Ashtoreth, or Artemis, venerated by those New Agers who believe in the resacralization of the earth.

"Declaration of Interdependence": A globalist document, drafted by the World Affairs Council in 1975, representing the New Age agenda by stating the world cannot survive

unless mankind recognizes "the necessity for collaborative regulation by international authorities."

Equivalency: A socialist concept that insists no nation should have an overabundance of resources, that commerce and substance should be distributed equivalently.

Ferguson, Marilyn: Prominent New Age theorist and author of the movement's classic *The Aquarian Conspiracy,* as well as publisher of the *Mind/Brain Bulletin* (see Chap. 12).

Fuller, Buckminster: Author, architect, inventor (geodesic dome), and futurist who has championed the "small is beautiful" ethic of globalism.

Globalism: Political and religious ideology that views the earth and its people as an interrelated organism that can survive only through reciprocal consent on objectives and equally allocated amounts of all resources.

Harmonic Convergence: A globalistic event held in summer of 1987; attempted to organize a "critical mass" of the world's population to enter altered states of consciousness to abolish war and inaugurate an era of world peace.

Hinduism: The dominant religion of the Indian subcontinent, it teaches that God is impersonal and unknowable and that man's ultimate purpose, after the effect of his bad deeds has been dissipated, is to re-emerge into the oneness of the inexplicable.

Holism: A unitary philosophy that claims organic or environmental systems consist of undifferentiated parts, which are integrated as a whole.

Humanism: A doctrine that supposes mankind is the ultimate essence of worth, and no divine being exists to determine the ideals and values of humanity.

Monism: From *mono,* meaning "one," it suggests that all creation emanates from a solitary energy source that pervades all animate and inanimate matter.

Muller, Robert: Former assistant secretary-general of the United Nations in charge of economics and social services and the cooperation of thirty-two specialized United Nations agencies and world programs (see Chap. 12).

Pantheism: The theological belief that God and his creation are not different in substance but that all is one, creation and Creator, so that to revere what exists is akin to worshiping God.

Plan, The: New Age reference to a "conspiracy" that would replace present religious, political, and economic systems with an intuitive thrust for planetary harmony.

Price, John Randolph: Author of *Practical Spirituality* and president of The Quartus Foundation for Spiritual Research, Inc., a nonprofit organization dedicated to research regarding the divinity of man.

Theocentricity: Belief that God is central to the propositions of man and omnipotent in his control of history's destiny.

Shamballa: Legendary kingdom of spiritually developed adepts (similar to the occult concept of Atlantis), proposed by Tibetan Buddhist theology and believed to be both an actual locale and an aspect of astral existence.

World Healing Meditation: A December 31, 1986, gathering of New Agers to meditate for peace under the inspirational tutelage of John Randolph Price.

IN MY OPINION

Globalism is altruism in action, noble but ignoring man's ignobility. It's also old hat. It was tried by Marx, Lenin, and Stalin. Like contemporary globalists, they, too, longed for worldwide social and political dominion. Today, Soviet Russia still abides by globalistic goals of centralized control. But maintaining that system has cost the lives of millions who have died in gulags of horror. Why flirt with a system that massacred innocent children in the Afghanistan mountains? Why consider a concept that erected the Berlin Wall as an "economic barrier" to prevent East Berliners from fleeing globalistic Communism?

Globalists have poor memories. They forget that many of their utopian models are also molded on the Third Reich's thousand years of predicted prosperity. Do the gas ovens of Buchenwald say nothing to the humanist who professes consummate faith in man's nobility? Perhaps we should ask the Jews of the Warsaw ghetto if globalism works. Maybe we should consult the citizens of Poland and Hungary about interdependence.

Globalism superstitiously assumes that abstractly articulated ideals will somehow hold in check man's voracious greed. History attests that man yearns for individuality, not the socialized sanctity of federal domination. He yearns to be a unique creature in the scheme of the universe, not an indistinguishable part of the whole. Globalism is also monism, the doctrine that all is one and that God, man, and nature are part of the same essence. This failed philosophy has produced only hunger, violence, and overpopulation in the Eastern societies where it has predominated.

The emerging world religion accompanying globalism insists that all religions teach basically the same truth. If Buddha and Jesus had differences, they were accidental doctrines, since both had the same intent. The New Age goal of globalism is to minimize distinctions between religions and humanistically focus on the man-centered aspect of all world faiths. While globalists speak romantically of one planet, one people, one government, one currency, and abounding brotherhood, the Bible promises a city where these ideas will reign for eternity—the New Jerusalem.[21] While New Agers speak of finding enlightenment through an altered consciousness that manifests itself in a transformed social structure, Jesus declares unequivocally, "I am the way, the truth, and the life."[22]

"Life is a process of becoming"; that New Age maxim epitomizes the optimism of globalists, who see current consciousness-raising activities as the precursor to a better life. They are convinced that beliefs now languishing on society's periphery will soon become mainstream American thought. It's only a matter of time until the ethos of a growing cadre of the movement is accepted by those in authority worldwide.

What would mainstreaming of transcendentalism on a global scale mean? For one thing, mystical fable would become more important than verifiable reality. Tough decisions and unwanted deductions would be harder for people to handle. Cultural escapism would increase. As cases in point, imagine a New Ager who creates his own reality as an air traffic controller or a military negotiator at a summit conference, or a committed metaphysician in charge of an atomic reactor or a critical care ward. Each of these individuals would make vital decisions without the guidance of objective criteria.

Isis, Diana, Aphrodite, Artemis, and their ilk do not represent a golden age of feminine supremacy. That conclusion ignores historical and anthropological fact. Matriarchal religions of antiquity made possible patriarchal exploitation of women. In the name of religious devotion, ritualistic sex merely excused legalized prostitution. By deifying femininity, women were demoralized and exploited. They were demoted to sex objects and childbearers without regard for true feminine self-esteem.

Jesuit philosopher Teilhard de Chardin, revered by New Agers, proposed that mankind would eventually reach an "Omega Point" at which a world consciousness would unify all individualized thought. Who would choose to live in such a homogenous civilization? Only those who espouse political socialism. What powers of state would be required to enforce such cooperation and unselfishness? Unthinkable forces of totalitarianism. What cost to personal freedoms would be required to establish the New Age of communal consciousness? Complete loss of privacy and the ability to live and travel unrestricted.

"I am the Alpha and the Omega, the Beginning and the End,"[23] Christ declares. Mankind's Omega Point is not a convergence with cosmic consciousness. It is Judgment Day when, according to Revelation 21:8, sorcerers "shall have their part in the lake which burns with fire and brimstone." The New Age Movement, with its proclivity for the occult, is sorcery of the first order, punishable by eternal condemnation, an inharmonious convergence with hell.

Chapter 12

NEW AGE PEOPLE, PLACES, AND PRACTICES

Straight Answers on Who's Who in the New Age

PEOPLE

Babbitt, Elwood: Known as "the medium from Massachusetts," Babbitt claims to channel Mark Twain, Einstein, and Wordsworth. He also asserts that he is the repository of channeled truth by the gods themselves, including Jesus Christ and the Hindu deity Lord Vishnu. Audio tapes are available of the entities' messages, and their missives are also in such books as *Voices of Spirit* and *Talks with Christ.* The message of Christ through Babbitt is, "You, in your own individuality, are a division of the Soul of Being, yet in all of your members you are united as one, the one and only great universe of Self."[1]

Bailey, Alice: Based on the teachings of Djwhal Khual, a spiritually Ascended Master, the writings of Alice Bailey form a compendium of Theosophical beliefs and New Age concepts. Bailey was born in England and communicated with spirit entities when very young. Her first husband was an Episcopalian clergyman, her sister a devout Christian physician.

Bailey, who founded the Arcane School to investigate and disseminate esoteric philosophy, includes the Great Invocation with her writings. It declares, "Let Light and Love and Power restore the Plan on earth." Bailey believes The Plan will be instituted after a global crisis when the Christ returns, representing the spiritual hierarchy. At that time, a new world religion will be instituted. Through her work with World Goodwill and the Arcane School, Bailey shed an earlier affinity for Christianity to become a prominent spokesperson for Theosophy, Eastern mysticism, and the New Age.

Besant, Annie: A radical English activist, Annie Besant joined the Theosophical Society and became its co-head with Col. Henry Steel Olcott in 1891. When H. P. Blavatsky, founder of the Society, died, Besant took over because of her oratorical skills. While American Theosophists adopted a less Eastern view of occultism, Besant insisted on a more metaphysical interpretation of cosmic spirituality, emphasizing karma and reincarnation.

Besant promoted the idea of past lives. In 1909, she prophesied that a young Indian named Krishnamurti would become a great World Teacher.

Blavatsky, H. P.: Helena Petrovna Blavatsky was born in 1831 of an aristocratic Russian family and exhibited psychic abilities at an early age. While visiting the United States, she became intensely interested in spiritualism and astral projection. Blavatsky claimed that during one of her astral journeys, she made contact with disembodied spiritual masters, whom she called *mahatmas*. In 1875, she helped form the Theosophical Society. Her first book, *Isis Unveiled,* became the Society's central document. She also articulated its central teaching: "There is no religion higher than truth."

Blavatsky promoted psychic phenomena, including apports (supernatural dematerializations), trance mediumship, and spirit manifestation. Her book *The Secret Doctrine* is considered Theosophical canon. Blavatsky was accused of being a magician, hypnotist, and charlatan. The British Society for Psychical Research pronounced her claims unverifiable. In 1891, she died a lonely, obese, and miserably sick woman, considered a fake and deserted by most of her followers.

Castaneda, Carlos: While in Mexico experiencing the influence of hallucinogens, anthropologist Carlos Castaneda explored sorcery under apprenticeship to a personage he calls Don Juan. This led to several best-selling books, including *Journey to Ixtlan, The Power of Silence,* and *The Fire From Within.* Castaneda experienced a dead branch as a living animal and communicated with a talking, bilingual coyote. According to Don Juan, in *Journey to Ixtlan,* "Coyotes talk and so do deer, as I once told you, and so do rattlesnakes and trees and all other living things. . . . Not to believe that coyotes talk is to be pinned down in the realm of ordinary men."[2]

Critics say Castaneda disregards the boundaries of anthropological objectivity by personally adopting the beliefs and practices of those he investigates. He is seldom seen and seeks no personal publicity. Little is known about Castaneda except that he was a UCLA Ph.D student and currently lives in Los Angeles. Even former supporters question whether the occult experiences of his south-of-the-border sojourns actually occurred since his credibility has been seriously challenged in recent years.[3]

Clarke, Arthur C.: A best-selling science fiction writer, Clarke is revered by many New Agers. His PBS-TV series on the supernatural helped introduce psychic phenomena to the viewing public. His *2010,* a follow-up book and movie to the immensely successful *2001: A Space Odyssey* depicted a millennialistic perspective that has inspired many Movement followers. At the conclusions of the book and movie, a voice intones, "Someday, the children of the new sun will meet the children of the old, and you can tell your children of the day when everyone realized . . . we have been given a new lease from the landlord." The landlord, a brightly shining new sun in the sky, is named Lucifer. Christians were understandably cha- grined by this blatant espousal of devotion to Satan, but New Agers were pleased since the Light Bearer (Lucifer) is considered a patron of the New Age.

Cole-Whittaker, Terry: A Doris Day look-alike in her late forties, Terry Cole-Whittaker was a rising star of the religious electronic media. Her weekly half-hour television program beamed her prosperity gospel to more than a million viewers in major markets. The one-time third runner-up in the Mrs. America contest gained her religious scholarship in Ernest Holmes's School of Ministry, a Religious Science sect. Her California-style enthusiasm for the good life began in the San Diego-area La Jolla Church of Religious Science. She eventually formed her own group, the Science of Mind Church International.

Cole-Whittaker combined pop psychology, New Age concepts, and ideas borrowed from est to declare, "God doesn't forgive; you've never been judged except by your own thoughts." Among the disciplines she advocated were group rebirthing, a breathing technique based on yogic principles, body massage, affirmations, and study of *A Course in Miracles*. Mastering the techniques of her rival fundamentalist counterparts, she spoke of her "prayer ministry" and "love offerings" and published a tabloid entitled *The Good News*. Her somewhat hedonistic approach to life was formalized in her best-selling book *How to Have More in a Have-Not World*.

After her empire crumbled in the early 1980s, Cole-Whittaker resigned from apparent exhaustion. She resurfaced in 1986 as a revitalized New Age advocate with her book *The Inner Path from Where You Are to Where You Want to Be*. In it she declared, "God is That Which Includes All Beings. God is All of it and the Everything, and God cannot be apart from any of it any way."[4] Her new interests are more esoteric: exploring goddess and Mother Earth energies, guided meditations, and channeling higher "knowingness" as pursuits of her Adventures in Enlightenment Foundation.

de Chardin, Pierre Teilhard: A Jesuit priest and paleontologist, Pierre Teilhard de Chardin is a virtual patron saint to the New Age Movement. Marilyn Ferguson's New Age classic, *The Aquarian Conspiracy,* quotes him liberally. Jean Houston speaks of him as a man who was "pure integrated organism/environment."[5] In *New Genesis,* Robert Muller devotes an entire chapter to this enigmatic Frenchman, referring to the "Five Teilhardian En- lightenments." Muller admits, "Much of what I have observed in the world bears out the all-encompassing, global, forward-looking philosophy of

Teilhard de Chardin."[6] The Catholic Church censured de Chardin for apostasy, restoring him to the church's good graces only shortly before his death in 1955. De Chardin's idea that mankind is destined to achieve an eventual recognition of world unified consciousness is still rejected by Catholic theologians.

Ferguson, Marilyn: Author of the movement's classic *The Aquarian Conspiracy,* Marilyn Ferguson is a premier spokesperson for the New Age. From education to health and politics, Ferguson addresses what she believes are the personal and social transformative issues of our age. *The Aquarian Conspiracy* has been published in several foreign countries and is used in some college courses. Ferguson publishes the *Mind/Brain Bulletin,* considered a continuing compendium on New Age thought. In Ferguson's estimation, "a leaderless but powerful network is working to bring about radical change in the United States. Its members have broken with certain key elements of Western thought, and they may even have broken continuity with history."[7]

While claiming the conspiracy is syncretistic, Ferguson is an avid apologetic for the Eastern view of life, advocating mystical meditation and imagery. She ridicules evangelical faith and optimistically proclaims:

> Every organized religion has been based on the claims of direct experience of one or more persons whose revelations are then handed down as articles of faith. Those who want direct knowledge, the mystics, have always been treated more or less as heretics. . . . Now the heretics are gaining ground, doctrine is losing its authority, and knowing is superseding belief.[8]

Houston, Jean: As past president of the Association for Humanistic Psychology, Jean Houston, trained at Union Theological Seminary, is well-positioned to promote New Age teachings within influential circles. As codirector of the Foundation for Mind Research in New York (with her husband, Dr. Robert Masters), Dr. Houston encourages the study of ancient Mystery School religions. The ten books she has written deal with self-induced states of altered consciousness, self-healing, and the development of psychic forces as part of what she calls sacred psychology, which involves past lives regression, including man's evolutionary past as an animal.

Houston has been heavily influenced by the teachings of theologian Paul Tillich and the French mystic Pierre Teilhard de Chardin. She was a personal friend and protégée of Dr. Margaret Mead. Her workshop publications describe Houston as "the Master Evocateur of our times." The use of theatrical devices to transform the consciousness of listeners during her lectures developed into what Houston calls "Therapeia . . . doing the work of the gods, the healing and wholing of person and planet." Dr. Houston believes, "Our minds are stargates, our bodies celled of mystery, which when unraveled, give us citizenship in a world larger than our aspiration, more complex than all our dreams."[9]

Hubbard, Barbara Marx: Buckminster Fuller, renowned architect and inventor, said of her, "There is no doubt in my mind that Barbara Marx Hubbard, who helped introduce the concept of futurism to society, is the best informed human now alive regarding futurism and the foresight it has produced."[10] As cofounder and director of the Global Family, her name was placed in nomination for the vice presidency of the United States at the 1984 Democratic National Convention. As a New Age theorist, she endorses the Quantum Leap in consciousness idea and was a guiding force behind the much-heralded World of Instant Cooperation on December 31, 1986.

To Hubbard, the devil is man's inclination to see himself as a failure. She advocates trance channeling, having written a guide on the subject, and teaches contacting one's Higher Self. Her system of futurism posits the idea that a new universal species of higher consciousness is being birthed on earth, based on "resonating cores" of those tuned in to their God-consciousness.

Krishnamurti, Jiddu: Annie Besant (see Besant entry above) believed Jiddu Krishnamurti was an incarnation of God. Born the son of a devout Brahman, he declared, "Discard all theologies and beliefs." Though Theosophists wanted to enthrone him as the new World Teacher, Krishnamurti repudiated the idea of his divinity. For over sixty years, he traveled and talked to audiences in the United States, England, and India, until his death in 1986. Krishnamurti taught that everything one needed to know about philosophy, psychology, and religion could be found inside oneself. His best-known books are *The Flight of the Eagle, You Are the World,* and *The Awakening of Intelligence.*

Kübler-Ross, Elisabeth: The Swiss-born psychiatrist is best known for her book *On Death and Dying.* Through her pioneering work in counseling terminally ill patients, she greatly expanded contemporary knowledge of thanatology, the study of death. Her thesis was based on analysis of characteristic attitudes in encounters with death, dividing them into five stages. In later years, Kübler-Ross has pursued more spiritistically oriented interests.

In addition to training people in the art of helping others to die, she shocked academia by declaring, "I know for a fact that there is life after death." Her assertion is based on occultism. At her Shanti Nilaya ("Home of Peace" in Sanskrit) teaching and healing center, Kübler-Ross has indulged in various forms of mediumship. She admits to conversations with a spirit guide named Salem and endorses spiritual-sexual unions with entities.[11] A distinguished doctor and scholar, her excellent work with the dying fell into some disrepute because of her abandonment of scientifically acceptable research for occult experimentation.

MacLaine, Shirley: A distinguished actress and dancer, Shirley MacLaine has become the undisputed cosmic superstar of the New Age. Her three books on the movement's preoccupations have sold more than 6 million copies. Such sales were followed by her on-the-road "Higher Self" seminars. In one month alone, her transcendental gatherings grossed more than $3 million. Attendees were told to sign waivers to absolve MacLaine and her organization from responsibility for psychological injury. During her sessions, some claimed to speak with departed loved ones. Others recalled past lives. Several experienced orgasm. MacLaine has revealed plans to establish a New Age spiritual retreat on 800 acres in southern Colorado.

Maslow, Abraham: Founder of humanistic psychology and transpersonal psychology (terms he coined), Abraham Maslow died in 1970. His concepts of self-fulfillment helped to spur today's interest in mystical experiences. Born in Brooklyn, New York, of Russian-Jewish parents, Maslow majored in psychology at the University of Wisconsin. He developed the theory of "self-actualization," living to one's full potential, as the means of achieving psychological health. His 1954 book *Motivation and Personality* recommended psychological investigation of unusual states of consciousness like ecstasy, mysticism, and elation.

Maslow studied works on Eastern religions, including Krishnamurti and Alan Watts, as well as the theories of C. G. Jung. In the late 1950s, he began research into peak experiences, feelings of awe, wonder, and happiness. With colleagues Richard Alpert (Ram Dass) and Timothy Leary, Maslow speculated on the value of hallucinogenic drugs. At the end of his life, Maslow abandoned his earlier fascination with Marxism and mysticism for what he called "plateau-experiences," extended periods of serenity. New Agers would not be comfortable with his assertion that man has a "dark side," a conundrum he was unable to resolve before his death at age sixty-two.

Montgomery, Ruth: Psychic Ruth Montgomery has written nine books by means of automatic handwriting. Each morning, she sits at her desk, pencil poised over paper, meditating into an "alpha state." She enters a slight trance and awaits the movement of her hand by unseen forces. Sometimes she uses a typewriter, allowing the entities to manipulate her fingers with incredible speed. Montgomery claims the sources of her inspiration, her "guides," are souls who lived previous lifetimes and now reside in a spirit plane.

The one-time syndicated Washington columnist introduced the concept of Walk-ins (entities who take over unwanted human bodies to rejuvenate them to help mankind) to the New Age Movement. Her books, such as *A Search for Truth, Here and Hereafter, A World Beyond,* and *Aliens Among Us,* circulate concepts of reincarnation and a prehistoric view of the world. Under the influence of her guides, Montgomery is convinced that "we are not our physical selves, but individual sparks of the Creator."[12]

Muller, Robert: For thirty-three years he served the United Nations, including time as assistant secretary-general in charge of economic and social services and the coordination of thirty-two specialized agencies and programs. He has garnered respect as an educator and self-proclaimed Christian and was considered the resident philosopher of the United Nations. Convinced that human beings represent an interconnected planetary consciousness, Muller believes that a Christ reappearance will usher in global harmony based on "divine or cosmic government."[13] His classic work, *New Genesis,* is subtitled "Shaping a global spirituality." Unlike evangelical Christians, who believe delusion and spiritual decline will mark the final days of our era, Muller insists the time has come to "prepare universal beings ready to flower to fulfill their divine lives or cosmic destinies."[14] Muller currently serves as chancellor at the University of Peace in Costa Rica, Central America.

Naisbitt, John: According to *Newsweek* magazine,[15] it was John Naisbitt's then-friend and now-wife, Aburdene, who first introduced the best-selling author of *Megatrends* to the New Age Movement. Aburdene, who had been in Werner Erhard's est cult, influenced Naisbitt to pepper his lectures and writings with New Age ideology. Both meditate daily and credit acceptance of reincarnation to explain their successfully symbiotic relationship, which John and Aburdene unabashedly refer to as a "New Age marriage." Although *Megatrends* doesn't specifically endorse New Age concepts, one major movement journal asserted, "Its conclusions, not surprisingly, coincide directly with projections of New Age thinking."[16]

Price, John Randolph: As head of the New Age Quartus Foundation and founder of the New Age Planetary Commission, John Randolph Price has become a major theoretician for the Aquarian Age. He has emphasized the importance of The Plan and its new order for humanity, founded on the coming Christ. In Price's theology, the Second Coming is not the literal event prophesied by the Christian church. Instead, it is each man's acknowledgment that he is a christ who will inaugurate this era.

His books tout the benefits of metaphysics, mystery schools, occult affirmations, and solicitation of spirit guides. Price teaches that mankind is evolving toward the cultivation of psychic powers by tapping into the superconscious of the supermind. As a mentor to the World of Instant Cooperation (which he called the International Healing Meditation), Price avidly opposes those who are "attacking progressive spiritual ideas and New Age concepts."[17]

His Quartus Foundation promotes remote healing, the development of a financial Prosperity Plan, and acceptance of the "New Birth of Christ Truth" to develop the "Twelve Doors" to spiritual mastery. Of spirit guide entities, Price promises, "Your true helper . . . will never guide you to do something contradictory to the Christ Standard."[18]

Ram Dass: Known by his anglicized name, Richard Alpert, Baba Ram Dass was an LSD-dropping contemporary of Timothy Leary. While traveling in India during the 1960s, he met a guru named Bhagwan Dass. Impressed by the aesthetic holy man, Ram Dass took up yoga, meditation, and a variety of Hindu disciplines. Ram Dass wrote *Be Here Now,* an early New Age document published before the popularization of the movement. In 1974, he founded the Hanuman Foundation, named after the Hindu monkey god. Ram Dass insists the truth of God resides in each person, but it can be realized only with the assistance of a spiritual teacher. He has also founded the Seva ("service" in Sanskrit) Foundation. Ram Dass has been a primary spokesperson for the assimilation of Eastern enlightenment into Western life.

Spangler, David: No newcomer to the New Age, David Spangler is a philosopher and educator who wrote and lectured on the subject for over twenty-five years. He was a codirector of the Findhorn Foundation, is currently president of the Lorian Association, and has been a board member of the Planetary Initiative. Strongly influenced by Theosophical thought and the writings of Alice Bailey, Spangler has obliquely referred to a "Luciferic initiation" and other occult doctrines. Such early references to esotericism were gradually replaced with more mainstream New Age ideology, as in his book *Emergence: The Rebirth of the Sacred.*

Spangler admits having talked with an entity who claims to be the New Age messiah. Like many New Agers, Spangler believes the Aquarian era will occur when all citizens of earth adopt an elevated Christ Consciousness. He even suggests that "Christ is the same force as Lucifer."[19] Today, Spangler sees the New Age as a more abstract manifestation of a transformative spirit rather than an actual event. Spangler seeks "a rebirth of our sense of the sacred, an inner impulse to understand and express our own divinity in co-creation and synergy with the divinity within creation."[20]

Sutphen, Dick: A self-described author, hypnotist, and seminar trainer, Dick Sutphen publishes a tabloid known as *Master of Life.* Sutphen traverses the country in his Silver Eagle customized bus, holding dozens of seminars on metaphysics. His wife, Tara, is director of Reincarnationists, Inc., a tax-exempt organization fostering karmic concepts. Video and audio cassettes, books, and miscellaneous metaphysical guides are offered through his extensive product promotion. An adamant opponent of religious fundamentalism, Sutphen's literature declares that "what is not moral is imposing your morality on someone else . . . that's fascism."[21] To Sutphen, "Christ is not the name of a person—it is a name for the ultimate state of consciousness. Jesus was one of many Christs, as were Buddha, Krishna, Lao Tzu, to name a few."[22]

Sutphen's seminars include "Higher Self Potentials," "Psychic Seminar," and "Past Life Therapy Professional Training." His video hypnosis series teaches viewers to balance chakras, attract a soulmate, develop psychic powers, and achieve financial success through subliminal suggestions. Audio cassettes offer hypnotic help with fingernail biting, weight loss, eyesight improvement, temper control, overcoming impotency, eliminating eating disorders, and telepathic communication with animals.

Yogananda, Paramahansa: With more than a half million adherents worldwide, the Self-Realization Fellowship owes its impetus to the late Paramahansa Yogananda. He taught that one must transcend the illusory world of matter by practicing Kriya Yoga. This discipline is said to circumvent the millions of reincarnations necessary to cleanse one's karma. He boasted that thirty seconds of Kriya Yoga could accomplish more than a year of normal spiritual seeking.

In his books, such as the best-seller *Autobiography of a Yogi,* Yogananda claims the true spiritual adept can perform miracles and achieve complete self-mastery of his body and spirit. While other yogis say spirituality is an arduous journey, Yogananda in his thirty years of lecturing in the West insisted that direct personal experience of God is possible through his advanced practices of meditation. Yogananda died in 1952, leaving the Self-Realization Fellowship Foundation to carry on his work.

Zen Master Rama: A controversial New Age guru, Zen Master Rama (Frederick Lenz) has been a target of those who suspect certain New Age leaders of irrational excess. The thirty-eight-year-old former college professor was a disciple of the Hindu yoga master Sri Chinmoy. Today, Lenz claims to be one of twelve enlightened masters on this planet. Several former disciples have accused him of administering drugs (LSD) and using sexual coercion on female followers. Lenz responds, "Naturally, I meet people who are interested in meditation, who share a high vibratory nature—evolved individuals—who I have something in common with and like to spend time with, whether it's going to the movies or going to bed."[23]

PLACES:

Arcane School: Original group formed to continue the work of occult Theosophist Alice Bailey. In spite of differences among her followers, it remains the largest of the so-called "full-moon meditation" assemblies. Local Arcane School gatherings can be found in most major American cities. Lessons administered by correspondence take students through varying degrees.

Association for Humanistic Psychology: Founded by Abraham Maslow and currently headquartered in San Francisco. It seeks to further the work of such psychologists as Maslow and Carl Rogers. Willis Harman, professor at Stanford University, has been a prominent guiding force. In its meetings and journals, occult and Eastern practices are frequently promoted, including shamanism, visualization, and trance states.

Astara: Bills itself as a "New Age Mystery School." Astara was founded by spiritualists Earlyne and Robert Chaney. Drawing from Masonic, Rosicrucian, and Theosophical beliefs, Astara seeks the assistance of spirit guides who represent the Universal Brotherhood. A monthly publication, *Voice of Astara,* conveys the messages of its primary entity, Kut-Hu-Mi.

Chidvilas Foundation: Carries on the United States work of Bhagwan Shree Rajneesh. Chidvilas publishes the books of Rajneesh and distributes a newspaper entitled *The Rajneesh Times of India.* Audio and video tapes are also available.

Club of Rome: Founded in 1968 by Aurelio Peccei, former Olivetti executive. Its aims are globalistic, enlisting the support of world business leaders to achieve international economic cooperation. The Club published a report entitled *The Limits to Growth* and advocated population control.

Esalen Institute: Located in Big Sur, California, Esalen has integrated mystical practices with behavioral sciences for more than twenty-five years. It was founded by Michael Murphy, an early leader in the Human Potential Movement. Mystical spirituality is encouraged, along with controversial therapies that allow participants to vent suppressed emotions.

Hunger Project: Originally started by Werner Erhard of est, with assistance from John Denver. Its initial goal was not to feed the hungry but to raise consciousness about the issue by declaring "the end of hunger is an idea whose time has come." Four-hour presentations on the problem of hunger encourage attendees to make a "personal commitment" to end hunger by the year 2000. Though self-described as a charitable institution, financial statements for one year revealed the Project's Canadian division spent 56 percent of revenues on salaries, benefits, and telephone calls.[24] Oxfam International, the Peace Corps, and other respected hunger-relief organizations have disassociated themselves from the Hunger Project. Though currently not directly affiliated with est, the Project is still influenced by Erhard's leadership.

Institute of Noetic Sciences: Founded in 1973 by Apollo 14 ex-astronaut Edgar Mitchell, who was raised in a Christian fundamentalist family. It seeks to explore frontiers of the mind and spirit by investigating ESP, telepathy, and other exceptional human abilities. Near-death experiences and occult healing techniques are also examined. Other interests include biofeedback research, assessing voluntary control of inner states, cancer research on the relationship of psychological facts of healing, and remote viewing of randomly selected targets inaccessible to normal modes of perception. Research and education regarding human consciousness are promoted by lectures and travel programs, based on the idea that anyone can cultivate psychic phenomena.

Regarding Christian concepts of heaven and hell, Mitchell says, "To me, that's all bull—."[25] In contrast, Mitchell declares, "The absolutes of good and evil that we have looked for in the universe simply don't exist. . . . We're an evolving species, evolving from family, to tribal, to national, to global citizens."[26] Currently, Mitchell is a management consultant on aerospace technologies, but he still serves on the board of directors of the Institute. Futurist Willis Harman is the director.

Findhorn Foundation: Founded in 1962 by Peter and Eileen Caddy, with Dorothy MacLean, to revere and communicate with devas (Sanskrit for "divine beings"), nature spirits inhabiting flowers and plants. (New Age spokesperson David Spangler has also been affiliated with Findhorn.) Believing in the organic nature of consciousness, Findhorn, with about 200 permanent residents, is located in Scotland and claims to grow oversized vegetables in its gardens.

This horticultural success, achieved by communion with "nature elementals," is seen as a model for the planetary cooperation of people. Talking to plants is encouraged to facilitate the energies and consciousness of man's leafy friends. According to Findhorn spokesman R. Ogilvie Crombie, fairies and elves are responsible for the autumn change of leaves. Such knowledge is said to come from direct inspiration of the devas, who also reveal gardening secrets.

The Foundation's purpose is stated as follows: "Humanity is involved in an evolutionary expansion of consciousness which will, in turn, create new patterns of civilization for all of society and promote a planetary culture infused with spiritual values."[27] According to Dorothy MacLean's spirit guide, "All forces are to be felt into, even the sun, the moon, the sea, the trees, the very grasses. All are part of My life. All is one life. Play your part in making life one again, with My help."[28]

Ken Keyes Center: One-day to three-month programs are offered at this Coos Bay, Oregon, center, intended to foster happiness. Keyes wrote the New Age classics *Handbook to Higher Consciousness* and *The Hundredth Monkey*. The human potential program offers what is called the Science of Happiness, encompassing exercise, nutrition, loving more, and serving. Participants are encouraged to develop Centers of Consciousness that provide sufficient love, joy, and peace for each situation. Seminars instruct participants in the "Living Love Methods."

Perelandra: Located sixty miles southwest of Washington, D.C., Perelandra with its "nature research" is similar to Findhorn in philosophy. (The name Perelandra was taken from the story of the same name by Christian writer C. S. Lewis, who used Perelandra as the name for Venus, planet of perfection.) Perelandra's leader is Machaell Small Wright, who claims to talk with fairies, commands moles to do her bidding, and says she has no insect problems in her gardens.

At Perelandra, residents cooperate directly with the intelligence of nature. Wright believes in the "vibrational reality" behind the form of plant life. To her, plant devas are "overlighting intelligences still consciously connected with God and part of the Original Pattern."[29] Wright says devas tell her what kind of seed to buy, what fertilizer to use, and how much space to leave between plants. She calls specific devas to her bidding by aiming her awareness at the deva's "vibratory pattern."

Perelandra's gardens consist of eighteen concentric circles near undisturbed brush, marked the Elemental Annex, where the nature spirits reside. According to Wright, "That which exists on the surface [plants] has begun to connect to and integrate with the heart and soul of the planet, which, in turn, is fully aligned with the heart and soul force of the universe."[30]

Planetary Citizens: Founded in 1972 by Robert Muller, editor Norman Cousins, and peace advocate Donald Keys. Among its goals is a federated world government by the year 2000. David Spangler and other Findhorn

Foundation associates helped develop its agenda. Other advocates include Edgar Mitchell and Willis Harman. Planetary Citizens has served as secretariat for the Planetary Initiative and investigates innovative economies, ecologies, and lifestyles. This inquiry includes a networking survey of such alternative communities as Findhorn. Donald Keys is the current president.

Planetary Initiative: Founded in 1981, its full title is Planetary Initiative for the World We Choose. Closely affiliated with the United Nations, it promotes global socialism and disarmament. It is an outgrowth of Planetary Citizens, also closely linked to the United Nations. Isaac Asimov, bestselling science fiction writer, has been a prominent leader of the Inititiatve. Adopting New Age rhetoric, the Initiative believes peace can encompass our planet if citizens of earth realize our globe's future lies in human hands.

Windstar Foundation: Founded in 1976 by John Denver, Windstar is a nonprofit education center located on a thousand acres near Aspen, Colorado. Peaceful conflict resolution, alternative technologies, and citizens' exchange programs are included on its agenda. Windstar sponsors a symposium each summer, reflecting on globalistic concerns and featuring a potpourri of New Age spokespersons.

World Goodwill: Political lobby located at the United Nations Plaza, similar in goals to Planetary Citizens.

PRACTICES:

Affirmations: To bring thought into reality, affirmations attest to what is believed to be true. These short statements of being or positive phrases of avowing usually begin with the personal pronoun *I*. "I am" frequently begins affirmations; for example, "I am that I am." Since metaphysics teaches that like attracts like, negative declarations are avoided. Positive affirmations keep the mind and spirit focused on one's higher consciousness, attracting its benefits. Some New Age sources suggest writing affirmations by hand.

Straight Answer

Affirmations may be blasphemous ("I am that I am") and a doorway to occult bondage. They are based on the Hindu idea that words have supernatural properties that affect reality. Through repetitious assault on the senses, many affirmations encourage trance states during which demons may possess the affirmer.

Aikido: This is the most overtly religious of all the martial arts. Literally,

247

it means "the road to a union with the universal spirit." All movements are intended to bring the practitioner into harmony with ki, the universal power of the cosmos. Founded by Morihei Uyeshiba, aikido seeks harmony among all souls and oneness with the universe. Though aikido is an effective means of self-defense, its ultimate purpose is to cultivate perfection of the spirit.

Straight Answer

Any practitioner of aikido should be careful that the instructor doesn't use physical exercises to introduce metaphysical concepts. Seeking to develop ki can lead to spiritual oppression.

Art: New Age art is intended to be a visionary glimpse into higher consciousness. Two separate paradigm realities are combined in a single expression. Transcendent images are commonly used, such as moons, temples, goddesses, lakes, spirit guardians, and manifestations of light. Nature spirits, gateways to consciousness, and softly textured colors are also common themes. New Age artists seek to touch the viewer's soul and psyche by infusing their art with their spirit's energy. Some art is considered transformative, affecting spiritual perceptions, while other art aims to heal and awaken a sense of awe about nature. Certain colors are employed to balance the brain or stimulate the body's chakras by providing a "color bath" to awaken spiritual forces.

Straight Answer

Some works of New Age art could affect the viewer through the emotional and spiritual intent conveyed by the artist. Psychologists are only beginning to understand how environments and colors impress the mind. Art deliberately based on anti-Christian concepts is a poor choice to associate with one's surroundings.

Astral Projection: In accordance with occult philosophy, New Agers believe the physical body has an etheric double. This spiritual body can be separated, maintaining contact through a thin, umbilical-like cord. Commonly referred to as astral projection or an out-of-the-body experience, the phenomenon is said to occur spontaneously while sleeping. Adepts seek to precipitate the occurrence at will and travel astrally to distant locations to reveal information unavailable through other means. Though it is said spontaneous astral projection may occur accidentally during stress or illness, New Age adherents seek the experience to ascend through astral levels for spiritual purification. Foremost proponents of the phenomenon are

Robert Monroe, author of *Journeys Out of the Body* and *Far Journeys,* and Gavin and Yvonne Frost, heads of the Church of Wicca (Witchcraft). Participants say they are conscious and are able to enjoy physical sensory perception during the experience.

Straight Answer

Astral projection may be hallucinatory. Whether it is an actual event or a perceived phenomenon, the spiritual dangers are equal. Willfully desiring to leave one's body neutralizes volition. Thus, during out-of-the-body experiences, demons may enter the participant's body, a form of spirit possession some Hindu yogis acknowledge.

Biofeedback: Dr. Green of the Menninger Foundation developed the procedure by investigating trance states of Hindu yogis, observing how they mentally controlled internal body functions during altered states of consciousness. Equipment was built to monitor physiological behavior and display it visibly on meters and light response devices. Patients use mental persuasion by viewing this apparatus to lower blood pressure, body temperature, and heartbeat to relieve stress. Many doctors and psychologists use biofeedback as adjunctive therapy when traditional means of relieving anxiety and pain are unsuccessful.

Straight Answer

There is nothing inherently evil or dangerous about biofeedback, though the original research was conducted under occult circumstances. Some patients undergoing biofeedback experience spontaneous psychic phenomena upon entering alpha wave states (the clairvoyant mind condition sought by psychics). Potential patients should ask the therapist if he is using the technique for physiological reasons or to alter consciousness.

Brain/Mind Development: Neurological research has uncovered the ways in which the two halves of the brain respond to stimuli. Functions of the left brain apparently are more analytical and routine. The right brain is believed to contain the creative, meditative, and artistic aspects of behavior. New Age brain/mind technology seeks to integrate the two to increase mental skills and intuitive responses and to expand awareness of the superconsciousness. Devices that aid left and right brain synthesis are flotation-isolation tanks, brain sound rooms, and brain/mind intensive devices whose sounds assault specific parts of the body.

An organization called Mentronics Systems, Inc. (produced by the Monroe Institute of Applied Sciences), provides audio tapes to synchronize brain hemispheres. Robert Monroe is a pioneer in the development of out-of-the-body experiences. His so-called Gateway Voyage program induces certain electrical patterns in the brain by bombardment with sound pulses that allow leaving the body to visit "other energy structures and realities." David Graham, a Canadian electrical engineer, devised what he calls the Graham Potentializer. An electrically charged piece of headgear supposedly creates an electromagnetic field to alter states of consciousness and produce "increased relaxation, inner peace, tranquility, significant personal insights, and mystical experiences."[31]

Current brain/mind research concentrates on achieving "synchrony," whole-brain thinking in which both hemispheres function in unison. Like exercise machines for the body, brain expansion machines are envisioned by New Agers as the way to increase brain size, regenerate dead cerebral cells, and create a superrace of citizens who are "imaginative, intelligent, adaptive, and capable of developing strategies to ensure the survival of the species."[32]

"Whole-Brain Learning" workshops are the brainchild of John-David, a neuroscientist concerned with left-right brain integration. He believes that ultra-intelligence is possible by sending certain tones and sounds at different frequencies to predesignated areas of the brain. In John-David's brain-sound rooms, one can receive a brain tune-up to improve memory. His Learning Institute also offers $5,795 float tanks, $3,700 brain-sync machines, and $6,500 alpha chairs, which surround the body with sound.

Straight Answer

Expanded awareness and proper use of mental capacities are laudable goals. But attempts to stimulate the right brain metaphysically as a center of the soul are deceptive. These techniques are a form of brain yoga, which lowers spiritual defenses and opens the mind to messages from evil forces. A philosophy of brain eugenics could form a new fascism whereby only those with expanded mental powers would be deemed worthy of the New Age.

Chakras: According to yoga, there are seven centers of psychic spiritual energy. (In Sanskrit, *chakra* means "energy center" or "wheel of the body.") These are located in ascending order, beginning at the base of the spine. Chakras are like batteries that store energy from the universal life force. Various exercises and spiritual disciplines are employed to awaken these loci. Some mediums claim the ability to actually see chakras as parts of the human aura. Certain spirit healers say they can manipulate the energy found in chakras to facilitate healing.

According to Hinduism, chakra power rises in the form of a serpent, the Kundalini force. It is represented at the base of the spine by the Hindu god, Shakti, who ascends to the seventh chakra, the crown chakra. There, she unites with Shiva (third member of the Hindu trinity) and a psycho-sexual merger occurs, conferring enlightenment. Each chakra claims a different color and vibratory property. Certain crystals and gemstones are believed to awaken specific chakras.

Straight Answer

Science has never proved the existence of an electromagnetic force field surrounding the human spine. Metaphysics is the only application of this theory. Awakening one's aura to heighten spiritual awareness is a substitute for repentance and submission to the will of a personal God. Those who experiment with chakra arousal are venturing into occult territory where strange supernatural occurrences may be precipitated by the interference of demonic forces.

Feldenkrais Method: An Israeli scientist with a Ph.D. in physics and engineering, Moshe Feldenkrais was crippled by a soccer injury. Seeking to restore his body's functions, Feldenkrais, a black belt in judo, combined his knowledge of anatomy, physics, and psychology to develop a system of body awareness. Known alternately as "Awareness through Movement" and "Functional Integration," the Feldenkrais Method seeks to use gentle body movements to stimulate exploratory learning natural to infants. Before his death at the age of eighty in 1984, Feldenkrais had produced thousands of lessons to re-educate people about neuromuscular patterns.

Straight Answer

The musculoskeletal aspects of the Feldenkrais Method must be evaluated on the basis of their anatomical benefits. One must also cautiously consider the attempt to integrate self with the body, a concept New Agers have adopted as a kind of Westernized yoga. Such mind-body connections can be dangerous if used as a way to release spiritual potentiality.

Isolation Tanks: Alternately referred to as isolation tanks and flotation tanks, these sensory deprivation devices place the patient in a weightless state, sequestered from the outside world. Water laced with Epsom salts creates buoyancy for the purposes of psychic exploration or simple relaxation. The idea is to shut down the conscious mind and enter a state of *samadhi,* deep contemplation. A dark, womb-like ambiance reduces all sensory input so the patient can enter a natural infantile state.

Straight Answer

Mystical tradition teaches that states of higher consciousness can be achieved through meditation and isolation, which silence the active mind. Some who have undergone isolation tank therapy report regression to prior lives, altered states of consciousness, and out-of-the-body experiences. Those who use isolation tanks to seek transcendence can trigger occult psychic experiences by such sensory denial.

Massage: Despite its recent association with prostitutes and pornographic parlors, massage has been used for millennia to relieve pain and promote health. This systematic manipulation of body tissues, performed with the hands, has several applications. Some masseurs concentrate on the structure of bones, muscles, and organs. Others are more exotic, relying on Eastern theories of energy meridians and electrochemical stimulation. Jin Shin Do, for example, is a kind of acupressure to release stagnant energy blocked in the body. Chi Lei Jung (also known as Taoist Massage) concentrates on cleansing organ energies.

Straight Answer

Massage as a means of relaxation to relieve muscular tension and improve circulation can be beneficial. Oriental massage performed for energy redistribution is a form of spiritualism. For example, Jin Shin Do supposedly opens spiritual channels to release the spirit to higher astral realms.

Near-Death Experiences: Since the 1970s, research into near-death experiences has been conducted through medical technology that resuscitates clinically dead patients. Stories of their experiences are remarkably similar. A peaceful feeling is followed by a buzzing sound that precedes the phenomenon of separation from the physical body. Voices of doctors, nurses, and loved ones can be heard. Then comes the sensation of floating through a dark tunnel. At the tunnel's end, the presence of a being who communicates telepathically is encountered. This being is usually luminescent and evokes a warm awareness. At that point, one can choose to continue the journey or return to life on earth. Before returning to the body, deceased loved ones and a realm of preternatural loveliness may be observed. The being of light usually conducts a life-review, asking the person what good has been accomplished during his time on earth. Classic works on the subject include *Life at Death,* by Dr. Kenneth Ring, and *Life after Life,* by Dr. Raymond Moody, as well as the writings of thanatologist Dr. Elisabeth Kübler-Ross.

Straight Answer

Ignoring the biblical truth of accountability to God after death, believers in near-death experiences substitute a nonjudgmental encounter with an unidentified presence for the moral responsibility of appearing before God's throne. Such encounters with an afterlife probably are hallucinogenic experiences based on spiritual denial, since unrepentant sinners would try to avoid recognition of eternal punishment. Carl Sagan, the noted astronomer, believes near-death experiences are a leftover memory of the birthing process. Most secular research has been influenced by the occult. Dr. Elisabeth Kübler-Ross consults with familiar spirits. Dr. Raymond Moody has frequently dabbled in the occult and psychic phenomena. He cites the *Tibetan Book of the Dead* as proof of his theories.

Numerology: Like other deterministic occult sciences, numerology holds to the fatalistic idea that birth is accompanied by precise conditions that govern all life. Numerology is linked with reincarnation, suggesting that life's purpose is to learn the lessons of karma according to precise mathematical calculations. Signs of the zodiac are assigned numerological designations to combine with the pseudoscience of astrology. Each number has a designated sacred significance, and cojoined numbers have compounded meanings.

Straight Answer

Scripture attaches significance to certain numbers, but it fails to give numbers intrinsic predictive qualities. That notion comes from occult tradition and is based on impersonal principles of fatalism that contradict the Christian belief that grace is an aggressive act of God's love.

UFOs: In New Age lore, unidentified flying objects are manifestations of superior, evolved beings. Whether existing on an astral plane or in another galaxy, these visitors are believed to be beneficient entities who warn of impending global disasters and offer to rescue man from his own destruction. Many channeled entities claim to be extraterrestrials. These space brothers say they wish to help humanity reach new levels of spiritual consciousness. New Agers assume that several religions were started by contact with extraterrestrials. New Age UFO advocates say this is an explanation for angels. The Urantia sect exploits this theory to explain Christ's appearance on earth.

Straight Answer

The origins of UFOs cannot be objectively determined, but it seems reasonable to conclude some UFO observers have seen a material or spiritual reality. Because extraterrestrial craft defy the laws of thermodynamics and are not subject to the confines of physical principles, such sightings are probably spiritual manifestations of extradimensional beings. Without exception, the message these visitors bring is consistent with New Age ideology concerning man's evolutionary ascent in spiritual consciousness and his divine inner nature. This refutation of biblical teaching indicates that extraterrestrials are demonic spirit beings, part of the delusion prophesied for the end of this age.

Past Lives Therapy: As a means of validating reincarnation, past lives therapy seeks to uncover the mystery of previous incarnations. The psychoanalytical approach assumes that current fears and phobias stem from events in past lives. By understanding unlearned lessons from previous lives, evolutionary development can be accelerated. Therapists using the technique of life regression seek to know the traumas hidden in one's deepest memories, especially circumstances of previous lifetimes. The goal is to release the unresolved negative emotions of experiences in another life.

Straight Answer

The idea of uncovering past-life problems that are expressed in the present is spiritually and psychologically hazardous. It expressly denies God's role as Supreme Judge of man's life after death by substituting an impersonal, karmic force of justice. Past lives therapy also ignores the moral results of actions in this life by assuming deeds in another incarnation are what affect current circumstances.

Plant Communication: Spurred by the work of such groups as the Findhorn Foundation, segments of the New Age Movement believe that "nature elementals" can be worshiped through nurturing plant life. Supernatural plant worship has long been acknowledged among primitive people. The early 1970s book, *The Secret Life of Plants,* by Peter Tomkins and Christopher Bird, advanced the idea that plants possess feelings and intelligence. Plants are said to respond to sensations of hostility toward them. This can be determined by attaching the plant to galvanometers. Plants are also thought to be affected by prayer, ESP, and the presence of evil.

Straight Answer

The underlying idea behind plant communication has nothing to do with a green thumb. It is pure pantheism. Some advocates suggest conjuring the Greek god Pan (*Lucifer* to Christians). Beyond the absurdity that plants are intelligent souls is the suggestion they are indwelt by devas, elemental spirits. This is animism, a dangerous, occult form of communication with demons.

Rebirthing: The New Age idea of remembering the first moment of birth and releasing its trauma is the basis of rebirthing. Its discoverer, Leonard Orr, experimented with the use of various devices to induce altered states, including hot tubs. Orr concluded that when a child at birth is deprived of his oxygen supply through the cutting of the umbilical cord, he must learn to breathe under frightening circumstances. This supposedly damages the breathing rhythm, which must be restored. Rebirthing allows grief, guilt, and primal pain to be psychologically and physiologically disengaged.

Advocates believe that during the process, which is induced by hyperventilative breathing techniques, one's own pure, divine life force removes the stains of error from the soul. Some refer to it as a spiritual bath. One proponent calls rebirthing the "science of letting in God's energy, wisdom and love . . . a biological experience of religion."[33] Certain rebirthers believe it cleanses the human aura.

Practitioners say an experienced rebirther must be present to direct the patient in the proper rhythms of inhaling and exhaling. Once the participant has mastered the technique, about an hour of the experience completely nourishes the mind and body. It also unleashes psychic powers and expands one's awareness of consciousness capabilities.

Straight Answer

Rebirthing is actually the Westernized Hindu practice of Maha Yoga, a variant of Hinduism that teaches breath is spirit and hyperventilation is a direct intuitive experience of God. Rhythmic ventilation of human breath is substituted for the redemptive work of Christ and the grace of God. The oversupply of oxygen often produces hallucinogenic experiences that are interpreted as instants of spiritual enlightenment.

Reiki: Its origin is in ancient Tibet, and its name is Japanese. Reiki (pronounced ray-key) is taken from *rei*, which means "universal," and *ki*, the vital life-force flowing through all living things. Sometimes referred to as the Radiance Technique, Reiki was rediscovered in ancient Sanskrit texts by Dr. Mikao Usui, a Japanese scholar.

Dr. Barbara Ray, the world's leading authority on Reiki, says, "The energy tapped by the Reiki system can't be seen or known through our five ordinary outer senses nor by our ordinary mental constructs."[34] According to Ray, "Reiki is a science of Light known for more than ten thousand years and passed through the centuries as part of the history of Light. Not by chance has this technique re-emerged at the dawning of the Aquarian Age—an age that will be characterized by science and spirit."[35]

More than 15,000 students have been led through Reiki's "attunement process," consisting of seven degrees. (Only a handful of Reiki masters have reached the fifth degree.) The first degree embodies twelve positions that balance and align the seven chakras (psychic energy centers). Moving from the top of the head downward to the base of the spine, hands are laid on the neck, eyes, pituitary gland, lungs, liver, and reproductive organs to stimulate universal life energy. Second-degree training conveys an absentee-healing technique. The student stands in proxy for the person to whom the healing is directed.

Straight Answer

Reiki's claim of tapping into a higher frequency of cosmic power is a New Age explanation for the ancient shamanistic method of infusing nature's life-force through the laying-on of hands. This procedure is an occult means of spirit transference, investing demonic power into one's body through conjuration. Reiki's so-called language of symbols involves talismans and the postures of Reiki, yogalike spiritual tuning techniques to prepare the body for demonic vulnerability.

Self-Healing: Some New Agers would abolish all medical practitioners for the sake of self-healing. Sounding like Christian Scientists, self-healers insist the mind controls every function of the body. Death, disease, susceptibility to infection, and immunological deficiencies are believed to be rooted in thoughts. Some self-healers even suggest that AIDS and leukemia can be cured by proper channeling of vital energies and concentrating on pure, happy thoughts.

Straight Answer

Self-healing assumes that the body is a pure organism fully capable of curing diseases without external intervention. That concept ignores the entire history of medical science and denies the Christian concept of healing through prayer to a beneficient God. The channeled energies could be demonic delusions that psychosomatically alleviate symptoms but fail to cure the real root of the disorder.

Self-Hypnosis: For relaxation, consciousness expansion, incarnation regression, and a variety of other New Age intents, some consider self-hypnosis the best tool for entering altered states of the mind. Movement catalogues offer subliminal devices to induce self-hypnosis, including audio cassettes that coach the subject into alpha states. For some, self-hypnosis is the pathway to rapidly releasing latent psychic powers. Practitioners are told to accept intuitively whatever images enter their minds under hypnosis. They are also warned to expect rebirthing stages and the possible intervention of entities seeking to use them as channels.

Straight Answer

As a therapeutic tool, hypnosis is technically neutral. But no one should attempt self-hypnosis without understanding its potential spiritual dangers. The spontaneous occult occurrences associated with hypnosis reveal that entering the alpha wave state creates spiritual vulnerability, during which volition can be manipulated. Attempting self-hypnosis without the guidance of a conscientious, licensed Christian practitioner can expose emotional memories too traumatic to handle alone. Careless use of self-hypnosis can also open the mind and body to evil spirit influence. Such trance states are too risky, even under guarded circumstances.

Yoga: This 5,000-year-old Hindu tradition is practiced today in YWCAs and New Age retreat centers. To most, yoga represents calming postures that improve physical fitness. But this Eastern science of living and spiritual discipline is far more complex than a few contortions of the torso. Breathing maneuvers, mental concentration, deep meditation, body purification, and cultivation of psychic energy are all involved. The ultimate intent of Hatha Yoga, the physical discipline known to most Westerners, is communication with one's higher self. Through development of vital breath, the participant learns to inhale the universal life force. In addition, the postures are designed to awaken chakras so the Kundalini power can be released.

Straight Answer

Yoga literally means "union with God." In this case, God is the impersonal, unknowable deity of Hinduism, Brahman. Though the initial calisthenics may provide some physical benefit, the student of yoga will be attracted to more spiritually dangerous stages of psychic development. Yoga seeks to deify man through intuitive spiritual enlightenment, an endeavor prohibited on any level to the conscientious Christian.

Notes

Chapter 1: Looking Out for Number One

1. Fergus M. Bordevich, "Colorado's Thriving Cults," *The New York Times Magazine*, 1 May 1988, p. 37.
2. "Peace Shield," *Time*, 25 April 1988, vol. 131, no. 17, p. 42.
3. Penelope Wang, "A Cure for Stress," *Newsweek*, 12 October 1987, vol. CX, no. 15, p. 64.
4. Otto Friedrich, "New Age Harmonies," *Time*, 7 December 1987, vol. 130, no. 23, p. 69.
5. Richard Watring, "New Age Training in Business: Mind Control in Upper Management?" *Eternity*, February 1988, vol. 39, no. 2, p. 30.
6. Ibid.
7. Annetta Miller, "Corporate Mind Control," *Newsweek*, 4 May 1987, vol. CIX, no. 18, p. 39.
8. Ibid., p. 38.
9. J. Yuitaka Amano, "Bad for Business," *Eternity*, March 1986, vol. 37, no. 3, p. 57.
10. John Bode, "The Forum: Repackaged est," *The Cult Observer* April 1985, p. 5.
11. Bob Larson, *Larson's Book of Cults* (Wheaton: Tyndale House, 1982), p. 275.
12. Bode, "The Forum: Repackaged est" p. 4.
13. "est Training Changed to the Forum," *The Cult Observer*, February/March 1985, p. 2.
14. "Erhard's 'Forum': Est Meets the Eighties," *Newsweek*, 1 April 1985, vol. 105, p. 15.
15. Bode, "The Forum: Repackaged est," p. 4.
16. McMahon, "MLA Selling Controversial Training," *Calgary Herald*, 14 January 1983, p. A1.
17. Neal Vahle, "Lifespring and the Development of Human Potential," *New Realities*, July/August 1987, vol. 6, no. 4, p. 22.
18. Pat McMahon, "MLA Selling Controversial Training," p. 2.
19. Vahle, "Lifespring and the Development of Human Potential," p. 21.

20. Neal Vahle, "John Hanley: Supporting Others to Produce Results," *New Realities*, July/August 1987, vol. 6, no. 4, p. 51.

21. Vahle, "Lifespring and the Development of Human Potential," p. 18.

22. "About . . . Life Training," promotional brochure, n.d., p. 3.

23. Ibid. p. 5.

24. Ibid.

25. Insight Transformational Seminars, "Do You Have *All* the Love, Joy, Confidence, Happiness and Success You Want In Your Life?", *The Awakening Heart Seminar*, promotional brochure, back cover.

26. Montogomery Brower, with Suzanne Adelson and Leah Feldon, "Cult Leader John-Roger, Who Says He's Inhabited By a Divine Spirit, Stands Accused of a Campaign of Hate," *People*, 26 September 1988, p. 121.

27. Ibid., p. 119.

28. Ibid., p. 120.

29. Insight Transformational Seminars, *Insight News* newsletter, p. 2.

30. Brower, "Cult Leader John-Roger . . . Stands Accused" pp. 119–120.

31. John-Roger, "The Awakening Heart: The Message of Insight," *The Awakening Heart Seminar*, promotional brochure, p. 2.

32. Insight Transformational Seminars, biographical note on John-Roger and his organizations, *The Awakening Heart Seminar*, photocopy of promotional brochure.

33. Brower, "Cult Leader John-Roger . . . Stands Accused," p. 120.

34. Ibid., p. 119.

35. Esalen Institute, photo caption, *The Esalen Catalog—25th Anniversary: The Early Years* (Esalen Institute: Big Sur, California, 1987), p. 9.

36. Michael Murphy, letter from the Esalen Institute, p. 1.

37. George Leonard, "First Visit to Esalen: February 1965," *The Esalen Catalog—25th Anniversary: The Early Years* (Esalen Institute: Big Sur, California, 1987), p. 8.

38. Murphy letter, p. 1.

39. Leonard, *"First Visit,"* p. 8.

40. Ibid., p. 8

41. Ibid., pp. 8–9.

42. Richard Leviton, "Job's Body: Deane Juhan Is Esalen's Philosopher of Bodywork," *East West Journal*, January 1988, p. 61.

43. *The Esalen Catalog—25th Anniversary: The Early Years*, back cover.

44. Ibid., p. 10.

45. Murphy letter, p. 2.

46. Murphy, letter from the Esalen Institute, pp. 1–2.

47. Mark Whitaker, with Gerald C. Lubenow and Joyce Barnathan, "Esalen's Hot-Tub Diplomacy," *Newsweek,* 10 January 1983, p. 32.

48. *The Esalen Catalog—25th Anniversary,* p. 3.

49. Sandy MacDonald, "The True Story of Esalen," *New Age Journal,* November 1983, p. 32.

50. Phil. 4:13.

51. Amano, "Bad for Business," p. 57.

52. John Enright, "Working with the Mentally Healthy," *New Realities,* July/August 1987, p. 19.

53. Jer. 17:9.

54. Vahle, "Lifespring and the Development of Human Potential," p. 19.

55. Ibid.

56. Clarus Backus, "New Age Religion," *Sunday Denver Post,* 3 May 1987, p. 10.

57. John Randolph Price, *Practical Spirituality* (Austin, TX: Quartus Books, 1985), pp. 18–19.

Chapter 2: Fired Up for the New Age

1. B. P. Elliot, "Hot Foot Therapy," *US,* 7 May 1984, p. 14.

2. David Handleman, "Tiptoe through the Embers," *Rolling Stone,* p. 26.

3. Carolyn Kortge, "Fighting Fear with Fire," *Register Guard,* Eugene, Oregon, 18 March 1984, p. E1.

4. Bernard J. Leikind and William J. McCarthy, "An Investigation of Firewalking," *The Skeptical Inquirer,* Vol. 10, No. 1, Fall 1985, pp. 23–26.

5. Ibid., pp. 29–30.

6. Ibid., p. 30.

7. Ibid., p. 31.

8. Ibid., pp. 31–32.

9. Ibid., p. 32.

10. Ibid., p. 33.

11. Michael R. Dennett, "Firewalking: Reality or Illusion," *The Skeptical Inquirer,* Vol. 10, No. 1, Fall 1985, p. 40.

12. Leikind and McCarthy, "An Investigation of Firewalking," p. 34.

13. Paul Zuromski, ed./pub., *The New Age Catalogue* (New York: Island, 1988), p. 208.

14. "Discoveries through Inner Quests," product catalogue, Institute of Human Development.

15. Heb. 11:1.

16. John W. White, "What Is Meditation?" *New Realities*, September/October 1984, vol. 6, no. 5, p. 46.

17. Ibid., p. 45.

18. Prov. 23:7.

19. Gen. 3:1.

20. Rom. 8:28.

21. Acts 10:38.

22. Matt. 6:7.

23. Matt. 4:7.

24. Isa. 43:2.

25. White, "What Is Meditation?" p. 50.

26. Ps. 19:14.

Chapter 3: The Whole Truth about Holism

1. Lee Aitken, "You Don't Need a Crystal Ball to See That New Age Rocks Are Clearly on a Roll," *People*, 15 June 1987, vol. 27, no. 24, p. 70.

2. Scott Sutphen, "Increasing Crystal Power," *Masters of Life*, January 1987, p. 14.

3. Martha Smilgis, "Rock Power for Health and Wealth," *Time*, 19 January 1987, vol. 129, no. 3, p. 66.

4. Marcia Gervase Ingenito, *National New Age Yellow Pages*, First Annual 1987 Edition, Fullerton, California, p. 38.

5. "Chatter," *People* 17 May 1976, vol. 5, no. 19, p. 102.

6. Barbara Brown, "Mind Over Body," *New Realities*, 1980, vol. 3, no. 3, pp. 48–50.

7. Ronald Kotzsch, "Acupuncture Today," *East West Journal*, January 1986, p. 61.

8. Anna Quindlen, "The Healing Touch," *McCalls*, May 1981, vol. CVIII, no. 8, pp. 134–37.

9. Dolores Krieger, Erik Peper, and Sonia Ancoli, "Therapeutic Touch: Searching for Evidence of Physiological Change," *American Journal of Nursing*, April 1979, vol. 79, no. 1–6, p. 660.

10. Paul C. Reisser, Teri Reisser, and John Weldon, *New Age Medicine* (Downers Grove, Ill.: InterVarsity, 1987), p. 45.

11. "The Psychic Surgeons—Are They Frauds or For Real?" *Lifestyle*, Calgary Herald, p. 17.

12. N. O. Brown, "Brazil's Psychic Surgeons," *Omni*, vol. 7, no. 7, April 1985, p. 96.

13. Acts 10:38.

14. Richard Miles, "What Is Holistic Health?" *Holistic Health Review*, Fall 1977, p. 4.

15. Gen. 3:4.

Chapter 4: Eye, Ear, and Foot Doctors

1. "Pair Claim AIDS Cured," *Rocky Mountain News*, 27 May 1988, p. 84.

2. Paul Zuromski, ed./pub., *The New Age Catalogue* (New York: Island, 1988), p. 143.

3. "Michio Kushi's New Deal," *East West Journal*, January 1976, p. 22.

4. Ibid., p. 23.

5. Ibid.

6. Ibid., p. 24.

7. Bruce Swain, "Homeopathy on Trial," *East West Journal*, June 1986, p. 38.

8. Dana Villman and Stephen Cummings, "The Science of Homeopathy," *New Realities*, Summer 1985, vol. 6, no. 6, p. 23.

9. Ibid., p. 50.

10. E. M. Oakley, "The 'Ayes' Have It/Iridology," *New Realities*, November/December 1984, vol. 6, no. 3, p. 44.

11. Chris Gainor, "Polarity Therapy Restores Body's Energy Balance," *The Vancouver Sun*, 15 September 1982.

12. Polarity Health Institute brochure, n.d.

13. Dr. Randolph Stone, *Health Building: The Conscious Act of Living Well*, CRCS Publications, Sebastopol, California, 1982.

14. Polarity Health Institute brochure, "The Polarity Balancing System: It's Origin and Development," p. 2.

15. Ibid., p. 3.

16. Bruce Miller, "Natural Healing through Naturopathy," *East West Journal*, December 1985, p. 55.

17. Ibid., p. 57.

18. Ibid.

19. Larry Brown, "He's Letting Nature Heal," *Rocky Mountain News*, 15 November 1985, p. 10.

20. "Chatter," *People*, 17 May 1976, p. 102.

21. Polarity Health Institute brochure, pp. 2-3.

22. Acts 10:38.

23. Paul C. Reisser, Teri Reisser, and John Weldon, *New Age Medicine* (Downers Grove, Ill.: InterVarsity, 1987), p. 45.

24. Rom. 1:24–25.

Chapter 5: Trancing in the Light

1. Shirley MacLaine, *Dancing in the Light* (New York, Bantam, 1985), p. 10.

2. Monica Collins, "Not Some Spaced-Out California Concept," *USA Today*, 16 January 1987, p. 1A.

3. Susan Jean Gifford, ed. *Choices and Connections '88-89* (Boulder, Col.: Human Potential Resources, Inc., 1987), p. 405.

4. Paul Zuromski, ed./pub., *The New Age Catalogue* (New York: Island, 1988), p. 3.

5. Ibid., p. 4.

6. Ibid., p. 5.

7. Ibid.

8. Ibid., p. 1.

9. Gifford, *Choices and Connections*, p. 401.

10. Brooks Alexander, "Theological Twilight Zone," *Christianity Today,* 18 September 1987, vol. 3, no. 13, p. 22.

11. Jim Myers, "Channels, The Latest in Psychic Chic," *USA Today,* 22 January 1987, p. 2D.

12. George Hackett, "Ramtha: A Voice from Beyond," *Newsweek,* 15 December 1986, vol. 108, no. 24, p. 42.

13. Zuromski, *The New Age Catalogue*, p. 4.

14. Caroline Young, "Woman Priest Quits in Dispute with Bishop," *Seattle Post Intelligence,* 28 July 1986, p. A1.

15. Alan Vaughn, "The Thinking Man's Channel," *New Realities,* May/June 1988, vol. 8, no. 5, p. 33.

16. Christina Garcia, "And Now, the 35,000-Year-Old Man," *Time,* 15 December 1986, vol. 128, no. 24, p. 86.

17. Hackett, "Ramtha: A Voice from Beyond," p. 42.

18. Ibid.

19. 2 Cor. 4:4.

20. Isa. 14:12–13.

21. Zuromski, *The New Age Catalogue*, p. 8.

22. Lev. 19:31; Deut. 18:10–11; 1 Chron. 10:13; 2 Chron. 33:6; Isa. 8:19; Gal. 5:19–21; 1 Tim. 4:1.

Chapter 6: Extrasensory Deception

1. Paul Zuromski, ed./pub., *The New Age Catalogue* (New York: Island, 1988), p. 216.

2. Ibid., p. 12.

3. Norm Bowles and Fran Hynds, *PSI Search* (San Francisco: Harper and Row, 1978).

4. Ibid.

5. Owen Davies, "Anti-Matter: Hidden Hoax," *Omni,* May 1985, vol. 7, no. 8, p. 90.

6. Robert Neubert, "The Institute of Noetic Sciences," *New Realities*, December 1982, vol. 5, no. 2, p. 88.

7. Bowles and Hynds, *PSI Search*.

8. "Psychic Makes Unborn Babies Vanish," *Sun*, 13 May 1986, p. 7.

9. Art Levine, "Mystics on Main Street," *U.S. News & World Report*, 9 February 1987, vol. 102, no. 5, p. 67.

10. Ibid., p. 69.

11. Casey McCabe, "CISCOP: Binding Men with Science," *New Age Journal*, October 1985, p. 11.

12. Col. 2:18 (NIV).

13. Jacques Moreau, "French Police Ask Psychics to Help Track Down Bank Robbers," *Astrology and Psychic News*, 24 August 1987, vol. LXVI, no. 13, p. 14.

14. Zuromski, ed./pub., *The New Age Catalogue*, p. 216.

15. Gen. 3:5.

Chapter 7: New Age Oracles

1. Joseph Henderson, "The I Ching," *New Realities* January/February 1985, vol. 6, no. 4, p. 31.

2. Susan Jean Gifford, ed. *Choices and Connections '88-'89* (Boulder, Col.: Human Potential Resources, Inc. 1987), p. 397.

3. *The Denver Post* 25 August 1978, p. 6BB.

4. Kris Mullen, "Astrology as a Tool," *Dallas Times Herald,* 4 July 1985.

5. Jefferson Graham, "Astrologers Chart Their Ascendencies," *USA Today* 18 July 1986, p. 1D.

6. Jennifer Bolch, "Biorhythms: A Key to Your Ups and Downs," *Reader's Digest,* September 1977, pp. 63–67.

7. Eric Pement, "Biorhythms: Facts and Fantasies," *Cornerstone,* vol. 7, no. 45, pp. 3–8.

8. Paul Zuromski, ed./pub., *The New Age Catalogue* (New York: Island, 1988), p. 65.

9. *The Washington Post,* 23 October 1983.

10. Deut. 29:29.

11. Dan. 2:28.

12. "Full Moon Theories Sheer Lunacy, CSU Scientist Says," *Rocky Mountain News,* 21 March 1986, p. 47.

Chapter 8: The Grateful Dead

1. John Stark, "A Would-Be Mummy Mogul," *People,* 28 July 1986, vol. 26, p. 85.

2. Ibid., p. 86.

3. Charles Leerhsen, "Out There with Shirley," *Newsweek*, 21 October 1985, vol. 106, no. 17, p. 78.

4. Shirley MacLaine, *Out on a Limb* (New York: Bantam, 1983), p. 5.

5. Ibid., p. 37.

6. Ibid., p. 97.

7. John W. White, "What Is Enlightenment?" *New Realities*, March/April 1985, vol. 6, no. 5, p. 58.

8. John Dart, "Can Churches Resist the Pull of the Paranormal?", *Los Angeles Times*, 14 February 1987, sec. 2, pp. 22–23.

9. John 1:9.

10. 2 Cor. 11:14.

11. 2 Cor. 5:4.

12. 1 Cor. 2:9.

13. Col. 1:16.

14. Eph. 1:18.

15. White, "What Is Enlightenment?" p. 58.

16. John 5:24.

17. White, "What Is Enlightenment?" p. 60.

18. John 8:12.

Chapter 9: It's All in the Selling

1. Deirdre Donahue, "Are These Beliefs?" *USA Today*, 4 June 1987, p. 1A.

2. Ibid., p. 2A.

3. Michael Walsh, "New Age Comes of Age," *Time*, 1 September 1986, vol. 128, no. 9, p. 83.

4. Robert Neubert, "Bergman's Musical Odyssey," *New Realities*, January/February 1987, vol. 7, no. 3, p. 11.

5. Paul Zuromski, ed./pub., *The New Age Catalogue* (New York: Island, 1988), p. 204.

6. Ibid.

7. Suzanne Doucet, "Success Has Diluted New Age Music," *Billboard*, 18 June 1988, vol. 100, no. 25, p. 9.

8. John Denver, "Creating Is Being, Being Is Creating," *Windstar Journal*, Summer 1987, p. 7.

9. Shirley MacLaine, *Dancing in the Light* (New York: Bantam 1985), p. 61.

10. Ibid., p. 111.

11. Ibid., p. 119.
12. Ibid., p. 122.
13. Ibid., p. 210.
14. Ibid., p. 272.
15. Ibid., p. 351.
16. Ibid., p. 357.
17. Shirley MacLaine, *It's All in the Playing* (New York: Bantam, 1987), p. 20.
18. Ibid., p. 21.
19. Ibid., p. 34.
20. Ibid., p. 69.
21. Ibid., p. 38.
22. Matt. 4:21.
23. MacLaine, *It's All in the Playing* p. 147.
24. Ibid., p. 222.
25. Ibid., p. 231.
26. Ibid.
27. Ibid., p. 329.
28. Ibid., p. 172.
29. Ibid., p. 335.
30. Ibid.
31. Ibid.
32. Ibid., p. 337.
33. Ibid.
34. Shirley MacLaine, *Out on a Limb* (New York: Bantam, 1983), p. 92.
35. Ibid., p. 188.
36. Ibid., pp. 356–57.
37. Zuromski, *The New Age Catalogue,* p. 204.
38. Heb. 9:27.
39. Luke 16:26.
40. Deut. 18:10–11.
41. 1 Chron. 10:13.
42. Exod. 3:14.
43. Kevin McKinney, "The Arts," *Omni,* September 1986, vol. 8, no. 12, p. 24.
44. Gal. 1:8.
45. Pat Rodegast and Judith Stanton, *Emanuel's Book* (New York: Bantam, 1987), p. 78.

Chapter 10: The Second Coming

1. Susan Jean Gifford, ed. *Choices and Connections '88-89* (Boulder, Col.: Human Potential Resources, Inc. 1987), p. xxiv.

2. "Introduction" to *A Course in Miracles,* vol. 1, (Framingdale, NY: Foundation for Inner Peace, 1975).

3. Robert Skutch, "The Incredible Untold Story Behind A Course in Miracles Part Two," *New Realities,* September/October 1984, vol. 6, no. 2, p. 15.

4. James Bolen, "William N. Thetford, Ph.D., Exclusive Interview," *New Realities,* September/October 1984, vol. 6, no. 2, p. 23.

5. *A Course in Miracles,* p. 61.

6. Ibid., p. 69.

7. Letter from Foundation for *A Course in Miracles,* 21 November 1984, p. 1.

8. William Plummer, "Turmoil in California Camelot," *People,* 1 July 1985, vol. 24, no. 1, p. 76.

9. Ibid., p. 76.

10. Clyde Bedell, *Concordex of the Urantia Book,* (Santa Barbara, Calif: Clyde Bedell Estate) 1986, p. 21.

11. Ibid., p. 23.

12. Tara Center brochure.

13. Tara Center advertisement, *Los Angeles Times,* 25 April 1982, p. 31.

14. Benjamin Creme, *The Reappearance of the Christ and the Masters of Wisdom* (London: Tara Press, 1980), p. 14.

15. Benjamin Creme, "Maitreya's Mission," *Share International,* Special Issue, 1986, p. 13.

16. "Network News," Tara Center Newsletter, April/May 1987.

17. "Network News," Tara Center Newsletter, May 1988.

18. John 16:8.

19. Isa. 40:8.

20. John 16:13.

21. Gal. 1:8.

22. "Maitreya Message No. 81," 12 September 1979, reprinted in *Share International,* Special Issue, 1986, p. 2.

23. Rev. 17:5.

24. Peter Liefhebber, "Jesus of Nazareth and Maitreya the Christ," *Share International,* Special Issue, 1986, p. 14.

25. Caryl Matrisciana, *Gods of the New Age* (Eugene, Ore.: Harvest House, 1985), p. 15.

26. Gen. 3:4.

27. 2 John 7.

Chapter 11: The Big Picture from the Wrong Angle

1. Dr. Ed Rowe, *New Age Globalism* (Herndon, Va.: Growth Publications, 1985).
2. Richard G. Chrisman, "Letters to the Editor," *Time*, 17 November 1986, vol. 128, no. 20, p. 7.
3. "More on a New Humanist Manifesto," *The Humanist*, March/April 1973, vol. XXXIII, no. 2, p. 36.
4. Yuitaka J. Amano, "Bad for Business," *Eternity*, March 1986, vol. 37, no. 3, p. 55.
5. Paul Zuromski, ed./pub., *The New Age Catalogue* (New York: Island, 1988), p. 219.
6. Susan Jean Gifford, ed. *Choices and Connections '88-'89* (Boulder, Col.: Human Potential Resources, Inc. 1987), p. 424.
7. Price, John Randolph, *Practical Spirituality*, (Austin, TX: Quartus Books, 1985), p. 18.
8. Ibid., p. 19.
9. Ibid., p. 21.
10. "More on a New Humanist Manifesto." p. 36.
11. Paul Kurtz, ed., *The Humanist Manifesto II* (New York: Prometheus, 1973).
12. Henry Steele Commager, "Declaration of Interdependence," World Affairs Council of Philadelphia, 1975.
13. Doug Groothuis, "The Greening of America," *Eternity*, November 1985, vol. 36, no. 11.
14. Marilyn Ferguson, *The Aquarian Conspiracy* (Los Angeles: J. P. Tarcher, 1980), pp. 428–29.
15. Dave Hunt, *Peace and Prosperity and the Coming Holocaust* (Eugene, Ore.: Harvest House, 1983), p. 208.
16. Texe Marrs, *Dark Secrets of the New Age* (Westchester, Ill.: Crossway, 1987), p. 98.
17. Constance E. Cumby, *A Planned Deception* (East Detroit, Mich.: Pointe Publishers, 1985), pp. 46–47.
18. Rev. 13:17.
19. Rev. 17:5.
20. Rom. 1:25.
21. Rev. 21:10.
22. John 14:6.
23. Rev. 1:8.

Chapter 12: New Age People, Places, and Practices

1. Paul Zuromski, ed./pub., *The New Age Catalogue* (New York: Island, 1988), p. 6.

2. Carlos Castaneda, *Journey to Ixtlan: The Lessons of Don Juan* (New York: Pocket Books, 1974).

3. Richard de Mille, ed., *The Don Juan Papers: Further Castaneda Controversy,* (Santa Barbara, Calif.: Ross-Erikson, 1980).

4. Zuromski, *The New Age Catalogue,* p. 44.

5. Susan Jean Gifford, ed. *Choices and Connections '88-89* (Boulder, Col.: Human Potential Resources, Inc., 1987), p. 7.

6. Robert Muller, *New Genesis,* (New York: Image Books, 1982), p. 160.

7. Marilyn Ferguson, *The Aquarian Conspiracy* (Los Angeles: J. P. Tarcher, 1980), p. 23.

8. Ibid., p. 37.

9. "Jean Houston Master Evocateur," promotional brochure for workshops with Jean Houston (The Oasis Center, 1986), p. 2.

10. Gifford, *Choices and Connections,* p. 416.

11. "The Other Side of Death," *Cornerstone,* vol. 6, no. 39, p. 5.

12. Ruth Shick Montgomery and Joanne Garland, *Herald of the New Age* (Garden City, N.Y.: Random, 1986).

13. Muller, *New Genesis,* p. 164.

14. Ibid., p. 152.

15. David Gelman, "The Megatrends Man," *Newsweek,* 23 September 1985, pp. 60–61.

16. Zuromski, *The New Age Catalogue,* p. 217.

17. John Randolph Price, *Practical Spirituality* (Austin, Tex.: Quartus Books, 1985), p. 136.

18. Ibid., p. 93.

19. Texe Marrs, *Dark Secrets of the New Age* (Westchester, Ill.: Crossway, 1987), pp. 36–39.

20. Zuromski, *The New Age Catalogue,*

21. Bob Mendel, "Sex and Spirituality," *Masters of Life,* no. 36, p. 12.

22. Ibid., p. 14.

23. Cherri Senders and Kathleen Maloney, "The Rama Drama," *New Age Journal,* May/June 1988, vol. 7, no. 5, pp. 20–22.

24. "Hunger Project Feeds Itself," *The Cult Observer,* April 1985, p. 15.

25. Lee Fowler, "From Outer Space to Inner Odyessy," *New Age Journal,* May 1985, p. 44.

26. Gifford, *Choices and Connections* p. 418.

27. Findhorn promotional brochure, 1984.

28. Ibid.

29. P.M.H. Atwater, "Perelandra: Cooperating Co-Creatively with Nature," *New Realities*, May/June 1988, p. 18.

30. Ibid., p. 48.

31. Michael Hutchison, "Mind Expanding Machines," *New Age Journal*, July/August 1987, p. 27.

32. Ibid., p. 33.

33. Zuromski, *The New Age Catalogue*, p. 83.

34. Robert Neubert, "Reiki—The Radiance Technique," *New Realities*, March/April 1987, vol. 7, no. 4, p. 19.

35. Reiki advertisement placed in New Age periodicals.

Bibliography

Secular Books

Argüelles, José. *Earth Ascending,* Santa Fe, NM: Bear & Company, 1984, 1988.

Capra, Fritjof. *The Tao of Physics,* New York: Bantam Books, 1975, 1983.

Ferguson, Marilyn. *The Aquarian Conspiracy.* Los Angeles: J. P. Tarcher, 1980.

Gifford, Susan Jean, ed. *Choices and Connections '88–'89.* Boulder, Col.: Human Potential Resources, Inc., 1987.

Harner, Michale. *The Way of the Shaman,* New York: Bantam Books, 1980.

Houston, Jean. *The Search for the Beloved.* Los Angeles: Jeremy P. Tarcher, Inc., 1987.

Hubbard, Barbara Marx. *The Evolutionary Journey,* San Francisco: Evolutionary Press, 1982.

Ingenito, Marcia Gervase. *National New Age Yellow Pages,* First Annual 1987 Edition. Fullerton, Cal.: National New Age Yellow Pages, 1987.

MacLaine, Shirley. *Dancing in the Light.* New York: Bantam, 1985.

———. *It's All in the Playing.* New York: Bantam, 1987.

———. *Out on a Limb.* New York: Bantam, 1983.

Muller, Robert. *New Genesis.* New York: Image Books, 1984.

Price, John Randolph. *Practical Spirituality.* Austin, Tex.: Quartus Books, 1985.

Raphael. *The Starseed Transmissions,* New York: The Talman Company, 1982.

Ram Dass. *Journey of the Awakening,* New York: Bantam Books, 1978.

Rodegast, Pat and Judith Stanton. *Emanuel's Book.* New York: Bantam, 1985.

Shakti Gawain. *Creative Visualization,* San Rafael, CA: *Whatever Publishing, Inc., 1978.*

Zuromski, Paul. ed. and pub. *The New Age Catalog.* New York: Island, 1988.

Religious/Evangelical Books

Chagall, David and Juneau. *The Sunshine Road.* Nashville: Thomas Nelson, 1988.

Chandler, Russell. *Understanding the New Age,* Dallas, Tex.: Word Publishing, 1988.

Cumbey, Constance E. *A Planned Deception.* East Detroit, Mich.: Pointe Publishers, 1985.

———. *The Hidden Dangers of the Rainbow.* Shreveport, La.: Hunting House, 1983.

Groothuis, Douglas R. *Unmasking the New Age.* Downers Grove, Ill.: InterVarsity, 1986.

———. *Confronting the New Age.* Downers Grove, Ill.: InterVarsity Press, 1988.

Hunt, Dave. *Peace, Prosperity and the Coming Holocaust.* Eugene, Ore.: Harvest House, 1983.

Hunt, Dave, and T. A. McMahon. *America: The Sorcerer's New Apprentice.* Eugene, Ore.: Harvest House, 1988.

———. *The Seduction of Christianity.* Eugene, Ore.: Harvest House, 1985.

Hoyt, Karen. *The New Age Rage.* Old Tappan, N.J.: Revell, 1987.

Lewis, C. S. *Mere Christianity.* New York: Macmillan, 1943, 1945, 1952.

Marrs, Texe. *Dark Secrets of the New Age.* Westchester, Ill.: Crossway, 1987.

———. *Mystery Mark of the New Age.* Westchester, Ill.: Crossway, 1988.

Reisser, Paul C., Teri K. Reisser, and John Weldon. *New Age Medicine.* Downers Grove, Ill.: InterVarsity, 1987.

INDEX

Index

Index